THE DORDOGNE, THE LOT AND THE TARN

D1634306

THE WHICH? GUIDE TO

THE DORDOGNE, THE LOT AND THE TARN

By ANDREW LESLIE

CONSUMERS' ASSOCIATION

Which? Books are commissioned and researched by
Consumers' Association and published by
Which? Ltd, 2 Marylebone Road, London NW1 4DF

Distributed by The Penguin Group:
Penguin Books Ltd, 27 Wrights Lane, London W8 5TZ

First edition 1995

British Library Cataloguing-in-Publication Data
Leslie, Andrew
Which? Guide to the Dordogne, the Lot and the Tarn
I. Title
914.4704839

ISBN 0 85202 547 5

Editor for *Holiday Which?* Anna Fielder
Additional research Liz Piccin

Cover photograph by Spectrum Colour Library
Designed by Paul Saunders
Illustrations by Madeleine David
Maps by Perrott Cartographics
Index by Marie Lorimer
Typeset by Saxon Graphics Ltd, Derby
Printed and bound in England by Clays Ltd, St Ives plc

CONTENTS

ABOUT THIS GUIDE

This guide to one of the most popular regions of France has been researched by the *Holiday Which?* magazine team. It is intended for both first-time visitors looking for an ideal holiday spot and those who are already familiar with the busier parts of the Central Dordogne and the Lot valleys but who want to explore further afield. There are four chapters devoted to the relatively little explored areas of Cantal, Corrèze, Aveyron and Tarn, and Aubrac and the Western Cévennes – all of which are within one- to three-hours' drive from the well-frequented tourist areas. The guide also includes the cities of Bordeaux and Toulouse, the former a perfect weekend break destination, the latter an important gateway and well worth a visit. All chapters include a summary of the good bases in the area. The map on p.9 shows how the region has been divided. You will find a separate map of each area at the beginning of each chapter. A city map of Bordeaux is included in the chapter on Bordeaux and its wine regions, and a map of Toulouse in the Aveyron and Tarn chapter.

Where to stay, eat and camp

At the end of each chapter is a list of our recommended hotels – all inspected first-hand and chosen for their comfort, service and value for money. We also include hotels that are worth considering but, in our opinion, do not merit a wholehearted recommendation. Most recommended hotels have restaurants that offer good meals; we also mention other restaurants in the descriptions of towns and villages.

In the Central Dordogne and Lot chapters we include a selection of recommended campsites near the rivers – the cheapest way to spend a holiday fortnight in these well-frequented areas. All hotels and campsites are marked on our maps.

Hotel fire safety

Consumers' Association has long campaigned for an EC Directive on fire safety in hotels. At the moment there are agreed standards throughout the EC, but they are not legally binding, and standards vary from country to country.

One of the biggest dangers in a fire is smoke. When you arrive at a hotel, always:
- Find out where the nearest exits to your room are and check that the exit doors open easily
- Find out where the nearest fire alarm point is and read the instructions
- Find out how to open the windows in your room and look for ledges and balconies that might help you to escape
- Read any emergency information available.

If a fire breaks out:
- Do not panic
- Report fire or smoke to reception immediately
- Never use the lift
- Never try to go through thick smoke

A useful leaflet, *About Hotel Fire Safety*, is available free with an SAE from the Fire Protection Association, 140 Aldersgate Street, London EC1A 4HX.

Opening times

Times given were correct when we went to press, but many are liable to frequent change, so double-check, particularly if you are visiting out of season or during a public or winter/Easter school holiday, when normal hours change for most sights: some may open up, others may close.

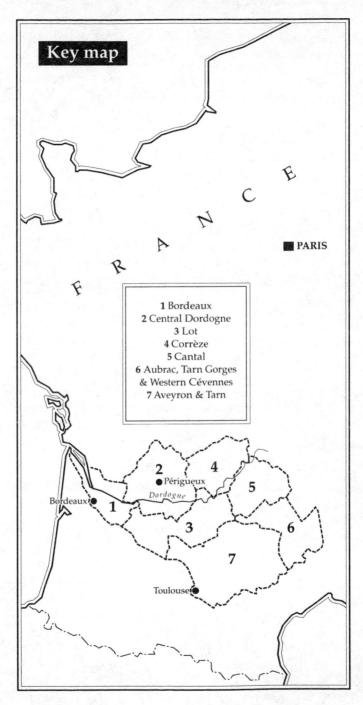

Key map

1 Bordeaux
2 Central Dordogne
3 Lot
4 Corrèze
5 Cantal
6 Aubrac, Tarn Gorges
& Western Cévennes
7 Aveyron & Tarn

■ PARIS

F R A N C E

Périgueux

Dordogne

Bordeaux

Toulouse

INTRODUCTION

The long-standing love affair between British holidaymakers and the Dordogne valley shows no signs of waning. Stand in the town of Uzerche in Corrèze on any Saturday in July or August and you will see the main road packed with British cars, loaded down with children, sailboard and cool-boxes, heading determinedly southwards towards a favourite cottage or campsite. It is not fashion that brings them. It is more the kind of addiction, not easily understood by those who have never been to the area, which led André Breton, a French surrealist poet and critic, to write of St-Cirq-Lapopie, *'J'ai cessé de me désirer ailleurs'* ('I have stopped wanting to be anywhere else').

The huge area of Aquitaine, which in medieval times stretched from Gascony to the highest peaks of the Massif Central, was once a possession of the Plantagenet kings of England, familiar to generations of English archers, sailors and merchants – and to the Scottish troops who fought on the French side to drive them out. Perhaps those 400 years of tramping across south-west France instilled something into the British blood which drives descendants of the medieval venturers to cross the Channel again and again to the banks of the great rivers of the area: the Dordogne, the Lot and the Tarn.

The golden towns and villages of these rivers are surely a place to come home to. There is so much to be found here that has long been missing from grey old Britain – real markets, hot summers and countryside which is both cared for yet is in places wild enough to suit the most determined of wilderness-lovers. There are ruined castles on high cliffs above limpid or rushing rivers, villages straight out of a story-book, walnuts, *foie gras*, full-bodied red wines. . .

Most British visitors pack themselves into the narrow confines of the central Dordogne and Lot valleys, where the region's most famous sights are to be found. Here, expatriates and second-home owners rub shoulders uneasily with their compatriots on holiday, hunching themselves into the corners of restaurants and pretending not to speak English. July and August are intolerable, they complain. Roll on the autumn when everyone else goes home.

It is true that in high season there are now simply too many people (French and Dutch as well as British) trying to see the castles, caves and villages of the Dordogne and Vézère valleys. Hotels are booked solid, there are lengthy queues for the best sights and the local markets feel like Sainsbury's on a Saturday morning.

Yet the countryside to the north, south and east of this small area remains comparatively deserted. It is as if visitors and tour operators have a mental map labelled 'The Dordogne' and are reluctant to explore beyond its boundaries. Why spend two hours queuing for an undistinguished cave near Les Eyzies when, in the same amount of time, you could be watching the swallows circle the extraordinary brick cathedral of Albi, or be walking on the deserted pine-scented footpaths of Corrèze?

There is far more to the south-west of France than the well-trodden stretches around Sarlat. The Dordogne, Lot, Tarn and their tributaries run through a countryside of astonishing diversity. From the heathery Cévennes or the high green pasture-lands of Cantal the rivers flow past sun-baked villages, through canyons carved in limestone plateaux, in wooded gorges, or over land where orchards of peaches and plums ripen. On all sides lie towns, villages and landscapes not one whit less interesting than those in the Central Dordogne valley.

For this reason we have drawn the boundaries of this book to include the whole river system of the Dordogne, Lot and Tarn. We recommend that the time to explore the caves and castles between Bergerac and Argentat is outside the peak holiday season, and that July and August are for exploration further afield. There is much to explore: it is hard to think what this region of France lacks except the seaside (but there are plenty of rivers and lakes for watersports) and mountains high enough to carry snow all year round.

City-lovers have the choice of Bordeaux or Toulouse. The former is an ideal short-break city, with glittering shops, fine museums and of course the wine merchants and the vineyards to browse through. Toulouse feels youthful and energetic, yet its history goes back to the days when its counts were an independent power, ruling from the Spanish border to Provence.

People who enjoy high, lonely country are spoilt for choice. The limestone plateaux above the fearsome gorges of the Tarn, the Jonte or the Dourbie are virtually uninhabited expanses with wide skies and long views. The grassy peaks of the Cantal mountains are ideal for long days ridge-walking among alpine flowers. The bare plateau of Aubrac and the forested hillsides of Corrèze are little-visited regions, where you can spend time digging yourself into local life. Then there are the rugged, barren ridges of the Cévennes, which conceal tiny villages and wayside churches.

A gentler, hotter landscape is to be found east of Toulouse, where rambling farmsteads crown low hills and the villages nestle in antiquity. The upper Aveyron valley, where villages seem lost among the foldings of rolling country, is lush and beautiful, yet how many visitors to the region travel to see it?

If you already enjoy rural France, or want to discover a new part of it, this region, and this book, are for you. We will guide you not only to the best of the sights on every tour operator's itinerary (and warn you of the worst), but will also lead you into some of the lesser-known corners of south-west France along the course of the rivers, great and small, all of whose waters meet the Atlantic near Bordeaux. Along the way we point you to the best-value and most interesting places to stay, tell you what is, and what is not, worth your time and money, and enthuse or criticise in equal measure.

RECOMMENDED SELF-CATERING AREAS

You can find cottages for rent throughout the area covered by this book (see Practical Information at end of book), although they are thinly scattered in the more isolated or mountainous areas. The following are areas of countryside which we would recommend for your shortlist.

Dordogne valley

The country to the east of the Montignac-Sarlat road (D704) is less densely wooded than to the west and is rich in small, isolated villages. This is a popular area, however, as it is within easy reach of the area's main sights, and you should ensure you book well in advance for it.

The broken, hilly country to the east of the Causse de Gramat around St-Céré is less frequented. Views from the hillsides are good. For exploring the Upper Dordogne or venturing into the mountains, this area makes a good base.

Lot valley

The village of Cajarc, between Cahors and Figeac, is a popular base for exploring the river valley. The limestone *causses* to the north and south are more or less deserted and sprinkled with tiny, half-depopulated villages. These make good hunting grounds if you want isolation but also want to explore the sights. You will be unlikely to find sophisticated accommodation.

Aveyron valley

The prettiest country in the Aveyron valley lies upstream of Villefranche-de-Rouergue. The valley is very steep here, but the rolling uplands on either bank are unfrequented and washed in sunshine. This is not an especially good area to tour from, but would be perfect for a do-nothing holiday.

Further south, try the fringes of the Forêt de Grésigne, west and south-west of Cordes. The uplands are wooded or patch-worked with hayfields; vineyards fill the landscape further down. This area is within easy reach of Albi.

Tarn valley

Most of the Tarn valley is too rugged to be good for self-cater-ing. In the Lower Tarn, try the dry, sun-baked hills north-east of Moissac. The Middle Tarn, the Rance valley and the area immediately around Ambialet are the best places to look. The valley of the Tarn where it flows through the Cévennes between Florac and Pont-de-Montvert is probably its most attractive stretch.

Bordeaux vineyards

The Entre-Deux-Mers region between the Garonne and the Dordogne and the area immediately around St-Emilion are the two best areas for relaxed touring and also have the best of the countryside.

Cantal

The weather is unpredictable around the high mountains, and self-catering properties are inclined to be thin on the ground. Try the area south-west of Aurillac: it is rolling and wooded and within reasonable distance of the sights of the Upper Dordogne.

ACTIVITIES

Walking

In addition to the long-distance footpaths (*Grandes Randonnées*) which wind through the south-west of France, almost every village has a network of short waymarked paths. For hill-walking proper, go to the Cantal mountains, whose long ridges provide lots of opportunity. In the uplands of Corrèze, or the Sidobre, east of Toulouse, most paths run through forests, but are not heavily frequented. The Tarn and Jonte Gorges have spectacular walks along the edge of canyons; the flat scrublands of the high *causses* between provide less dramatic but equally pleasurable walking. In the Lot and the Dordogne valleys, the best walks are the small circuits running from the villages along the banks. The Cévennes National Park caters well for walkers. The going can be fairly tough here, with paths winding over dry rocky ridges, but there are many easier options too.

Boating

The two most popular areas for seeing the scenery by water are the Dordogne valley between Argentat and St-Cyprien, and the Tarn Gorges around La Malène or Le Rozier. There are river-trips, and on both rivers you can hire kayaks and canoes. There are river-trips on the Lot, too, but fewer stretches of spectacular scenery for canoeing. Pleasure-boats chug up and down the lakes formed by the dams on the Upper Dordogne and the Truyère; there are opportunities for sailing and windsurfing on the man-made lakes of Corrèze, and most towns with water nearby will have landscaped a *plan d'eau* for picnicking and swimming.

Wildlife

If you want to see a vulture, head for the gorges of the Jonte. Other good areas for sighting birds of prey are the high moorlands of the Cézallier and Aubrac plateaux. The same areas are wonderful places for wild flowers – almost anywhere in the Cantal mountains can be added to them. For limestone-loving flora, try the Causse Noir – early May is the best time – above Millau. The Cévennes National Park is the best-organised place for in-depth introductions to local ecology and geology.

15

Anglers should make for the rivers of Cantal or Corrèze, where, among some excellent scenery, there is some superb fishing for wild trout.

TOP SIGHTS

These are the sights which we consider to be particularly worth taking time and trouble to see. We recommend that in high season you avoid those marked with an asterisk.

* *Lascaux II* (Central Dordogne) Facsimile of famous prehistoric painted cave.

* *Font-de-Gaume* (Central Dordogne) More splendid prehistoric art.

Château de Beynac (Central Dordogne) The best of the many castles on the river.

Château de Montal (Lot) Wonderful Renaissance stone carving.

Musée d'Aquitaine (Bordeaux, Bordeaux and the Wine Route) Much the best archaeological/historical museum in the region.

Musée de l'Automat (Souillac, Lot) Computer-controlled collection of working models.

Cathédrale Ste-Cécile (Albi, Aveyron and Tarn) Severe exterior shrouds marvellous Gothic interior.

Musée Toulouse-Lautrec (Albi, Aveyron and Tarn) Extensive collection of the artist's work.

Musée de Cuzals/Musée en plein air du quercy (Lot) A highly idiosyncratic open-air folk museum.

Aven Armand (Aubrac, the Tarn Gorges and the Western Cévennes) The best rock formations of all the caverns.

Taxiway (Toulouse, Aveyron and Tarn) Unique, well-organised tour of an aircraft factory.

Abbey church of St-Pierre (Moissac, Aveyron and Tarn) The very best Romanesque carving in the region.

TOP VILLAGES

Not all of these are famous, but all are among the most beautiful in their area. Those marked with an asterisk draw large crowds.

* La Roque-Gageac (Central Dordogne)
* St-Cirq-Lapopie (Lot)
* Domme (Central Dordogne)
* Collonges-la-Rouge (Lot)

Autoire (Lot)
★ Monpazier (Central Dordogne)
Gimel-les-Cascades (Corrèze)
Ségur-le-Château (Corrèze)
Salers (Cantal)
Lherm (Lot)
Belcastel (Aveyron)
Estaing (Aubrac, Tarn Gorges and Western Cévennes)

HISTORY

The fact that the south-west of France was where the science of prehistory was pioneered gives the region the prestige of having a history one can trace back to the Ice Age. The early millennia are inevitably shrouded in speculation, however, and it is not until the Roman conquest of Gaul that the story begins to take shape.

Like most of France, this is an area that has been marked by armed conflict. The earliest wars were mostly between the north and the south; by medieval times, the long-drawn-out struggle against England had shifted the battle to an east–west one. The Wars of Religion found communities across the region in internecine warfare. It is hardly surprising that the country is so liberally sprinkled with castles and fortifications.

The Romans

By the time Julius Caesar undertook his conquest of Gaul, much of the southern part of the country was already heavily under Roman influence – especially through the trade in Italian wines. The Gaulish tribes around the Tarn and Aveyron joined in the resistance to the invader with less ferocity than their neighbours to the north, the inhabitants of today's Périgord and Quercy. Nevertheless, the site of the last Gaulish resistance, at Uxellodonum, is somewhere in the area, though no one knows exactly where (there are several rival candidates). Under the Romans, Cahors, Périgueux, and especially Toulouse became flourishing cities, while the countryside was scattered with luxurious villas. Close to Millau pottery factories produced earthenware for half the empire.

The Barbarians

During the third century, invasions of Germanic tribes from the north became increasingly frequent. The Visigoths swept through the region on their way to Spain. In 415 the Emperor Honorius, making virtue of necessity, employed them as peacekeepers, and they returned to the south-west to settle. As the Roman Empire disintegrated, the Visigoths set up their own semi-Romanised kingdom, which stretched from Spain to the frontiers of Roman Aquitaine, and made a glittering city of Toulouse.

However, the Visigoths were in their turn displaced by the Franks sweeping down from the north. In 507 the Frankish king Clovis won the Battle of Vouillé, bringing much of the south-west under a new regime. Invasions from the east by Saracens brought further chaos, as did ceaseless wars between the successors of Clovis. In particular, the campaign by Pépin le Bref against the self-styled duke of Aquitaine, Waiffre, reached its climax in 766.

Charlemagne and Aquitaine

Charlemagne, crowned Holy Roman Emperor in 800, succeeded in reuniting France. His system for ensuring stability was to establish his most loyal followers in power in the regions. During his reign the counts of Toulouse and the dukes of Aquitaine emerged as powerful barons, subject of course to the emperor's will. Charlemagne's empire did not last long. It was destabilised by Viking invaders, who travelled up the rivers, laying siege to Toulouse in 864, and also by the growing independence of the regional barons. By the year 1000 the count of Toulouse was styling himself 'by the grace of God', and his lands embraced most of Quercy. To the west a grouping of smaller barons, the counts of Périgord among them, were still nominally part of Aquitaine.

The Albigensian Crusade

The crusade called by Pope Innocent III in 1209 (see box) devastated the land again. The Cathar heresy was most firmly established in the lands of the count of Toulouse and when the crusade to extirpate it got under way, these were the areas to suffer most. Under Simon de Montfort, however, the crusaders ranged far into the Dordogne valley, destroying towns and fortresses alike. There were rich pickings to be had from being on the side of the righteous. Although the land of the count of Toulouse itself was not absorbed by the French crown until 1271, most of the old Cathar families lost their possessions, which were snatched up by the invaders from the north.

The Plantagenets

The marriage of Henry Plantagenet and Eleanor of Aquitaine in 1154 began the long conflict between England and France. Eleanor brought the dowry of Aquitaine to Henry, who was already duke of Normandy and Anjou, and was to become king of England only a few months later. The Treaty of Paris in 1259 brought a certain measure of stability to the relationship between France and England, whereby the Plantagenets paid homage to the French king for their possessions in Aquitaine. In the years following the treaty the *bastide* (fortified) towns were rapidly established, as both French and English marked out their territories by settlement. The trouble was that the feudal relationship between king of France and king-duke of Aquitaine brought complications that endless legal wrangles were powerless to resolve. The duchy of Aquitaine was 'confiscated', given back and confiscated again. Truces were broken and patched up. But the most important consequence was Edward I of England's agreement to marry his heir to Isabella, daughter of Philip IV of France.

The Hundred Years' War

In 1327 Edward III came to the throne of England. He was grandson (by his mother) of Philip IV of France. When Charles IV (Philip's brother) died, Edward had a good claim to the French throne. Tension increased; the French chose Philip of Valois as their king and he proceeded to confiscate Aquitaine again in 1337. In retaliation, Edward claimed the French crown and in 1340 formally styled himself king of France.

The first episodes of the Hundred Years' War were fought in Brittany and Normandy, ending with the English victory at Crécy in 1346. In 1356, the Black Prince (the eldest son of Edward III), on a raid out of Aquitaine, defeated the French at Poitiers and the French king was taken prisoner. In 1360, the Treaty of Brétigny gave the English much of what they demanded, including all of Aquitaine, although the clauses stipulating full English sovereignty over Aquitaine in exchange for Edward's renunciation of the French crown were never put into effect. In 1369 war broke out again. This time the French succeeded in nibbling chunks out of the English-dominated south-west. Towns were 'liberated' or simply declared that they had changed sides. A further failure to reach a peaceful settlement ended in a truce in 1396.

The accession of Henry V to the English throne changed matters. In contrast to his predecessors, who were largely using force to establish what they saw as their feudal rights, Henry embarked on a conquest of France. He was successful enough, especially owing to the Battle of Agincourt in 1415, to enforce the Treaty of Troyes on the French (helped by his allies among the French nobility). This treaty preserved France as a unity, but recognised that Henry should succeed to the French crown on the death of the current king, the sick Charles VI.

However, many French people were still loyal to the dauphin, son of Charles VI, and Joan of Arc believed utterly that his succession was a cause worth fighting for. Her conviction helped to turn the tide of the war. Starting with the raising of the siege of Orléans, Franco-Scottish armies gradually reconquered much of the northern part of France. In 1435 the Duke of Burgundy, the most powerful of England's allies, changed sides. By 1450 only Calais in the north remained loyal to the English.

Aquitaine fell last. The French invaded in 1442, took Bordeaux in 1451 and, despite regaining control of that city, the English were defeated in 1453 at the Battle of Castillon in the Dordogne valley, effectively putting an end to 400 years of English domination of the south-west of France.

The shape of the conflict in Aquitaine

If the Hundred Years' War was complicated on the level of conflict between countries, it was far more so on a regional level. One of its more bewildering features is the rapidity with which people and towns changed sides – through an awoken sense of renewed loyalty in some cases, but just as often through self-interest, bribery, the effects of faraway treaties or local antagonisms. For this was not until its last stages a 'nationalistic' war. Landowners threw in their lot with their feudal overlord – it was merely a question of which overlord had the better claim to their loyalty.

Nor was it a war of pitched battles. The sequence of armed raids mounted by both sides was less an attempt to destroy the enemy than to expose his weaknesses. The virtually impregnable castles were seldom worthwhile targets. It was the towns and villages that suffered.

The various periods of truce produced large numbers of unoccupied soldiers. No longer employed, they merely banded together and continued to plunder for themselves. The menace posed by these so-called 'free companies' was, if anything, worse than that of the properly constituted armies, for they owed allegiance to no one except themselves. Much energy was expended by both French and English in pursuing the robber-barons and the footloose soldiers in their wakes.

It was this constant raiding, whether in the name of the king or the name of plunder, which turned much of the Dordogne basin into a wilderness, leaving the towns girdled with walls, the churches fortified as refuges for the villagers and every clifftop crowned by a castle. These may be romantic and beautiful things to explore today, but they were created out of cruel necessity.

The Wars of Religion

Lutheran and Calvinist doctrines spread through France as fast as they did through the rest of Europe. By the mid-sixteenth century, the south-west of France was split. Montauban and Toulouse and much of the old lands of the count of Toulouse were Protestant, Périgueux and Cahors were Catholic. The outbreak of war in 1562 led to 37 years of bloody turmoil in the south-west. Périgueux suffered especially badly; it fell to the Protestants in 1575 and its old church of St-Etienne was pillaged. Cahors endured a three-day siege before falling in 1578. Throughout the region, it was again the small towns and villages that came off worst. Fortified churches were put to use again and old castles reoccupied. In 1598 Henri IV proclaimed freedom of worship under the Edict of Nantes, which at last brought peace. It was not until the reign of Louis XIV that religious trouble was to flare up again. His revocation of the Edict of Nantes provoked rebellion in the Cévennes mountains, leading to a period of guerrilla warfare and savage repression, while from the Protestant towns of Montauban and Bergerac hundreds of skilled workers were forced into exile.

From the Bourbons to the Second World War

One result of the centralising tendencies of the great Bourbon monarchs, Louis XIII, XIV and XV, was the neglect of the provinces. All the brilliance and all the intrigue were to be found in Paris or Versailles, and by and large the rest of France was left to contribute the taxes to pay for the palaces, the courtiers and the wars of conquest. One destructive (to our eyes) feature of the *ancien régime* was the determination with which the demolition of old castles and fortifications was undertaken. Again and again we read of walls destroyed or fortresses demolished on the orders of Cardinal Richelieu. Louis XIV, ever mindful of the tendency of the great nobles of France to seek their own interest, was determined to deprive them of their strongholds.

The Revolution came to the countryside of the south-west in the tradition of the peasant revolts (the *Jacqueries* and the *Croquants*) which had exploded from time to time whenever the repressions of the landowning classes had become too much to bear. Whatever troubles it brought in its wake, it at least left many of the peasants owning their own land for the first time, a tradition which has continued to this day.

Bordeaux played a leading role in the Revolution, for it was from that city that the 'Girondin' faction stemmed. The Girondins' idea of a federalist France proved insufficiently radical and they were deposed and hunted down by fiercer rivals. Two of their deputies took refuge in caves near St-Emilion until their eventual discovery and execution.

During the nineteenth century and the beginning of the twentieth, the countryside of the south-west became increasingly depopulated. This haemorrhage of people was the result of many factors including the difficulty of making a living from tiny parcels of land, the ease of transport provided by the railways and the lure of employment in the growing cities. The First World War took its toll on the young men, as can be seen by looking at any village war memorial. Added to this, the disease of phylloxera devastated the vineyards, causing thousands to migrate or to seek employment elsewhere. A census of 1851 gives the population of the Lot as 300,000. In 1946 it had fallen to 155,000. Outside the cities, the same pattern repeated itself all over the south-west, especially in the harsh terrain of the *causses*, Lozère and Auvergne.

The Resistance

As a result of the invasion of France and the capitulation of 1940 German troops were installed in Bordeaux. The remainder of the region was part of the unoccupied zone – which lasted until 1942. Parts of the south-west, especially the forests of Corrèze and the Truyère gorges, were ideal for partisan warfare, and the French Resistance was especially strong in these areas.

The particular tragedy of the Dordogne basin was the role played by its *maquis* in seeking to delay the SS armoured division 'Das Reich' from moving north against the Allied landings in Normandy of 1944. In a series of actions throughout towns and villages from Figeac to Limoges, small groups of inadequately armed resistance men confronted the tanks and half-tracks of the Germans. They were successful in so far as the whole division was ordered from its prime task to suppress the 'banditry' that threatened the German hold on the south, but the reprisals were terrible. On your travels, you will find dozens of monuments to those taken hostage and deported, or simply shot by the roadside.

BORDEAUX AND ITS WINE REGIONS

All the waters of south-west France carried by the Dordogne and the Garonne meet at the long incision of the Gironde estuary at whose head stands the city of Bordeaux. For centuries the trade on these rivers has revolved around the city. The alluvial gravels from the Pyrenees and the Massif Central on the banks of the Garonne and the Dordogne have brought another enormous benefit to the area, for on the banks of the rivers has evolved one of the world's greatest wine-growing regions. Bordeaux is now synonymous with wine, but it was in Britain where this wine first gained a high reputation, and Britain remains its most steadfast enthusiast. Go round the Médoc or the St-Emilion wine regions at any time of year, and among the wine professors from German universities and Japanese and American buyers, you will discover the British amateur with a cellar to fill back home and a booklet of tasting notes under one arm. Tours of vineyards and cellars are offered, from the most prestigious châteaux to the smallest proprietors, to suit all tastes and all levels of experience.

Without its wine, the Bordeaux region might be easy to write off as a haunt for tourists. In comparison with what lies further upstream, the scenery is not remarkable, while St-Emilion is the only town outside Bordeaux that merits a journey.

Bordeaux itself, however, is a city worth getting to know well. Its centre features splendidly grand architecture from the eighteenth century, and its older quarters have plenty of fascinating shops and cafés. It is an elegant and prosperous place.

Because of the temptations of the Dordogne valley, visitors often sweep around Bordeaux on the efficient ring road and ignore the city. Our advice, however, is to spend time in the town. Its museums and galleries are as good as its shops and its shops are as good as its street life.

For 300 years, Bordeaux was the capital of Plantagenet Aquitaine (corrupted by Anglo-Saxon tongues into 'Guyenne'), court of the Black Prince and arsenal of the Hundred Years' War. Aquitaine came into Plantagenet hands in 1154 as the dowry of Eleanor, only daughter of William, Duke of Aquitaine. She had previously been married to the French king, Louis VII, who got rid of her in one of the most politically inept divorces ever. With her went her dowry, and Henry Plantagenet, already Duke of Normandy, was not slow to snatch up the neglected bride. A mere two months later, Henry inherited the throne of England as Henry II.

The devastation of the Hundred Years' War was inflicted on communities far and wide throughout south-west France but did not affect Bordeaux until the very end. Prospering on its wine, which was already much in demand for Plantagenet ceremonial occasions, the city never really suffered and the final departure of the English did nothing to diminish their taste for Bordeaux wine.

BORDEAUX

In spite of its monumental neo-classical buildings and ruler-straight boulevards, the centre of Bordeaux is a curiously homely place, little more than a meeting point of four streets in front of the beautifully proportioned façade of the Grand Théâtre. A little way to the east, the Garonne curves gently towards the sea, but the old city seems firmly to turn its back on its river, keeping many of its splendours hidden from passing boatmen. Until 1965 only one bridge crossed the water, and even that was completed only in 1822. This is not to say that town planners, particularly those of the eighteenth century, have not sought to alter this perspective. The centrepiece of the city ought to be the huge Esplanade des Quinconces, a gravelly rectangle bordered by whole parklands of trees linking river bank to city centre, with the lofty gilded monument to the Girondins rising above it. As often as not, however, the esplanade is turned into a fun-fair with a huge Ferris wheel dominating the skyline while cars park under the trees.

A little way to the east, the Place de la Bourse ought to be equally imposing – a crescent of mid-eighteenth-century buildings receding gently from the river – but the traffic whizzes past and there is no real reason to linger. A riverside revival scheme is mooted, but whether even this will make the Bordelais pay any attention to their waterway must remain in doubt.

Meanwhile, all the life of the city goes on away from the Gironde, as it has done since Roman times. All around the Grand Théâtre, where the forum once stood, street cafés mix with the mansions given over to the wine trade. The Cours de l'Intendance plunges westwards from here, with chic shoe shops, furriers, lingerie and leatherwork salons vying for the money of the well-heeled. The less moneyed cross the Cours de l'Intendance and shop in the pedestrianised, restored streets of old Bordeaux, where, among the music stores and the Galeries Lafayette, they are propelled past shops selling

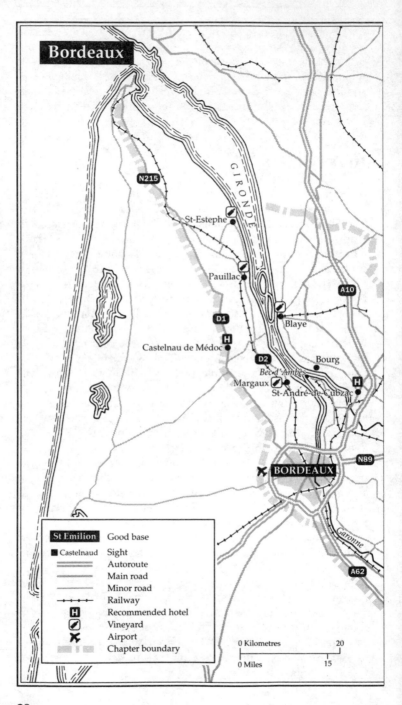

Bordeaux

G I R O N D E

N215

St-Estephe

Pauillac

Blaye

A10

D1

H

Castelnau de Médoc

D2

Bourg

Bec d'Ambès

Margaux

St-André-de-Cubzac

H

BORDEAUX

N89

Garonne

A62

St Emilion	Good base
■ Castelnaud	Sight
	Autoroute
	Main road
	Minor road
	Railway
H	Recommended hotel
◪	Vineyard
✈	Airport
	Chapter boundary

0 Kilometres — 20
0 Miles — 15

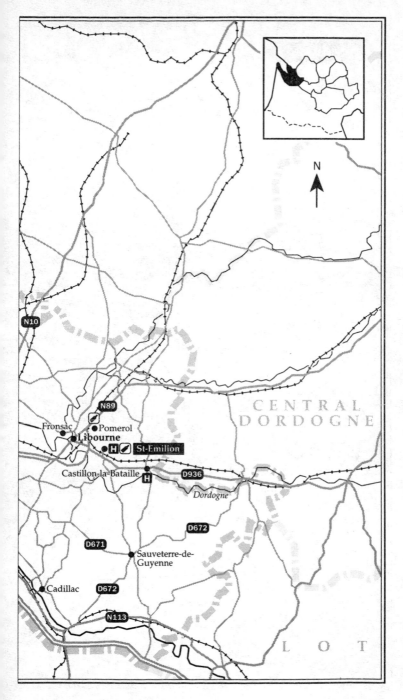

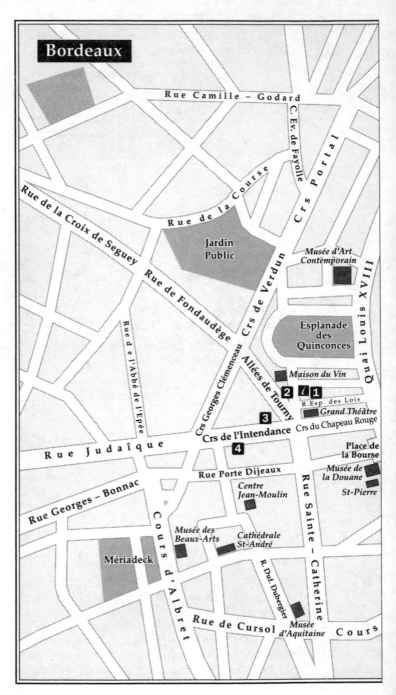

Bordeaux

Rue Camille – Godard

C. Ev. de Fayolle

Crs Portal

Rue de la Course

Rue de la Croix de Seguey

Rue de la Course

Rue de Fondaudège

Rue de l'Abbé de l'Epée

Crs de Verdun

Jardin Public

Musée d'Art Contemporain

Esplanade des Quinconces

Quai Louis XVIII

Crs Georges Clémenceau

Allées de Tourny

Maison du Vin

2 *i* **1**

R.Esp. des Lois

Grand Théâtre

3

Crs de l'Intendance

Crs du Chapeau Rouge

4

Rue Judaïque

Place de la Bourse

Musée de la Douane

St-Pierre

Rue Porte Dijeaux

Centre Jean-Moulin

Rue Georges – Bonnac

Cours d'Albret

Musée des Beaux-Arts

Cathédrale St-André

Rue Sainte – Catherine

Mériadeck

R.Duf. Dubergier

Rue de Cursol

Musée d'Aquitaine

Cours

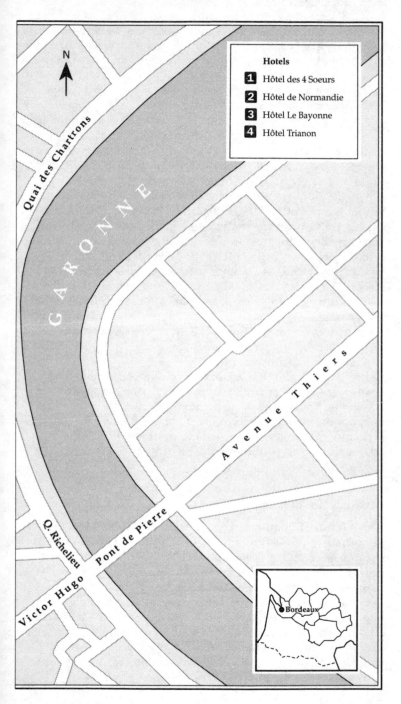

31

chocolates and carnival masks, old books and white porcelain until they emerge exhausted before the gaunt massive shape of the Cathédrale St-André, primed for a coffee and a snack in the Café Français opposite.

Those with more leisure stroll through the narrow streets behind the church of St-Pierre to the east of the shopping zone, gazing in the windows of antiquarian booksellers and summing up the rival merits of English writing desks and Louis XVI chairs before settling down to a brandy and the newspaper in the quiet and beautiful Place du Parlement, once the Marché Royal, and surrounded by Louis XV houses.

On the northern side of the Esplanade des Quinconces, a further tranche of Bordeaux life can be explored. Once a fashionable area for eighteenth-century high life, the streets behind the Quai des Chartrons declined in the nineteenth, but are being injected with new life. Here is the Cité Mondiale des Vins et des Spiritueux – a wine merchants' meeting house and market. Here, too, is the Musée d'Art Contemporain in a cavernous warehouse of brick and glass. Not to be missed is the Village des Antiquaires in the Rue Notre-Dame. And if you come in October at the time of the new vintage, you may see barrel-rollers racing in the streets, twirling wine casks one-handed around the market place.

Bordeaux is unusual in having a number of good-value hotels right in the centre, making it a relaxing city to explore. Everything you are likely to want to see is easily reached on foot, but there are buses in plenty if you need them. Parking in the centre is expensive if you want to stay more than an hour or two; it may be worth leaving the car further out and taking a bus.

Around the centre

The **Grand Théâtre**, architectural star of Bordeaux, was completed in 1780 on the site of a Roman temple, whose remains were pulled down to make way for it. Appropriately enough, the building's exterior imitates a classical shrine, with a large peristyle of 12 columns surmounted by statues of muses and goddesses. It is easier said than done to get into the interior – tour times vary and you must book in person at the tourist office – but visit if you can to see the frescoed ceiling and the enormous single chandelier which dangles over the stalls. A profusion of carved and gilded wood, numerous swags and statues complete the impression of opulence.

If the theatre is the shrine of the arts, a second, secular shrine lies diagonally opposite in the shape of the **Maison du Vin,** housed in an eighteenth-century building of considerable splendour. The *Grand Salon* on the ground floor, a formal place of pillars, tapestries and stained glass, is open to the public. Do not be put off by the hushed atmosphere – the institution exists to publicise the wine industry, and the range of leaflets available is so comprehensive that you need go nowhere else for information. The various *appellations* which make up the Bordeaux wine region each produce lists of châteaux open to visitors, and all these lists are available here. There is also a video, and maps and address lists, with telephone numbers of vineyards throughout the region. The only problem is sifting through all the information and deciding exactly what you want to do with it. At 11 and 3 there are free wine tastings, and more sophisticated two-hour sessions (a charge is made) operate according to demand.

A third place worth a stop in the city centre is **La Vinothèque**, a wine shop sandwiched between the Grand Théâtre and the tourist office on the Cours du 30 Juillet. This claims to sell over 200 Bordeaux wines, at prices to suit all pockets; even a quick stroll past the crates and racks is enough to give you an intimation of the size of the wine industry here.

Lastly there is the Bordeaux tourist office, a very efficient example of the breed. This is the place to book tours, both of the city and of the vineyards (the latter in half- or full-day versions). If you do not know much about wine, taking one of the vineyard tours makes an excellent introduction.

A short walk north of the Grand Théâtre takes you to the Esplanade des Quinconces (incidentally an extremely convenient, if expensive place to leave a car). The monument commemorating the Girondins at its western edge is part pillar and part fountain, the fountain a gargantuan creation involving sea-horses, chariots and multiple gushes of water. The unfortunate Girondins were a powerful faction during the early days of the French Revolution, who got their name because several of their leaders were from the Bordeaux area. They eventually fell from grace and were executed for favouring a federal rather than centralist state.

The most interesting eating place in the immediate area is the Brasserie 'La Belle Epoque' at 2 Allées d'Orléans (tel 56 44 75 37), where you can eat well under a splendid painted ceiling in an inimitable turn-of-the-century interior.

A short walk south-east along the river on the Quai de la Douane brings you to the elegant architecture of the Place de la Bourse, rather out of place behind the riverside highway. One wing houses the **Musée des Douanes** (open all year, daily exc. Mon 10-12, 2-5, 6 in summer), a curious place given over to the history of the French Customs and its officials, and altogether rarefied in tone. Among bills of lading, uniforms, muskets and anti-smuggler devices rests a tiny collection of confiscated works of art, some of them, if genuine, by artists more usually found in fine arts museums.

Behind the Place de la Bourse, the **Quartier St-Pierre** is a maze of narrow streets and largely unrestored houses. This is one of the oldest quarters of Bordeaux, settled during medieval times and still retaining something of the atmosphere of the days before boulevards and neo-classical architecture. The Eglise St-Pierre was heavily renovated in the nineteenth century and is not especially interesting. The pleasures of this quarter lie more in the variety of small shops along its streets and in glimpses of what remains of the old city gates, of which the **Porte Cailhau** (1495) and the **Grosse Cloche** are impressively medieval and spiky.

There are four excellent eating places round here. Chez Gilles, at 6 rue Lauriers (tel 56 81 17 38), is modern and friendly and makes a great spot for lunch. Didier Gélineau, 26 Rue Pas-St-Georges (tel 56 52 84 25), is more elegant and intimate, with fresh flowers. The duck is particularly recommended. La Chamade is close by, at 20 Rue Piliers-de-Tutelle (tel 56 48 13 74). Close to the Place de la Bourse at 7-8 Place Jean Jaurès is Jean Ramet (tel 56 54 12 51/56 52 19 80), which has the best reputation in Bordeaux and would make an excellent place for an evening out. It is not large inside so book in advance. A longish walk or a taxi journey towards the Gare St Jean will bring you to La Tupina at 6 Rue de la Porte Monnaie (tel 56 91 56 37).

The goal of this southward wandering should be the **Musée d'Aquitaine** (open all year, daily exc Mon 10-6). Thoroughly up to date in presentation and extremely cleverly thought out, this is probably the best archaeological and historical museum in the whole of the Dordogne basin. One particular strong point is the excellent collection of Stone Age artefacts, including some delicate engravings from caves and rock shelters too fragile to leave in their original positions. Another is the assembly of Roman remains from Bordeaux itself, organised thematically with an especially lucid display of Roman burial customs and funerary rites. The Stone Age and the Romans are followed by early medieval and high Gothic sections, and so on down the ages.

What is inspiring is less what the collection contains than the way it is put together. Walking through gives a clear sense of historical progression, so that an archway or a column is presented to you again and again – one Roman, another Gothic, and so on, enabling you to perceive the evolution of objects, customs and buildings from our earliest ancestors onwards. Clever use of spotlights helps to stress particularly important objects, while split levels, recesses and well-positioned chairs with books or pamphlets piled beside them create an atmosphere belonging more to a sumptuous art gallery than to a conventional museum. All in all, this is a place not to be missed.

Around the cathedral

The big **Cathédrale St-André** (not much smaller than Notre-Dame in Paris) is rather a muddled building, partly because its construction and reconstruction lasted for more than 400 years, from the eleventh to the fifteenth centuries, and partly because it was not too well built in the first place and needed a great many supplementary props and buttresses to keep it upright. It is an impressive whale of a place, long and thin on the outside and garnished with a distinguished spire, bare and grey and peaceful within, with a lofty chancel illuminated by stained glass. The Gothic tympanum above the Porte Royale entrance has a carving of the Last Judgement – an interesting contrast in style if you have been saturated with the Romanesque art further inland.

Opposite the cathedral, the **Centre Jean-Moulin** (open all year, Mon-Fri 2-6) commemorates one of France's greatest Resistance heroes, the man who was chosen to unify the Resistance network within France but who was betrayed to the Gestapo and executed. This is one of the better Resistance museums, with ample documentation, an especially good collection of photographs, including many of wartime Bordeaux, and a graphic and nasty portrayal of the fate of French deportees in the Nazi camps.

The municipal centre of Bordeaux lies west of the cathedral, where the restrained, classical town hall is complemented by a colourful and shady garden (open until 9pm). At the far end of the garden, the **Musée des Beaux-Arts** (open all year, daily exc Tue 10-6) owes much of the importance of its collection to Napoleon, who handed over some of his looted artworks in 1801. Under restoration (full opening projected for 1995), the museum currently hangs only its best works – and all in a single gallery, but a glance at the Titian, Vasari and Veronese shows the strength of the Italian Renaissance works, while from Flanders and the Netherlands there is Jan Brueghel's spirited *Wedding Dance* and a typically well-balanced van Ruysdael landscape. Delacroix' *Greece on the Ruins of Missolonghi* is the gallery's best-known Romantic work, but there is, too, the gory *Fire on the Steamer Austria* by Isabey. Boudin represents the Impressionists, and from the modern period Picasso, Matisse and Kokoschka are the most noteworthy. The museum is worth visiting even in its current state; once the restoration is complete it will be unmissable.

The **Musée des Arts Décoratifs** (open all year, daily exc Tue 2-6) is less exceptional but still interesting if you are at all keen on furniture (of which there is a lot), apothecaries' jars, glasswork or pottery. All is brought together in the *salon Bordelais*, a homely interior from the early nineteenth century full of tasteless clutter.

Quartier des Chartrons

Taking its name from an ancient monastic foundation, this is the district sandwiched between the Cours Portal and the Quai des Chartrons. Wine merchants wishing to be near the port built fine mansions here, and the trade with the colonies added warehouses. Today this quarter is a maze of small streets running off the Rue Notre-Dame. Its chief attraction for the visitor is without a doubt the **Village des Antiquaires** in Rue Notre-Dame, a labyrinth of shops and stalls, some seemingly roofed by carpets, others selling brass elephants, full of antiques and charm in equal proportions. A happy morning's browsing can be spent here, followed by lunch at the Crêperie du Port, 73 Rue Notre-Dame (tel 56 51 17 01), which is more of a passage lined by second-hand books than a restaurant, but with bags of atmosphere and *crêpes* and good fish soup.

The enormous glass and steel **Cité Mondiale du Vin** is worth viewing, although the inside is given over to the professionals. However, the **Musée des Chartrons** (open all year, daily exc Sun and Mon 10-12.30, 2-5.30), housed in an eighteenth-century Irish merchant's house, is a more interesting affair. In the old bottling room there is an exhibition of all the peripheral objects associated with the wine trade, in particular labels and bottles, together with a description of how Bordeaux wine was shipped and traded through the centuries. This museum is often a stop on various wine tours, so beware of having to visit it twice!

On the way back to the centre, visit the **Musée d'Art Contemporain** (open all year, daily exc Mon 11-7) where, in a warehouse-like interior, striking exhibitions are held – perhaps colourful frenzies of paint or rows of greying-white hospital beds.

THE VINEYARDS

The Bordeaux wine-growing region extends along both banks of the Garonne and the Dordogne from close to the Pointe de Grave at the mouth of the Gironde to the departmental boundary. While the surface area is large, it is manageable enough: nowhere in the area is more than a couple of hours' journey by car from Bordeaux. The problem lies more with the complexities of the various *appellations* and in the sheer number of wine-producers: there are over 50 different *appellations* and the number of properties runs into the thousands.

The professional who knows exactly what he or she is in search of and where it is likely to be found has less difficulty in getting satisfaction out of touring the Bordeaux vineyards than the ordinary tourist, who may well have drunk the occasional bottle of claret and have heard of names of châteaux, such as Mouton-Rothschild or villages, such as Margaux, but will be bewildered by the sheer number of things to explore. Our advice would be:

● Start by going on one of the organised wine tours. Most provide a good introduction to the history of Bordeaux wine and the process of making it, together with visits to châteaux. There is usually an English interpreter, and it is possible to take in a lot of information in a short space of time. Tours are organised by the Bordeaux tourist office (tel 56 44 28 41).

● Get one of the excellent maps of the Bordeaux vineyards (the Bordeaux Maison du Vin is a good source). This shows all the different *appellations* and the areas covered by them.

● For a gentle do-it-yourself tour, choose the Entre-Deux-Mers region, not, perhaps, an area with the most interesting wines, but with gently pretty scenery and many small properties. For a short, intense visit, try St-Emilion, starting with the excellent Maison du Vin in the town itself. To gaze at grand châteaux and make lists of famous names, drive through the Médoc (though do not expect inspiring scenery), and for a general mixture of all of these, make for the Pomerol and Lalande-de-Pomerol areas.

● If you want to buy wine in small quantities, your best bet is either one of the many shops in Bordeaux itself or else the Maisons du Vin in the centre of the various *appellations* (St-Emilion has an especially good one). Prices in the latter will not be much more expensive than at the châteaux themselves, and someone will be on hand to give you advice. If you visit individual châteaux, it is considered polite to buy at least one bottle as a small thank-you for the owner's time, especially if it is a small, family enterprise.

The Médoc

The Médoc is the area on the west bank of the Gironde which runs north-west from Bordeaux. To the west lies the sandy, pine-forested area of the Landes. On the bank of the river and immediately inland, the Médoc is an area whose soil – poor and gravelly with outbreaks of chalky clay – has proved perfect for some of the world's greatest wines. To see the big names in wine and to visit the ostentatious (and often vulgar) châteaux that go with them, this is the place to come. Half a day's drive will take you from the western side of town out to the limits of the wine-growing area.

It has to be said that there is not much to see except for the ranks of vines, the occasional lavish château or gateway, and a series of villages where the housing looks distinctly run down for such a prosperous area. The further from Bordeaux you venture, the more rural the scenery becomes.

Visiting many of the best-known châteaux can be arranged only by appointment. Some are snooty with it, others are not. There is no harm in trying for an appointment at Château Mouton-Rothschild, a very opulent but visitor-friendly property, with a good personal collection of wine-related *objets d'art*. Indeed, you may be able to be squeezed into a group if you just turn up. A good place to make preliminary enquiries is the tourist office in Pauillac, self-styled capital of the Médoc and with a long history as an intermediate port on the way in or out of Bordeaux.

A typical tour of one of the more famous châteaux does not differ much from one of the smaller properties. You probably will not see much of the interior of the château. Instead, you will tour the cellars (known locally as *chais*), see the wine in vats, casks or bottles, be taken through the process of grape-growing and wine-making, and then be allowed to taste the local product. However, it's worth noting that the more famous the château the less likely there is to be a free glass of the best vintage.

If you need a meal while in the Médoc, several restaurants are designed for lunching wine merchants and are therefore plush places. Better for the casual visitor is either the Lion d'Or in Arcins (tel 56 58 96 79), an excellent roadside family-run place, or else the simple but extremely friendly Les Glycines in Lamarque (tel 56 58 94 79).

Rather than return down the peninsula the way you came, take the ferry across the Gironde from Lamarque (a board with sailing schedules is by the pier) and return down the east bank from Blaye. Blaye itself is rather too industrial to be pleasant, but is graced by a citadel of considerable size designed by the famous military engineer Marquis de Vauban. The whole medieval town had to be destroyed to make room for it!

The east bank of the Gironde is far hillier than the Médoc and correspondingly much more attractive to tour through. Wine properties are a good deal less pretentious too, and this is a much better area in which to visit small growers with a view to tasting the product and enjoying a chat. Other diversions apart from the wines include the **Roman villa at Plassac**, south of Blaye (open daily June-Sept 9-12, 2-7), where there are some superb mosaics.

Bourg, a hilltop village with a separate port on the Dordogne beneath, is the place from which to look out over the junction of the Garonne and the Dordogne.

St-Emilion and around

There is nowhere in the whole of the Bordeaux region to match St-Emilion for beauty or atmosphere, which is why, paradoxically, the town is best avoided in the height and heat of summer when the tourists throng the streets. It is at its best in the evenings, when the lights of the houses sparkle all around the natural amphitheatre in the hills where the town is sited. This setting is mostly what makes St-Emilion what it is: from the rim of the amphitheatre you can gaze down on the roofs of the houses and the narrow market place before picking your way down the steep, cobbled streets towards one of the town's many restaurants.

St-Emilion is at the centre of a prime wine *appellation*; it is prosperous and clean, with vineyards stretching up to the walls of the houses. Its fame dates back to antiquity, for it was near here that the Latin scholar and poet Ausonius lived, writing to his friends that he could not bring himself to leave his beloved patch of country in order to visit them. Today's town owes its name to a hermit-saint who lived in a cave among the chalky cliffs.

A lot remains from the medieval period in St-Emilion, and a stroll through the town (it is far from large) will take you past the most interesting monuments. Chief among these is the **Eglise Monolithe** (guided tours nine times a day in summer, eight in winter), a semi-subterranean church carved out of caves and tunnels between the eighth and twelfth centuries. From the outside, little can be seen except windows carved into a rock wall with a huge fifteenth-century spire built on top. Inside, however, a triple nave has been carved out of the rock, leaving rectangular pillars to support the vault. The weight of the tower above made emergency underpinning a necessity some years ago. The same stroll takes in the **Chapelle de la Trinité**, a small Gothic chapel built over what is assumed to be the original cave where Saint Emilion lived, complete with his bed, his chair (carved from rock) and a source of fresh water. Further caves and tunnels were once the catacombs; you can see the tombs carved out of the soft rock.

On the top of the slope to the west, the **Château du Roi** is a small cubic keep, possibly built in the thirteenth century. There is not much to see, but the view of the town from the base of the old castle is probably the best there is.

Balancing the secular with the religious, the other dominant building on the skyline is the **Collégiale**, a very large church indeed for such a small town. Its Romanesque nave and its Gothic choir are less of a draw than the fourteenth-century Last Judgement sculpted above the main doorway, which, although much mutilated, is still worth finding.

A last ecclesiastical sight is the **Cloître des Cordeliers,** now little more than a sequence of ruined fourteenth-century archways and walls, in the middle of which fork-lift trucks loaded with crates of wine may suddenly appear.

After the sightseeing, descend to the Place du Marché to see the street life. The town is geared towards tourism – more so than anywhere else in the region – and there is plenty to watch and buy. The Maison du Vin has a lucid description of wine-making and a wide range of St-Emilion wines. The macaroons here are renowned, and plenty of shops sell them. For eating, you will not do better than at Francis Goullée at 27 Rue Guadet (book in advance: there are not many tables. Tel 57 24 70 49).

Close to St Emilion, **Libourne** has long outgrown its *bastide* origins, and is now a big commercial town with shops of every sort and plenty of colourful flower-beds. A short distance west, **Fronsac** has extensive views over the Lower Dordogne, and Château Fronsac is recommended as a good spot for a *dégustation*. The tiny geographical enclaves forming the *appellations* of **Pomerol, Lussac-St-Emilion** and **Montagne-St-Emilion** lie north-east of Libourne and are a good area for wine-lovers to drive around. Here, the vineyards are exceptionally neatly groomed, with carefully cut verges and deep drainage ditches beside the roads. The villages are little more than a clump of cottages and a church among a sea of vines.

Entre-Deux-Mers

The wide, trapezoidal stretch of country lying between the Garonne and the Dordogne east of Bordeaux is, for our money, the most attractive of all the Bordeaux wine districts for the amateur to explore. This is partly because the rolling, soft countryside is full of small, hidden corners and partly because there are one or two old towns whose attractions go beyond the culture of wine.

The star is probably **Cadillac**, down on the banks of the Garonne. This is a thirteenth-century *bastide*, and its ramparts are still in existence, as is its small central square. It lacks the quaintness of the *bastide* towns further east, but is well worth stopping for. On its outskirts, the large **Château des Ducs d'Epernon** (open all year, daily 10-12, 2-6 or 7) dates from the late sixteenth century. Like many another property confiscated during the Revolution, the castle has done its time as a prison. Still, its remarkable fireplaces remain, as do the vast, vaulted cellars.

Beyond Cadillac, **Ste-Croix-du-Mont** is raised above the river on the edge of an escarpment, with good views from the terrace in front of the caves that are used as cellars. This is a very pleasing spot in which to sample a glass of the local produce (very sweet) in the shade.

A short way inland, **Verdelais** is the village where Henri Toulouse-Lautrec lies buried in a simple grave in the cemetery.

He spent several years at the nearby **Château Malromé** (open Apr-June, Sat and Sun 10-7; June-Sept Sat and Sun 10.30-7; rest of year by appointment), and died here, aged 37. It is a particularly beautiful place, and reproductions of Toulouse-Lautrec's drawings are on show in its rooms. The local inn, the Hostellerie Saint-Pierre (tel 56 62 02 03) has a genuine sketch which Toulouse-Lautrec roughed out on one of the walls. This is a friendly family place, recommended for lunch. It has simple rooms if you want to stay overnight.

A trip across the river to **Langon** brings you into the Sauternes area, home of Bordeaux' most famous sweet white wines, with Chateau d'Yquem widely agreed to produce the best. For any other reason than wine-touring, this area and the Graves *appellation* which encloses it are best left alone, for the scenery and the villages are dull.

Instead, head north on the D672, making for **Sauveterre-de-Guyenne**, an unassuming, indeed workaday place, but with

BORDEAUX APPELLATIONS

The Appellation d'Origine Contrôlée (AOC) is a legal guarantee as to the origin of a wine. It has been much refined since its introduction in 1935, and a producer wishing his wine to be allowed to bear an *appellation* must meet strict criteria over such matters as degrees of alcohol, amount of natural sugar, density of planting, grape varieties and so forth. The AOC demands the highest level of conformity to standards – the lesser *appellation* of Vin Delimité de Qualité Supérieure (VDQS) is less demanding, while the Vin de Pays *appellation* allows growers much more flexibility in grape varieties and in blending. Below Vin de Pays is Vin de Table.

In the Bordeaux area there are two regional *appellations*: Bordeaux and Bordeaux Supérieur. Any producer who wishes to can make wines under these AOC. Then there are sub-regional *appellations*, such as Entre-Deux-Mers or Côtes de Blaye. These are territorially strictly defined areas, but may cover quite a large stretch of country. Finally, there are the 'communal' *appellations*, which are limited to perhaps just one village or group of villages, for example Margaux or Pomerol. The Médoc area has the complete hierarchy, with two sub-regional *appellations* (Médoc and Haut-Médoc) and then a series of

its *bastide* origins firmly displayed as a huge central square and four narrow fortified gates. West of here the vines clothe hilltops and slopes as far as the eye can see, with wooded patches breaking the monotony. It is a good region for aimless wandering, looking out for grape-picking machines like mobile car-washes, scenting the wine in the small villages you pass through, and dropping in on any château that takes your fancy.

WHERE TO STAY AND EAT

Key: ✦ = 0-250FF, ✦✦ = 251-450FF, ✦✦✦ = over 451FF; prices are per room without breakfast, which costs around 40-65FF extra. Some hotels insist on half-board during high season. Unless we say otherwise, all have rooms with bath or shower and accept the major credit cards.

communal *appellations*, but other areas may just have the sub-regional or the communal. All these *appellations* will have their own strict definitions, and it will be up to the producer, in areas where he has a choice, which *appellations* he chooses to submit his wines for.

As if this were not enough to take in, there is additionally, the system of classification (established in 1855) of the best château-bottled wines into 'growths', ranging from first (the top) to fifth, with humbler and less expensive *cru bourgeois* wines below them. The first growths are as well-known as they are expensive: Château Lafite, Latour and Mouton-Rothschild in Pauillac, Château Margaux in the village of Margaux and Château Haut-Brion to the south in Graves. The sweet white wines of Sauternes and Barsac were also classified at the same time, while Graves and St Emilion were classified more recently using a simpler system.

Another factor to complicate matters is that many châteaux may regularly produce two wines, the best sold under the château's own name and the second wine (from less favoured parts of the vineyard or younger vines) under another – Château Latour's second wine, for instance, is called Les Forts de Latour.

Recommended hotels

BORDEAUX

Hôtel Trianon
5 Rue du Temple
33000 Gironde   *Tel: 56 48 28 35; Fax: 56 51 17 81*

The Trianon is on a narrow street off the Cours de l'Intendance. Although central, the hotel is sufficiently distant from Bordeaux's main thoroughfare to be free from traffic noise. The interior is simple and the public rooms include a light, airy breakfast area in pastel shades and a more sombre *salon* which appears little used. Bedrooms are of a good size and tastefully decorated, and all are clean and quiet. Rates are very reasonable for the superb central location.

Early Jan-end Dec; no restaurant; 18 rooms

Hôtel le Bayonne
15 Cours de l'Intendance
33000 Gironde   *Tel: 56 48 00 88; Fax: 56 52 03 79*

This well-maintained, eighteenth-century building is ideally located just a five-minute stroll from the Grand Théâtre and within easy walking distance of all the main sights. The hotel has recently been refurbished to include modern facilities, although the public rooms are limited to a small but pleasantly decorated breakfast area next to reception, done out in 1930s style. The bedrooms themselves, although a little small, are well-equipped with modern furnishings.

Early Jan-end Dec; 36 rooms

Hôtel de Normandie ◆◆-◆◆◆
7 et 9 Cours du 30 Juillet
33000 Gironde   *Tel: 56 52 16 80; Fax: 56 51 68 91*

The position of this hotel is unbeatable – opposite the Grand Théâtre and next to the Maison du Vin. It is not as characterful as the 4 Soeurs opposite (see below), but it has been thoroughly refurbished in a modern if somewhat bland style. The bedrooms tend to be on the small side, but it is a civilised, clean and a good value option.

All year; no restaurant; 100 rooms

Hôtel des 4 Soeurs
6 Cours du 30-Juillet
33000 Gironde   *Tel: 57 81 19 20; Fax: 56 01 04 28*

Local legend has it that Wagner stayed here in 1850 and to prove it his portrait takes pride of place in the half-panelled reception area. The public areas include a bar (open to non-residents) and are decorated in exuberant, high-camp style – all dark wooden panelling, elaborate plasterwork, huge mirrors and red velvet. The result is thoroughly over the top but highly characterful. In the bedrooms furnishings have a more modern feel, though each is individually decorated. Room sizes vary considerably – some are a little cramped so it is worth asking to see a room first. The greatest advantage here is the price, as room rates are low for such a superb location.

All year; 35 rooms

CASTELNAU DE MEDOC

Château du Foulon
33480 Gironde   *Tel: 56 58 20 18; Fax: 56 58 23 43*

A chocolate-box setting, ideal if you want to escape the hustle and bustle for a day or two. This beautifully maintained nineteenth-century château is owned by Viscomte J. de Baritault du Carpia and is set amid 50 hectares of woodland, close to the Médoc's famous vineyards and to beautiful pine forests. The setting is truly idyllic and incredibly peaceful, the only sound from the peacocks roaming the grounds. The atmosphere is unexpectedly informal – guests are free to explore the estate and breakfast is a communal affair. The rooms are beautifully decorated in traditional style – bare wooden floors scattered with rugs, huge, elaborately carved beds, gilt mirrors and bureaux stuffed with antique books. Sumptuous accommodation at very reasonable prices.

Early Jan-mid-Dec; no credit cards accepted

CASTILLON-LA-BATAILLE

Château Lardier   ◆-◆◆
Ruch
33350 Gironde   *Tel: 57 40 54 11; Fax: 57 40 70 38*

The exterior of the hotel is in better shape than the interior – a stony track leads to the ivy-covered building situated in the heart of beautiful, undulating countryside. The terrace to the rear has some splendid views and is ideal for relaxing after a hard day's sightseeing or wine-tasting, though the château has its own cellar (*chai*) which is open to residents. Rooms are practical, comfortable and sensibly priced though some furnishings have seen better days and bathrooms are not recommended for visitors who suffer from claustrophobia. Sloping floors and crooked door-frames lend some extra character.

March–mid-Nov, closed Sun pm, Mon in low season; 9 rooms

ST-ANDRE-DE-CUBZAC

Château du Vieux Raquine
Lugon
33240 Gironde   *Tel: 57 84 42 77; Fax: 57 84 83 77*

Although there are just ten rooms, the hotel covers an entire hilltop, which gives an impression of space and provides wonderful views of the surrounding countryside. To the front a small terrace is set among beautiful gardens with mature trees and lawns the size of snooker tables, while to the rear a larger terrace overlooks the meandering Dordogne and sloping vineyards. The bedrooms are all at ground-floor level and look out on to terraces; feature windows in the public areas have panoramic views. The bedrooms are light, airy, good-sized, tastefully decorated with plain walls and bold fabrics, and comfortably furnished.

All year; 10 rooms

ST-EMILION

Auberge de la Commanderie
Rue des Cordeliers
33330 Gironde   *Tel: 57 24 70 19; Fax: 57 74 44 53*

The hotel is housed in two golden stone buildings on either side of a narrow cobbled street. The older part dates from the twelfth century, though most of the rooms are in the main building, which has been done out with a mixture of modern and traditional furnishings. The rooms are clean, comfortable and tastefully decorated, and some have excellent views over St-Emilion. Two family rooms are in the old annexe, which has yet to be refurbished – the décor here is a little dated though this is reflected in the prices.

Mid-Feb-mid-Jan; no restaurant; 17 rooms

Hostellerie de Plaisance
Place du Clocher
33330 Gironde   *Tel: 57 24 72 32; Fax: 57 74 41 11*

Superbly located opposite the tourist office and beneath the bell-tower, with spectacular views over the rooftops of the town and its nearby vineyards, the Hostellerie de Plaisance is immaculately maintained both inside and out. The hotel is set in a small but beautifully verdant garden with an attractive terraced area, and has a distinct character and elegant feel: low peach sofas, tangerine drapes and bare stone walls. All the bedrooms are named after famous châteaux and again have an individual style, perhaps with fabric-covered walls and a mixture of old and new furnishings. Bathrooms are a particular feature.

Feb to Dec; 12 rooms

THE CENTRAL DORDOGNE VALLEY

Between Bergerac and Souillac lies the golden heart of the Dordogne valley. Now the *département* of Dordogne, this is pre-Revolutionary Périgord, a countryside marked as no other by the conflicts that have plagued French history and above all by the Hundred Years' War.

This is a countryside that approaches perfection – one of the reasons why it is enduringly popular with holidaymakers. The landscape has been tamed by man but not trampled upon, and towns, villages and farmhouses are of just the right size and have just the right blend of tradition, prosperity and beauty. However, there is more to the Central Dordogne than this; there is the sense that life here has a quality that is missing elsewhere. It is not possible to pin down this aura of quality that separates out the Central Dordogne from its neighbours to any particular feature. Sunshine, fertile soil, superlative buildings, the peculiar loveliness of the river, the thickness of the light – all these play their part.

This is a region whose pleasures have more to do with a gentle do-it-yourself exploration of half-forgotten byways than with a frantic attempt to see everything there is to see. That said, of all the areas covered by this book, it is the Central Dordogne that has the most to offer by way of conventional sightseeing; it also has the most variety. At the top of the list come the great prehistoric sites of the Vézère valley, notably the painted caves where neolithic man covered walls and ceilings with representations of the animals he lived amongst. Then there are the many castles, spanning all periods from the twelfth to the eighteenth centuries, and the 500 or so Romanesque churches. Museums of all kinds, a distinctive wine region, poultry farms, gardens and Roman remains round off the list. The towns of Bergerac, Périgueux and Sarlat are large enough and historic enough to be worth the better part of a day's exploration, while the *bastide* towns south of the Dordogne river form a small sightseeing circuit of their own.

This wealth of things to see has its own perils. In July and August the area close to the Dordogne valley becomes distinctly overcrowded, not yet to the same degree as the Mediterranean coast perhaps, but badly enough to cause queues for the best sights, fully booked hotels and a shortage of desirable *gîtes*. Very little of the country away from the river is affected by the crowds, however, and if conditions are intolerable in the caves or the castles, it is easy enough to escape. All that is needed is the strength of will to stay away from the most famous sights and to reserve them for a future occasion. May, June or September are the best times to go sightseeing in the Dordogne. However, if you have no choice but to go in high season, it is perfectly possible to have an enjoyable time by booking accommodation well in advance, arriving at sights as soon as they open, and relaxing during the hottest part of the day.

The area's popularity does bring some advantages with it. For a start, you are likely to find some allowance made for visitors who do not speak French. There are guided tours in English (they are not always frequent), English translations of menus and information leaflets and English newspapers in the village shops. If you require this kind of support system, the Central Dordogne is the place to find it.

It is also an excellent region for walking, cycling, or canoeing. The best walking in the Central Dordogne valley is on short circuits out of villages, leading through the scrub woodland or up the river banks, past farms, castles or prehistoric sites. Every tourist office is awash with leaflets and booklets that are full of suggestions for walks – many of them printed in English.

No introduction to the area can ignore the food. Périgord is the home of *pâté de foie gras*, truffles and walnuts. Poultry of all kinds are reared; the strawberries are magnificent and the wild fungi rich in variety and aroma. Probably the best place to sample these things is in one of the many *fermes auberges*, which are strewn throughout the area. To eat a huge and rich lunch in a farm kitchen, where the produce is fresh from the fields, is an experience that ought not to be missed. All tourist offices have lists of participating farms; it is then merely a matter of reserving a table and arriving on time.

There are also farms that you can visit to see how geese and ducks are fattened for *pâté de foie gras*. This process (*gavage*) involves force-feeding the birds with large quantities of maize. It is worth noting that if you are sensitive the sight may not be pleasurable and you may have to forswear one of France's great delicacies in future.

If you eat out extensively in restaurants, you may find the menus here too similar to one another for prolonged enjoyment. The food is rich to a degree almost forgotten in health-conscious Britain, and poultry dishes almost always take up 90 per cent of the menu. When you become sated, the local markets come into their own; shopping in them is a pleasure, and picnics something to be relished.

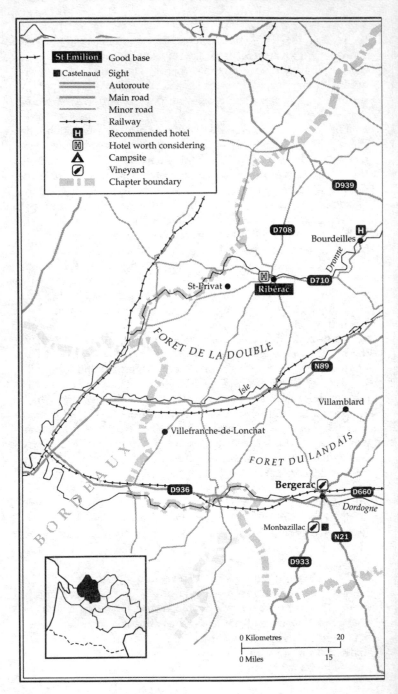

St Emilion	Good base
Castelnaud	Sight
	Autoroute
	Main road
	Minor road
	Railway
H	Recommended hotel
H	Hotel worth considering
▲	Campsite
	Vineyard
	Chapter boundary

D939

D708

Bourdeilles H

Dronne

St-Privat ●

H Ribérac D710

FORET DE LA DOUBLE

N89

Isle

Villamblard ●

● Villefranche-de-Lonchat

FORET DU LANDAIS

B O R D E A U X

D936

Bergerac ▱

D660

Dordogne

Monbazillac ▱ ■

N21

D933

0 Kilometres   20

0 Miles   15

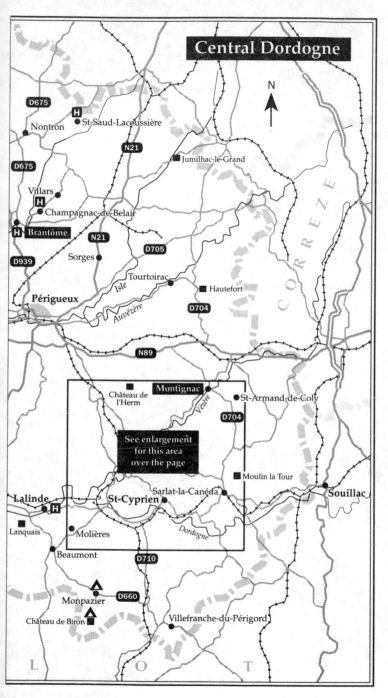

Central Dordogne

D675
Nontron
H St-Saud-Lacoussière
N21
Jumilhac-le-Grand
D675
Villars
H
Champagnac-de-Belair
H Brantôme
N21
D705
Sorges
D939
Tourtoirac
Isle
Hautefort
Périgueux
Auvézère
D704
N89
Château de
l'Herm
Montignac
St-Armand-de-Coly
Vézère
D704
See enlargement
for this area
over the page
Moulin la Tour
Lalinde
St-Cyprien
Sarlat-la-Canéda
Souillac
H
Lanquais
Molières
Dordogne
Beaumont
D710
D660
Monpazier
Château de Biron
Villefranche-du-Périgord
L   O   T

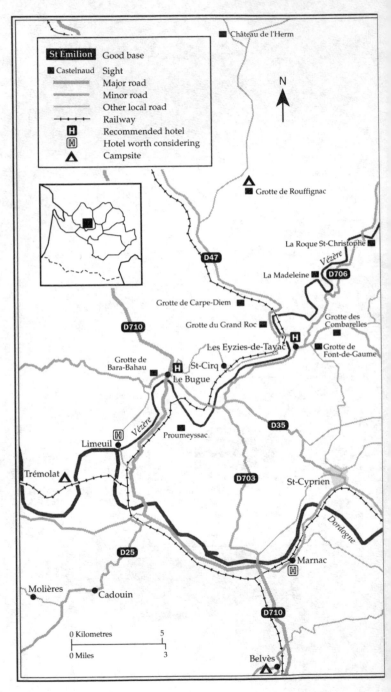

St Emilion — Good base
Castelnaud — Sight
Major road
Minor road
Other local road
Railway
Ⓗ Recommended hotel
Ⓗ Hotel worth considering
△ Campsite

N

Château de l'Herm

△ Grotte de Rouffignac

La Roque St-Christophe ■

Vézère

D47

La Madeleine ■   D706

Grotte de Carpe-Diem ■

D710

Grotte du Grand Roc ■

Grotte des Combarelles ■

Les Eyzies-de-Tayac ● Ⓗ

Grotte de Bara-Bahau ■   Ⓗ St-Cirq ●

Grotte de Font-de-Gaume ■

Le Bugue

Vézère

Proumeyssac ■

D35

Ⓗ Limeuil ●

Trémolat △

D703   St-Cyprien

Dordogne

D25

Marnac ●
Ⓗ

Molières ●   Cadouin ●

D710

0 Kilometres   5
0 Miles   3

Belvès ●
△

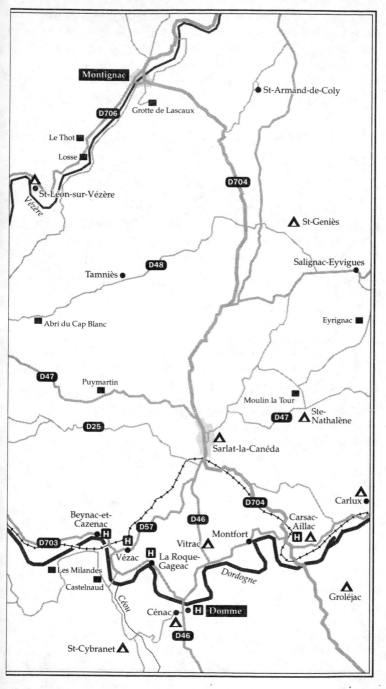

Montignac

St-Armand-de-Coly

D706

Grotte de Lascaux

Le Thot

Losse

D704

St-Léon-sur-Vézère

Vézère

St-Geniès

Salignac-Eyvigues

Tamniès

D48

Abri du Cap Blanc

Eyrignac

D47

Puymartin

Moulin la Tour

D25

D47

Ste-Nathalène

Sarlat-la-Canéda

Carlux

Beynac-et-Cazenac

D57

D46

Montfort

Carsac-Aillac

D703

Vézac

H

Vitrac

D704

H

La Roque-Gageac

Dordogne

Les Milandes

Castelnaud

Céou

Cénac

H Domme

Groléjac

St-Cybranet

D46

Beware of the truffle. This strange fungus, looking like a blackened owl pellet is not only incredibly expensive but is also often abused: Dordogne menus are rich in dishes with slivers of truffle added – notably the omelettes – but such dishes are very seldom worth the extra cost. Put off spending money on truffles until you find a restaurant with an excellent chef.

THE DORDOGNE FROM BERGERAC TO SOUILLAC

This is a long stretch of river, but most of its visitors cram themselves into the comparatively short section between St-Cyprien and Souillac, where it is undoubtedly at its most beautiful, and where all the best villages and castles are found. The area around Bergerac, and certainly the town of Bergerac itself

Good bases

● **Ribérac** This town on the Dronne is at the heart of a popular self-catering area in the gentle countryside to the north-west. The town itself has little historical interest but is renowned for its market.

● **Montignac** At the upper end of the Vézère valley, Montignac is preferable to the over-exploited Les Eyzies-de-Tayac as a base from which to explore the nearby prehistoric sights. It is a small town with enough character to be interesting. For self-catering, the country immediately to the east is some of the most attractive in the Dordogne river basin.

● **Brantôme** The 'Venice of Périgord' lies on the Dronne within easy reach of Périgueux. The town, tucked into a bend of the river, is lovely and has a fair range of accommodation. The countryside immediately south of the river is the place to look for cottages to rent.

● **Domme** This fortified town on the edge of the Dordogne valley is one of the most beautiful in Périgord. During the summer holidays it becomes appallingly overcrowded, but if you use it as a base (it has a good hotel; see Where to Stay) you catch it at its best in morning or evening. The countryside to the south is attractive too. It is well positioned for exploring the chief sights of the Dordogne valley.

forms a worthwhile stop on the way into this Dordogne heart-
land; but immediately upstream of Bergerac there are only a
few scattered sights, while the river has lost most of its shingly
appeal and has begun to take on the sluggish aspect of a river of
the flatlands.

Bergerac

Bergerac lays claim to be the capital of south-west Périgord and
is at the centre of the tobacco-growing industry as well as of its
own wine region. So even if the river trade and the pilgrimage
routes, both of which were important to the town in earlier
days, no longer exist, it is still a busy place. It was once the
Protestant intellectual stronghold of the south-west. When the
Edict of Nantes was revoked, and freedom of worship no
longer tolerated, many of its people emigrated to the
Netherlands and England.

For visitors, all the interest of the town lies in the old quarter. This compact area lies on the north side of the river and has
been excellently restored, with cars banished from most of its
narrow streets and squares. At the centre of this labyrinthine
area, the Place de la Myrpe is a suitable starting point for exploration. At one end is a statue of Cyrano de Bergerac, the long-
nosed romantic hero created by the playwright Edmond
Rostand in 1897. His central character was based on a seventeenth-century eccentric philosopher-writer, but this 'real'
Cyrano had nothing to do with the town from which he took
his name – not that this has prevented Bergerac from basking in
his reputation.

At the western end of the Place de la Myrpe, the **Musée de
la Batellerie et de la Tonnellerie** (open all year, daily exc.
Sat pm, Sun and Mon, 10–12, 1.30–5.30; open Sun in high
season 2.30–6.30) is the most interesting museum in town. It
traces two elements of Bergerac's history, barrel making and
river transport, all admirably laid out and explained. Huge
casks, cauldrons, pots and tools form most of the first exhibit;
model boats, old photographs and maps most of the second.
The difficulties of the river traffic among the shallows and
shoals of the Dordogne are brought to life, and there is a
picture of the crew of the last *gabarre* on the river, grinning at
the camera beside their small boat.

The **Musée du Tabac** (open all year, Tue–Fri, 10–12, 2–6,
Sat 10–12, 2–5, Sun 2.30–6.30) in the Place du Feu is rather a
more higgledy-piggledy place, laid out on three floors of a fine

old house. Exhibits on the early history of the tobacco habit are fascinating, and there is a splendid collection of snuffboxes and pipes, but little from modern times is on show. Bergerac is the centre of the Dordogne tobacco-growing industry and if you want to know more about it, the **Institut du Tabac de Bergerac** (tel 53 63 66 00) is open during summer weekdays, with videos, fields of tobacco plants and a drying shed.

In the same building as the tobacco museum, the **Musée d'Histoire Urbaine** has assembled remnants of old Bergerac. The maps and old engravings show how much the town has changed.

Back in the Place de la Myrpe, the **Cloître des Récollets** was once a monastery and is now a wine institute. It is open in July and August for visits to the ancient cellars and to the modern Maison du Vin. The **Maison du Vin** is the place to start an exploration of the Bergerac wine region. Its most famous *appellation* is Monbazillac (see below); Pécharmant is the other wine to look out for. The region extends downstream almost as far as the junction with the Bordeaux vineyards and, while not very scenic, may make a good alternative to wading through the dense complexity of the Bordeaux wines.

Bergerac is full of small eating places. There's a good Moroccan restaurant, Le Sud (tel 53 27 26 81), on Rue Ancien Pont in the old town, and La Treine (tel 53 57 60 11) on Quai Salvette serves good regional food.

Around Bergerac

The **Château de Monbazillac** (open Oct–mid-Jan, mid-Feb–Apr, daily exc. Mon, 10–12 & 2–5; May, daily, 10–12, 2–6; June–Sept, daily 10–12.30, 2–7.30) stands on a hilltop due south of Bergerac. This is the home of the most famous of the Bergerac wines – a honey-coloured, highly flavoured dessert wine to match the best Bordeaux ones. The château dates from the sixteenth century, is styled midway between a fortress and a Renaissance home and is extremely picturesque, with round towers at the corners and pointed gables rising above the elaborate windows. The interior is remarkable only for its *grande salle*, which has a huge Renaissance fireplace, but the tour comes complete with a *dégustation*. Views from the hilltop are excellent.

Upstream of Bergerac, **Lalinde**, nowadays too industrial to be pretty, was once an English *bastide*. Here, in earlier times, lived a huge dragon called Coulobre, which preyed on the boatmen of the Dordogne until ordered by Saint Front to throw itself on a bonfire. A Romanesque chapel on the south bank marks the dragon's lair. At **Lanquais**, a short distance to the south-west, is another Renaissance château (open Apr–end Sept, daily exc Thur in low season, plus weekends in Oct, 10–12, 3–6) not dissimilar to Monbazillac, but with fewer elaborate windows and less pleasing proportions. The interior is worth seeing for the superb carving on some of the fireplaces.

Badefols-sur-Dordogne is dominated by the remains of a twelfth-century castle. This was once the haunt of Seguin de Badefols, the worst of the many robber-barons who terrorised the country during and after the Hundred Years' War. He even went as far as to attack the pope at Avignon before dying of poison.

At **Trémolat** the Dordogne circumscribes a great meander under limestone cliffs, prefiguring the even better ones to come. A viewpoint high on the cliff edge takes in the whole bend. There's a wonderful domed fortified church in the village, with enough space in the chambers above the vault to shelter the inhabitants of the whole village.

St-Cyprien to Castelnaud

All that remains of the once-powerful monastery at St-Cyprien is its massive church, complete with the fortified bell-tower known in these parts as a *clocher-donjon*. Around the church is the oldest part of the village, with some striking houses, especially the Renaissance presbytery; the **Château de Fages** above the village adds to the general charm of the place. There's good walking on the small lanes in the woods behind the village, with various châteaux or villages to act as goals, notably the castle of **La Roque**, a bizarre collection of architectural styles, and the tiny hamlets of Finsac and Baran.

A further village worth pausing in is **Bézenac**, just above the road (D703). A Romanesque church and a stone cross are all there is to see, but the situation is very fine.

Les Milandes

(Open Apr–end Sept, daily, 9.30–11.30, 2–6; July and Aug, daily 9.30–6.30.)
This late fifteenth-century château owes its fame less to any architectural merit than as the home of Josephine Baker, cabaret superstar, and her 'world village' of abandoned children whom she adopted. The château is full of mementoes of her

life, chronologically arranged from room to room, mixing rather oddly with various pieces of antique furniture belonging to the previous owners. The black marble bathroom is an unusual sight in a Gothic castle. For those interested in Josephine Baker and her life, this is a fascinating place; otherwise go elsewhere as it is pricey and the incidental attractions (some rather bedraggled falcons) are not up to much.

Beynac-et-Cazenac

Beynac, the first of the sequence of riverside villages built in the shadow of a looming precipice and crowned with a castle, is not to be missed. The immediate river frontage in summer is not the best part – half-naked canoeists and ice-cream eaters dodge among the souvenir stalls. Once into the village, however, things improve. Mounting the streets, which sometimes approach the vertical, you will find numerous terraced cafés in which to pause and take a breather, and shops selling craftwork of all kinds. The houses are mostly sixteenth- and seventeenth-century, and look it. The **Musée de la Protohistoire** (open Mar–mid-Nov, daily 10–6) has a rather tedious exhibition inside; its nearby outdoor archaeological park has reconstructed buildings from prehistory to Gaulish times and is much more fun, especially if you take children.

However, the **Château de Beynac** (open June–Sept, daily 10–12, 2–6; rest of year, daily, 2–5) is the most important sight in the village. The best approach is on foot up through the village, but you can also reach it by car. It is a tremendously strong castle, protected on one side by the 150-metre cliff overhanging the Dordogne and the village beneath, and on the other by a double barbican, double ditch and massive ramparts. What you see was built or embellished between the thirteenth and eighteenth centuries, but the history of Beynac as a stronghold and key to the Dordogne goes back much further – to the days when the castle was known as 'Satan's arch' on account of the cruelty of its barons.

The guided tours are excellent, full of interesting anecdotes and details, such as how the mules were sheltered along with the local inhabitants in time of war, or why pine resin was used as a supplement to boiling oil.

The most fascinating part of the interior is the oratory, where a playful medieval fresco shows the supper at Cena attended by Christ and various local worthies along with the Apostles. Rows of toes peep from beneath the diners' robes.

The tour takes you to the topmost and most vertiginous parapet of the place, from where you are encouraged to view the curling valley beneath and pick out the castle of Castelnaud in the middle distance.

Beynac (French) and Castelnaud (English) glared at each other across the river during the long wars between the countries. Each had its subsidiary castle – Fayrac stands opposite Beynac and surveys it; Marqueyssac is opposite Castelnaud. The English were never able to take Beynac – it is easy enough to see why.

Beynac is an excellent place to fix up a canoeing or kayaking trip. From Cénac, eight kilometres upstream, down to Beynac is probably the best section of the Dordogne to go boating on, in terms of both the scenery and the ease of passage. Numerous canoe-hire companies around Beynac will take you upstream and kit you out. The efficient tourist office in the village has full details.

Castelnaud

(Open Mar, Apr and Oct–mid-Nov, daily 10–6; May, June and Sept, daily 10–7; July and Aug, daily 9–8; mid-Nov–Mar, daily exc Sat, 2–7.)

On the opposite side of the river from Beynac and built on a similar precipitous site, Castelnaud is the least altered medieval fortress in the whole region. It is less well preserved than Beynac, having been abandoned at the beginning of the eighteenth century, but plenty remains to be explored. Huge curtain walls loom over the little village beneath and there is a massive round tower and further bastions to protect the drawbridge.

During the Hundred Years' War this was an English stronghold, contesting control of the river passes with Beynac. The English had a less easy time than the lords of Beynac, since they had to repossess Castelnaud five times after losing it to turncoats or military force. Perhaps to celebrate its English antecedents, it has a guided tour in English (12 noon – times may differ, so check beforehand. Tel 53 29 57 08). Alternatively, you can wander around on your own.

The castle, reroofed and restored, now houses a museum of medieval warfare. This is intriguing, since most of the weapons are positioned in the places where they might have been used. Crossbows are poised by arrow slits, and you can watch catapults being fired (only on video, alas).

The story you hear at Castelnaud is that of Anne de Caumont. She was born towards the end of the sixteenth century just before the Wars of Religion and was one of the richest heiresses in France. Her father was assassinated by his groom (poisonous mushrooms, it is said). Her mother brought her up in the fastness of Castelnaud, but at the age of eight she was kidnapped and forced to marry a thirteen-year old boy. He was killed in a duel, aged eighteen and Anne, by then twelve, was forced to remarry. But she was kidnapped again, by her mother's agents, and taken to Paris. Her second husband died, she was promised in marriage again, but this time eloped and married the man she wanted to. Unfortunately, he was worse than the others and abandoned her. Her furious mother had disinherited her and she retired to a nunnery, having lost her only son in battle.

On summer evenings Castelnaud hosts various events – details from the Beynac tourist office.

Castelnaud to Souillac

Just upstream and around the corner from Castelnaud lie two of the Dordogne valley's most popular villages, La Roque-Gageac and Domme. Before reaching them, or if the crowds are simply unbearable, explore the valley of the **river Céou**, which joins the Dordogne under the walls of Castelnaud. Almost at once you are away from the throngs and into a countryside of half-deserted villages. **Daglan** is the village to make for, complete with a fifteenth-century château and crumbling houses. It is also remarkable because of the number of dry-stone igloo-shaped huts (known locally as *bories*) built by generations of peasants on the boundaries of the fields to act as shelters or storerooms. Giving a date to these structures is difficult, but some are thought to go back to prehistoric times, while others may have been built in the nineteenth century. Driving along the lanes or peering over hedges will soon lead you to them – there are more than 300 in the immediate area.

La Roque-Gageac

This is the village that vies with St-Cirq-Lapopie for the title of prettiest village in France. Officially it has won that title, although we prefer its rival. Still, it is extraordinary and is the third most-visited sight in France (after Mont-St-Michel and Rocamadour), so expect crowds. The village is squeezed between river and cliff to such an extent that it would have seemed impossible to build more than a single house here, let alone a village. Yet the houses mount up the cliffside, layer on layer, seemingly part of the rock itself, until they abut the precipice. Even then, in place of a château, there is a troglodytic fort hollowed out of the cliff face.

At first glance the village is off-putting because of the traffic, which roars along the main riverside road beneath, while every house on the roadside has been turned into a café or a shop. But the village grows on you once you are inside it. The golden stone glows; the rock face bounces reflections and heat back from the river; the parade of cars and tourists become merely irrelevant distractions in the foreground of a view that embraces fields of sunflowers and the shimmering of the poplars by the water's edge.

Once it was an important place. It was never taken by any enemy, never belonged to any overlord. In recent times 200 river-boats moored here, trading salt, timber, wine and iron; now they have been replaced by hundreds of canoes, in a tourist village *par excellence*. Miraculously, it is little the worse for it.

Domme

Henry Miller thought Domme the closest place to paradise on Earth. He had obviously not seen it on a summer Saturday, when it more closely resembles the kind of hell reserved for tour operators. Small *bastides* such as this were not designed to welcome huge crowds within their close-set lanes and squares, and there are occasions when the old ramparts seem in danger of bulging under the pressure.

Domme is popular because it is exquisite. In setting, uniformity of architecture and medieval atmosphere, it ranks top of the Périgord *bastide* towns. It is therefore worth taking the trouble to see it at its best; in the early morning before the buses arrive, when the shops are just opening and the village breathes the cool freshness that precedes a hot day; or else in the thickening twilight of the evening, just before the swallows cease swooping over the battlements and while the sun still burnishes the stone. Better still, come in October, with a morning mist shrouding the valley beneath and with only the inhabitants for company.

Domme is built on the edge of a triangular plateau high above the south bank of the Dordogne. Sheer cliffs plunge down to the river on one side; its ramparts and its three forti-fied gateways guard it on the other. The town was founded in 1283; its strategic site was obviously ideal to defend, but its situation did not strike potential settlers as being a practical place in which to make a living, and it did not prosper for a long time. It came into its own in the Hundred Years' War, changing hands between French and English a number of times in the four-teenth and fifteenth centuries. It suffered more, however, during the Wars of Religion, when the Protestant captain, Geoffroi de Vivans, took the place by climbing the cliffs. The ancient castle was destroyed, and little more than fragments remain.

To get the best out of Domme, walk the ramparts on the southern side of town, making sure to see the Porte des Tours, the best fortified gateway you are ever likely to come across. Then walk through the geometric pattern of streets lined by sun-warmed cottages of no great distinction but of great beauty, and end up at the Place de la Halle – the central market square. Here are Domme's most distinguished houses, particularly the Governor's House, which is fifteenth century, and the seven-teenth-century covered market. The latter conceals the entrance to Domme's caves (which you can explore), 500 metres of underground passages, used as a place of refuge for the town's inhabitants for many centuries.

Finally, make your way past the parish church to the very edge of the cliff over the Dordogne valley. This escarpment is the Barre de Domme, and it gives what is without doubt the best view you can have of the valley. Downstream La Roque-Gageac, Castelnaud and Beynac are visible, while upstream the Château de Montfort stands high above its meander.

Close to Domme you will find a good Romanesque church at **Cénac**. Once part of a priory, the church has some very beautiful carved capitals in its interior – the monkeys, and Daniel and the Lions are worth looking out for.

Cingle de Montfort

This is the best known meander on the Dordogne, where the river describes a perfect semicircle beneath towering white and ash-grey cliffs. It is undoubtedly best seen from the water, but views from the road are not to be sniffed at. The bend is made interesting by the spectacular **Château de Montfort**, which seems to sprout from the cliff edge like a pine tree. For a place that has been destroyed and rebuilt six times, the château presents a remarkably harmonious whole – from a distance at least. It jumps into history under a Cathar lord of unlikely cruelty, reputed to have cut off the feet and hands of any Catholic who fell into his clutches. Simon de Montfort took the stronghold during the Albigensian Crusade, then came the Hundred Years' War and the Wars of Religion, both of which caused extensive damage to the château. The château is said to be haunted by the ghost of a woman burned alive during one of the numerous sieges.

At **Caudon**, on the opposite bank, there is a troglodytic chapel burrowed into the cliff face, together with holes used for burial; the tiny hamlet of **Turnac** has a good view, a fifteenth-century mansion and a troglodytic fort but not much else.

Upstream again, the **Château de Fénelon** (open Mar–Oct, daily exc Thur in low season, 10–12, 2–6, 7 in July and Aug), close to Ste-Mondane, is the birthplace of François de Fénelon, the author of *Telemachus*, the anti-Louis XIV tract that prefigured the philosopher Rousseau. The castle is a mixture of medieval and Renaissance, with three great towers and high gabled windows. At **Carlux**, itself a little-visited and pleasing village, there are the ruins of another huge castle, burned during the Hundred Years' War and finally demolished in the fifteenth century. A further castle, **Rignac**, close by, was struck by lightning in 1966, but has been restored to something approaching its original state and is worth casting an eye on.

THE VEZERE VALLEY

The river Vézère runs down from the hills of Corrèze, reaching the limestone plateaux of Périgord, west of Brive, and cutting its own wriggling canyon through the forests of scrub oak to join the Dordogne at Limeuil, west of St-Cyprien. It is a wilder river than the Dordogne, with less fertile land around it and with even more cliffs of water-worn peach-coloured stone bordering its valley.

These cliffs are riddled with caves, and their overhangs form ideal rock shelters. In prehistoric times our distant ancestors were here in force, hunting the mammoths, the reindeer and the wild horses that roamed the country, contesting the possession of the rocks with cave bears or sabre-toothed tigers, burying their dead in niches and leaving behind on the walls and ceilings of the caverns flowing paintings of the animals they lived among and enigmatic daubs and symbols, whose meaning we can only guess at.

Traces of prehistoric man are found all over Périgord and Quercy, but nowhere else is there such a concentration of sites. Scarcely a bend of the Vézère is without its rock shelter, burial site or cave. The valley is equally well supplied with castles and villages, smaller and cruder for the most part than those on the Dordogne, but equally worth seeing. The historical and prehistoric sights are supplemented by a number of modern museums and parks designed to set the prehistoric sights in context. Some are excellent; others rely on plastic mammoths for their appeal.

The traditional centre for exploration of prehistory is the village of **Les Eyzies-de-Tayac**, which has a dense grouping of hotels and eating places. It becomes desperately crowded in summer, and the village of Montignac at the northern end of the valley makes a preferable base. Overcrowding also affects the most famous sights. The painted caves of Font-de-Gaume and Lascaux II both restrict the numbers of visitors per day, as do several other caves with vulnerable paintings, and the summer demand usually outstrips the supply of places. Such caves sell timed tickets for the day's visits, and the only way to

PREHISTORY IN THE DORDOGNE

History is counted in centuries, prehistory in millennia – thus runs one definition. Whatever its other claims to fame, Périgord is where the study of prehistory as a science began, with the first systematic excavation of sites around Les Eyzies-de-Tayac in 1863. Other countries may have prehistoric remains as imposing as those in the caves and rock shelters along the valley of the Vézère, but the abundance of such remains, together with the art left behind by Stone Age man on the walls of the caves, gives Périgord a good claim to be the place where a species of man capable of culture (in the broadest sense) first lived.

The climate was very different. Between 200,000 BC and 10,000 BC, periods of glaciation left the Dordogne valley with an Arctic flora and fauna. Reindeer, mammoth, woolly rhinoceros and cave bears roamed the valleys. During the early millennia of this period, Neanderthal man inhabited the Vézère valley (five skeletons were discovered at Moustier). These people had learned how to use fire, while evidence of the attention given to burial suggests they also had

be certain of a place is to be at the ticket booth well before opening time and to queue to book a visit later in the day. Frustrating though this system is, it is manageable provided that your time is flexible and that you get up early enough to beat the coach-parties.

There are many other things to see, however, and it is easy enough to enjoy the Vézère valley without going near a cave. The museum and open-air prehistoric safari park (for want of a better term) at **Le Thot** is fascinating enough to take up most of a day, for example.

Limeuil to Les Eyzies-de-Tayac

This lowest section of the Vézère has a great concentration of prehistoric sites around Les Eyzies. The village of Limeuil is attractive mainly for the pattern made by its bridges crossing the Dordogne and Vézère. **Le Bugue** is larger but has little to see apart from arts and crafts exhibitions, an aquarium and a reasonable, if commercial, folk museum called **Le Village du Bournat** (open May–Sept, daily 10–7; Oct–Dec, daily 10–5; Feb–May, daily 10–5). However, it is the setting-off point for two nearby caves. At **Bara-Bahau** (open Feb–Mar daily 10–12,

some kind of religious sense. They seem to have been replaced by Cro-Magnon man around 35,000 BC.

It is during the Magdalenian period (which started about 25,000 years ago) that Cro-Magnon man perfected the artistic techniques which can be seen at their best at Lascaux. The first 'pictures' as such had appeared earlier, around 30,000 BC; the Lascaux paintings, which are generally held to be the highest point of achievement, date from around 15,000 BC.

The men of this time were skilled toolmakers as well as artists. Flint 'factories' existed, reindeer bone was shaped into deadly harpoons. But for all the evidence of their skill, the question of how they lived is still open to endless debate. Their paintings seem to have been ceremonial, worked deep under ground away from the rock shelters they inhabited. The distortions and exaggerations of their portraits, the rarity of human figures and the enigmatic symbols they used suggest a series of taboos or a kind of symbolic language – no one can ever be certain.

2–5; Apr–June, daily 9.30–12, 2–6.30; July and Aug, daily 9–7; Sept–Oct, daily 9.30–12, 2–6.30; Nov–Dec, Sat and Sun, 10–12, 2–5), a 100-metre-long cavern has prehistoric drawings scraped in the soft rock walls by flints, thought to date from 17,000 BC. Fairly crude outlines in some respects, they possibly predate the Lascaux paintings by about 2,000 years. One of the more fascinating things about this cave is the scratches made by a huge cave bear sharpening its claws on the wall thousands of years ago.

The **Gouffre de Proumeyssac** (open Feb–end Dec, daily 10–12, 2–5; June–Aug, daily 9–7) has no prehistoric art, but is a good cave to visit all the same, notably because of its crystalline rock formations and cheerful guides. It is busy in season, but there are facilities to keep you content until your numbered ticket reaches the head of the queue. Pottery placed under the drips in the cave gradually becomes sheathed in calcite, and you can see whole trays of jugs and such like laid out to be sold as souvenirs. Proumeyssac has been a tourist sight since 1924, and the old photographs and stories are part of the fun of the place. In its time, this hole in the ground was also used to dispose of hated overlords.

Les Eyzies-de-Tayac

In origin little more than a hamlet by the Vézère, whose inhabitants carved themselves refuges (from the Vikings) high in the monstrous yellow cliff rising behind the village, Les Eyzies now promotes itself as the World Capital of Prehistory.

There is still an argument about the size of the prehistoric population. The huge numbers of carved flints found suggest either a large population working over several years or a small one working over centuries. The essential element of the argument is how many people the local herds of game could support. The sophistication of the works of art and the fact that they are found in caves that were not otherwise inhabited suggest that this population was sufficiently unified to have developed ceremonial rites.

The current population of Les Eyzies is quite small, but swollen out of all proportion in summer by visitors. Hotel prices then are inflated above the norm, and rooms are hard to come by. For these reasons it is better to base yourself elsewhere and to visit the village only for an intensive bout of prehistoric sightseeing.

Musée National de la Préhistoire

(Open Mar–mid-Nov, daily exc Tue, 9.30–12, 2–6; mid-Nov–Feb, daily exc Tue, 9.30–12, 12–5.)

The old château of Les Eyzies has been a museum of prehistory since 1918 and it now contains, in its various extensions and galleries that range along the cliff above the village, around a million different items. There is also a statue of Neanderthal man, who stands on the cliff edge like something from *Planet of the Apes*.

This is a dry, academic museum: a glass case entitled 'Morphological Variations on the Theme of the Scraper' gives you an idea of the sort of thing you will encounter. In a way it is a pity that the museum is so heavily sold as an important sight, for the number of bored visitors (and even more bored children) usually outnumber the fascinated ones.

Still, there is no better place for learning about the various periods into which prehistory is divided, and seeing the long slow development of tools from the earliest shaped stones to the sophisticated reindeer-horn harpoons of the late neolithic period. Everything is arranged chronologically and explained in fairly dense French.

The best exhibits are the fragments of engraved stone or bone, or the larger bas-relief sculptures salvaged from sites all over the region. They are apt to be overwhelmed by the thousands of arrow-heads, scrapers, punches and other tools that surround them.

Visit the museum if you want a serious introduction to prehistory. Otherwise, Le Thot is more entertaining and fulfils much the same requirement.

Font-de-Gaume

(Open Nov–Feb, daily exc Tue, 10–12, 2–5; Mar and Oct, daily exc Tue, 9.30–12, 2–5.30; Apr–Sept, daily exc Tue, 9–12, 2–6; Numbers limited to 200 per day.)

Second only to Lascaux in the density and beauty of its prehistoric paintings, this long narrow cave is reached via a mere slit in the hillside. The paintings are so fragile and the humidity and carbon dioxide produced by visitors are so dangerous that there is constant talk of closing this cave and opening a reproduction, as had to be done with Lascaux. Still, for the moment, this remains a genuine prehistoric art gallery dating from around 12,000 BC.

The guided tours are scrupulous and intense, with little of the trumpet-blowing encountered in some of the smaller painted caves (France as the Birthplace of Art, and so forth). At Font-de-Gaume the guides are intent on pointing out the skill of the engravings and paintings and leave you to your own conclusions. As at Lascaux, the artists here have used the bulges of the rocks to give a third dimension to their animals. There are strings of mammoths, two beautiful reindeer locked either in combat or an embrace, bisons, more reindeer and horses. Somehow the narrow confines of the cave add to the vividness of the painting, it is almost as if you were passing down a narrow corridor between herds of beasts.

To visit Font-de-Gaume in high summer demands persistence. Come out of season if possible, but do be certain to visit.

Grotte des Combarelles

(Open Nov–Feb, daily exc Wed, 10–12, 2–5; Mar and Oct, daily exc Wed, 9.30–12, 2–5.30; Apr–Sept, daily exc Wed, 9–12, 2–6; visitors limited to 114 per day.)
In marked contrast to Font-de-Gaume, this cave contains only one painting, but over 800 engravings. The cave is narrow and sinuous, and prehistoric man must have had to crawl on hands and knees to reach the sections he wished to decorate.

The guided tours here are excellent, partly because groups are kept very small (making tickets even harder to come by). It is not always easy to pick out the engravings scratched on the walls, especially where one is superimposed on another, and you need the guide's help. Among the animals, horses predominate, some of which are very skilfully outlined. The cave also has a comparatively large number of human figures (their rarity throughout all the caves is something of a puzzle), most of them slightly distorted, suggesting that life-like representation was not permitted. Another feature is the number of symbolic signs, which are repeated sufficiently often for us to be sure they were not arbitrary.

Combarelles is not easy to get into, but it is a great cave for those seriously interested in the development of prehistoric art.

Grotte de Rouffignac

(Open early Apr–mid-June and Sept–Oct, daily 10–11.30, 2–5; July and Aug, daily 9–11.30, 2–6; limited tickets, which are sold in advance of morning and afternoon sessions.)

The scale of this cave makes it different from the narrow confines of Font-de-Gaume, as you explore 300 metres of it in a small electric train. The theme here is mammoths, of all shapes and sizes, some engraved, some outlined in black. The work is fairly late in the Magdalenian period, probably about 12,000 BC.

One of the most fascinating features is the great pits left in the soft floor of the cave by the bears that hibernated here. A veritable moonscape of these pits can be seen, along with numerous scratchings on the walls left by the animals' claws.

Other sights nearby

The **Abri du Cap Blanc** (open Apr–end June and Sept–mid-Dec, daily 10–12, 2–6; July and Aug, daily 9.30–7) is a rock shelter in the woods above the Beune valley, remarkable for the sculpted frieze of horses, bison and deer running along one wall. Picked out in bas-relief, the frieze uses the natural bulges of the rock in the same way as the paintings of Font-de-Gaume do.

In high season it can seem a long wait to see one frieze but, however, the history of the shelter, which was inhabited about 14,000 years ago, is lovingly outlined.

Nearby, the **Grotte de Bernifal** (open June–Sept, daily 9.30–12, 2.30–6; July and Aug, daily 9–7) and the **Grotte de la Grèze** (open Mar–mid-Nov, daily exc Tue 9.30–12, 2–6) have rock engravings; for enthusiasts only.

Two further caves near Les Eyzies contain interesting rock formations rather than paintings. The **Grotte du Grand Roc** (open Feb–end Mar, daily 10–5; Apr to June and mid-Sept–end Dec, daily 9.30–5; June–mid-Sept, daily 9–7) is particularly impressive because many of the stalactites grow side-thrusting crystals, turning the roof of the cave into something resembling a furry chandelier. The **Grotte de Carpe Diem** (open Apr–end Sept, daily 10–12, 2–6.30) contains a more conventional collection of stalagmites.

The **Musée de la Spéléologie** (open June–end Aug, daily 11–6), carved into the rock above Les Eyzies-de-Tayac, is a spin-off sight taking advantage of the crowds. The museum features a general history of cave exploration, but on the whole the setting is better than the museum.

The Vézère upstream of Les Eyzies

From Les Eyzies to Montignac is only 26 kilometres, but the journey seems much longer as you follow the tortuous curves of the river, with one precipice after another thrusting up above the oak woods.

High on the hillside opposite the village of Tursac is the site of **La Madeleine**, the prehistoric shelter where the implements discovered allowed an accurate dating of what is now called the Magdalenian period (between 15,000 and 9,000 BC). The prehistoric site is not open, but up here you will find a complete troglodyte village carved from the cliff; crowned by a ruined château from the fourteenth century. It all makes an excellent goal for a walk, and the views over the Vézère are excellent.

Forget the **Préhistoparc** beyond Tursac (it is not as good as Le Thot) and explore **La Roque St-Christophe**, a long gallery of a troglodytic fort reaching for five storeys up a huge overhang, but only if you have the time or want to admire the Vézère from far above.

Moving on to a later period, stop at **St-Léon-sur-Vézère** to see the Romanesque church, one of the most beautiful in Périgord, with its square bell-tower and rounded, turreted apse and side chapels. The village also possesses a fourteenth-century château squatting in the main square. Another château, **Losse** (open Easter–end Oct, daily 10–12, 2–6), lies upstream from Thonac. This is a Renaissance building on medieval foundations, in a lovely situation on the very banks of the Vézère. The interior is worth seeing for the fireplaces and the proportions of the rooms. The furnishings, mostly sixteenth and seventeenth century, are less interesting.

Le Thot

(Open Feb–end June and Sept–end Dec, daily exc Mon 10–12, 2–5.30; July and Aug, daily 9.30–7.)
Le Thot, admirably organised and staffed, is split into two parts: a museum and an outdoor park. It is closely linked to the painted cave of Lascaux, to which it acts as supplement and context-setter. Which you should visit first is debatable, but at Le Thot there are no problems with timed-tickets, and the exhibits can only whet your appetite for the cave. On the other hand, seeing Lascaux before the technical explanation of its creation in no way diminishes your sense of wonder.

A large part of the museum is given over to an explanation of how Lascaux II was constructed; it also carries reproductions of paintings and engravings found in the far corners of the original cave that were not incorporated in the replica.

Even more interesting is the exhibit on prehistoric art. This explains, without fuss and with convincing exhibits, the techniques used by early man as he decorated the walls of the caves. Lamps, pigments, tools . . . all are set out and explained, with more concise explanations and examples of the mysterious scratchings and symbols found in the caves than you are likely to hear on the guided tours of the caves themselves.

The outside section is equally enthralling, especially for children. Here are living specimens of the animals which are painted on the walls of the caves – reindeer, horses and bison. There are even mammoths which are sufficiently life-like to cause moments of anxiety, as you will discover when you trip the hidden sensors. A group of prehistoric dwellings from all over the world rounds off the exhibit. Look out for the Ukrainian hut constructed from the bones of mammoths.

Lascaux II

(Opening times as for Le Thot above; visitors limited to 2,000 per day.)

Lascaux is cited as the eighth wonder of the world. It is the apotheosis of the painted cave because, although even somewhere as rich as Font-de-Gaume has paintings scattered along corridors, parts of Lascaux have paintings covering the whole cave, roof and all.

The cave was discovered in 1940 by four boys hoping to find an underground treasure. As the original entrance had been blocked by a landslip, the paintings of Lascaux were as fresh as when they were first painted.

Unfortunately, when the cave was opened to the public, the polluting effects of humankind rapidly became apparent. 'Green sickness' (algae from the increased light) started to damage the paintings, while 'white sickness' (accelerated calcification from increased concentrations of carbon dioxide breathed out by visitors) began to cover them in a fine, chalky film. Lascaux was closed in 1963.

Ten years later the replica cave known as Lascaux II was opened. Computers helped measure the exact dimensions of the original, and these were reproduced, layer by layer, using steel, steel mesh and increasingly exact coats of cement and reconstituted stone. Once the new cavern was formed, it was painted, using only the pigments and techniques used by prehistoric man himself and following the precise dimensions of the original artworks. The replica is itself a wonder – perhaps the ninth of the world.

So precise is the reproduction that no effort of imagination is needed to feel yourself deep under ground in the original cave. Every surface seems to be covered with animals – it might be the grand parade of a circus – and some of them appear to be moving, an effect achieved by moulding their bodies around curving rock surfaces. Four huge bulls lumber among herds of deer, while a mythical beast strides off on his own, panther-skinned, bison-headed, horned . . . could it be a man clothed in skins performing some strange rite?

After this Hall of the Bulls comes an even greater marvel, the 'Sistine Chapel', so-called because the paintings cover both roof and walls. Realism is forgotten – a circle of cows' heads, a group of fleeing horses and further stylised horses with huge bellies and short legs. The animals' ears all seem to be in the wrong places – why?

The originals of these paintings were created at the beginning of the Magdalenian period, about 15,000 BC. As you visit this cave and others, you will sense the puzzle, never to be explained, of attempting to interpret the meaning, or even the existence of these paintings, which were executed such an unimaginable length of time ago. Every guide has his own theories, and so does every prehistorian, but in the end your guess is as good as theirs. This is part of the secret charm of visiting the great painted caves.

Montignac

This small town has a life of its own outside tourism, although with Lascaux so close, tourism plays a large part in its economy. It is a much bigger and livelier place than Les Eyzies, although it does not have quite the same number of hotels. In summer a folk festival animates the place, and there is usually something going on during the evenings. There is not a great deal to see in the town (which may be a relief), only some fine half-timbered houses beside the river, some of them on piles. The château here was once the most powerful in Périgord and was inhabited during the fourteenth century by a particularly rapacious family of robber-barons. After many a siege, the castle was taken and destroyed, which is why all that remains today is a single tower.

Montignac makes a pleasant base for the Vézère valley. Look for a cottage a little to the east if you are self-catering, for the countryside is very attractive there, with a scattering of honey-coloured villages.

BETWEEN THE VEZERE AND THE DORDOGNE

This triangular wedge of country with the town of Sarlat-la-Canéda at its southern fringe has the most attractive landscape of the Central Dordogne. It is ideal for self-catering holidays, for it is isolated enough to be free of crowds yet within easy reach of all the best sights. It also has several sights of its own that are well worth discovering. To the west, towards the meeting of the two rivers, the country is wooded and rocky; to the east it is gentler, more open and scattered with small villages, almost all of them blessed by a peach-coloured manor house, a tiny Romanesque church or a crumbling fortress.

Sarlat-la-Canéda

This is the best-looking town in Périgord by a long way, with a Gothic and Renaissance centre whose streets are lined with houses of great beauty. What makes the town notable is its combination of the light tan stone from which the buildings are constructed, the decoration of the Gothic windows and roofscapes and the network of small streets and squares.

Come into town on the arrow-straight Rue de la République, which was driven through it in the nineteenth century, and you will not see any of this, only a brawling hubbub of traffic, and pedestrians inching their way down narrow pavements. Through one of the narrow alleyways to the east, however, and you are into a haven where it is possible to wander in peace. Park on the edge of the centre to the south and walk in – it is not far.

Sarlat is one of those towns where there are no great sights, just an endless succession of pleasures. The cathedral is big and bony, but not desperately interesting. The twelfth-century tower (up the hill behind) known as the Lanterne des Morts is more fascinating. This enigmatic structure has a ground-floor room and another under the conical roof, but the latter is inaccessible and its purpose is not known.

Most of the cafés and most of the crowds are around the Place de la Liberté, where the seventeenth-century town hall and a sixteenth-century mansion stand, as well as the tourist office where you can pick up a good self-guided walk leaflet (in English). In summer theatrical performances are held in the square.

Sarlat gets crowded, hardly surprisingly, but it is the sort of town where this does not matter much, and where the ambience is improved when the streets are full of people. Come off-season and you will find the place almost dead, a kind of ghost town with the residents shut firmly behind their thick walls.

Not all of old Sarlat lies to the east of the Rue de la République. At the south-west side of town is a hidden quarter, much less restored and much more atmospheric than the area around the town hall. A tower from the old ramparts, a watch-tower built in among twisted old buildings, and the gardens of an old convent are here.

The Saturday market, famous throughout the region (there is a less touristy one on Wednesdays), makes the town seem as if it is bursting at the seams, with stalls spreading all down the streets. The Place des Oies is reserved for sellers of geese; there are vegetables in abundance, masses of poultry products, truffles in the winter, and of course a plethora of arts and crafts put together locally (many of them by expatriates). The market is a tourist attraction, and in summer the tourists often outnumber the locals, making it less authentic than most other Périgord markets. Authenticity is less important here than atmosphere, though, and there is plenty of that. Do not expect to do any serious shopping – inching through the crowds with bags of provisions is not a comfortable experience.

East of Sarlat

A tour around this country pays dividends in the beauty of its villages and rolling countryside, crossed by small, clear streams. From Sarlat, follow the valley of the river Enéa, past a fine old manor house at Mallevergne to Ste-Nathalène and then to the **Moulin de la Tour** (signposted). This is a walnut mill, where the oil is still produced by the old methods of crushing, slow heating and then pressing, using machinery that appears to go back to the Industrial Revolution. The enterprise is family-run, and even if the mill is not working (Wednesdays and Fridays offer the best chance of seeing it in action) you can catch a glimpse of the workings, chat to the owner about how to choose really good fresh walnuts, and buy tin upon tin (if you can carry them) of walnut oil and the even more pungent hazelnut oil.

At **Eyrignac** to the north-east, the eighteenth-century gardens of the manor house have been restored to their original glory (open Apr–June, daily 10–12.30, 4–7; July–Sept, daily 10–7; Oct–end Mar, daily 10–12, 2–dusk). Here are all the features beloved by the French creators of formal gardens, including hedges of clipped and sculpted hornbeam, patterns picked out in box or yew, and rows of conical cypress trees. It is a delightful spot in which to walk for an hour or so.

Salignac-Eyvigues is a crumbling hilltop village with thirteenth- and fourteenth-century houses, a covered market and a most curious castle, one of the oldest in the region, tucked into the cliff face underneath. It is best seen from a distance, although you can visit.

Around here is the area to search for villages, most of them tiny, where the houses clump together in a harmony of sagging roofs and haphazard gardens. A Romanesque church or a nearby château hidden among the trees completes the excitement of discovery. Try, for a start, **St-Geniès, Le Poujol and St-Crépin**, or try to catch a glimpse of the Château du Claud, hidden among the trees to the south.

Then head across country to **St Amand-de-Coly**, home of the best fortified church in the area. From a distance the church looks like a slab of rock with a huge mouth, which turns out to be the tall arch over the door, above which a chamber under the eaves allowed the defenders to hurl missiles and pour boiling oil on any attackers. A parapet walk below the roof and further defensive chambers complete the impression of impregnability. Whether the building is more like a church or a castle, especially since it is surrounded by a defensive wall, is hard to tell.

In its crumbling churchyard, with a minuscule hamlet of earth-brown houses around it (one shows a video about the church), the church seems a grossly large building. But it was once the defensive core of a large and rich twelfth-century abbey. This declined so fast that there were only two monks left by 1430. In 1575 the Protestants withstood a siege of continuous bombardment in the church for six days. Now the church stands almost forgotten, with a bare and simple interior and a cool wind blowing from its doorway.

If you feel like stretching your legs, use the car park at the edge of St-Amand as the starting-point for several round walks, mapped out on a board.

West of Sarlat

Once outside the town the country becomes higher and less welcoming than it is to the east, with the dark scrub oak alternating with outcrops of limestone. The château of **Puymartin** (open Easter–Nov, daily 10–12, 2–6.30) is a fifteenth-century structure of round towers, curtain walls and arrow slits, with a distinguished interior of coffered ceilings, panelling and fireplaces. North of here, **Marquay** is a pretty village hidden among the trees, and **Tamniès**, high above the Beune valley, another. The upper Beune valley is worth driving along (on the D48). It is like the Vézère in miniature, with a sequence of dark curling pools beneath precipices and houses or troglodytic dwellings squeezed into such space as there is.

Finally, off the busy D47 Les Eyzies to Sarlat road near Beyssac, a sign points to the **Cabanes de Breuil**, a cluster of beehive-shaped stone huts with curious round windows. These are part of a small working farm, and a gaggle of geese wanders freely around. The huts cannot be precisely dated, but they are almost certainly farmers' dwellings from medieval times – you can see the primitive set-up and a few implements inside one of them. A little downhill there is a campsite and a *crêperie* with tables laid out under shady trees – a good lunch stop.

SOUTH OF THE RIVER DORDOGNE

This is the country of the *bastide* towns, a pleasing area of small hills and open countryside, becoming more wooded as you head east. The best way to see it is to take a long slow semi-circle through it from Bergerac and rejoin the Dordogne near Domme. This is another popular self-catering area; if you want to rent a cottage here move fast and early in the year.

The bastides

The pleasure of visiting *bastides* is in discovering the different effects that the passage of time has had on them. Although those in Périgord were all founded within the period 1222 to 1373, to much the same design and for much the same purpose, they now vary hugely in size, state of preservation and overall atmosphere. Luckily, the group just south of the Dordogne gives a marvellous sense of this progress or decline over the centuries, and are best visited in sequence.

Molières, just west of Cadouin, is an example of a *bastide* whose population in 1365, at 1,200, was four times greater than it is today. It is a sleepy, tiny village, where the regular grid-pattern streets of the original foundation tail off into little country lanes. Nevertheless, the proportions of the central square and the huge fortified church are more in keeping with its original size.

Beaumont, south-west of Molières, was an English *bastide*, founded in the reign of Edward I. It is said to have been built in the shape of an H, in memory of the king's father, Henry. Here is a town that was very important in medieval times, and has remained sufficiently central to local commerce to have been altered and rebuilt over the centuries. Its state of preservation is less good than Monpazier, but the town is worth exploring, for it still has thirteenth- and fourteenth-century houses, while the Gothic church, more like a fortress, is one of the best in the area.

Monpazier is in the best state of preservation of all the Périgord *bastides*, having neither grown nor shrunk since its peak period of medieval prosperity. Glossy local guidebooks show a photograph of it from the air, which helps you understand how the town was laid out, how the building lots were divided up and how the market-place acted as the natural hub. At ground level the market-square is a wonderful place to dawdle in. The arcades around its edges, the covered market place with some of the original measures in position, and a strategically placed café tempt you to linger. Drop into the Gothic church for a glimpse of the carved choir stalls and visit the three remaining fortified gateways to the town.

Seven kilometres south-west of Monpazier, the bulky **Château de Biron** (open early Feb–end Mar, daily exc Mon 2–6; Apr–end June, daily exc Mon 10–12, 2–6; July–early Sept, daily 10–7; early Sept–mid-Oct, daily exc. Mon 10–12, 2–6; Mid-Oct–end Dec, daily exc Mon 2–5) was inhabited by the powerful Gontaut-Biron family for 24 generations. It was a Gontaut-Biron who founded Monpazier, and throughout French history the family was one of the most important in Périgord. The castle is a complex of buildings from every period between the twelfth and seventeenth centuries. As you may imagine, this can be a pretty exhausting tour, from medieval keeps and Renaissance chapel, through the courtyard of honour, reception rooms and cavernous kitchens.

Villefranche du Périgord, at the south-east corner of the Dordogne *département*, was founded in 1261. It was another English *bastide*, but changed hands several times during the Hundred Years' War. Like Monpazier, this is a well-preserved town, with arcades and a spacious central square. It is less busy with tourists and rather more busy with traffic. In autumn the Saturday market, usually a sleepy affair, turns into one of the great buying and selling spots for the wild *cèpes* that grow plentifully in the surrounding woods. The antique shops around the square are worth a browse, while the Hôtel du Commerce serves a decent lunch.

Crossing the departmental boundary westward brings you to a further clump of *bastides*, including **Villeréal, Castillonnès** and **Monflanquin**, all well-preserved large villages, and to **Rayet** (near Villeréal) which, by contrast, is little more than a few cottages.

Cadouin

Cadouin's **abbey** (open early Feb–Apr, daily exc Tue 2–5; Apr–July and early Sept–mid-Oct, daily exc Tue 10–12, 2–6; July–early Sept, 10–7; Nov–Dec, daily exc Tue 2–5) was founded in the twelfth century, and the village really owes its existence to it. It is a sunny place, in the Bessède forest, and if you are here during shopping hours there are stalls (expensive craftwork) close to the old abbey church, a café and a restaurant. The abbey owed its prosperity to its ownership of the shroud that apparently once wrapped Christ (records of it go back to 1117). The legends go back even earlier, to the seventh century, when a dispute over the shroud between Jews and Christians in the Holy Land was solved by a Muslim arbitrator; he threw it in the air to see which way the wind would blow it (towards the Christians as it happened). The shroud was plundered from Palestine in the First Crusade, brought to Périgord and placed in a silver reliquary at Cadouin, though it did suffer further trials and tribulations. Alas, an inquiry in 1932 revealed that the cloth carried an eleventh-century inscription invoking the name of Allah. All that fuss for a fake!

The shroud is on display, with the history explained in detail, inside the abbey, but the carved capitals in the cloisters are the main reason for visiting. You are handed an explanatory leaflet (in English, and very necessary), locked into the cloister and left to examine them at your leisure – bang on the door to be let out when you've finished. The capitals are very weathered and need close examination to reveal the small detail, such as monks attempting to avoid various temptations, musicians or a couple of merchants arguing over a goose.

Around the corner in a part of the old abbey buildings is an altogether different attraction – a bicycle museum with an idiosyncratic collection of models from every period of the machine's history, put together by an enthusiast.

Belvès

This old town, in marked contrast to the regularity of the *bastides*, has grown up haphazardly around its castle, its market-place and its church. A wander through the lanes around the remains of the château will suffice as a taste of the town's medieval flavour. Reserve your attentions for the extensive and authentic market (Saturday), a marvellous place to stock up if you are self-catering. Look out for extra-strong honey, butter and olives.

Among the villages south and east of Belvès, **Salle de Belvès** has a Romanesque fortified church, **Doissat** a walnut museum and **St-Pompont** the remains of a château.

THE ISLE VALLEY

The Isle is the least attractive of the Dordogne *département's* three big rivers. In its lower reaches, where it runs parallel with the Dordogne, the small towns along its banks – Montpon, Mussidan and Neuvic – have been spoilt for tourism by industry and traffic. Higher up, the river runs through the centre of Périgueux (see below), the capital of Périgord and a city not to be missed.

For much of its course through Périgord, the Isle is bounded on both banks by large areas of woodland – the Forêt du Landais to the south and the Forêt de la Double to the north. Both of these, but especially the latter, are favoured hunting-grounds for British people in search of property to buy. Equally, they make good areas to look for self-catering accommodation, though their distance from the main sights of the Dordogne valley means that they are more suited to those in search of peace and quiet than to those who wish to see the sights.

In the Forêt du Landais, Romanesque churches and the remains of old castles provide most interest. From **Villefranche-de-Lonchat** head east for the ruins of the château near **Carsac-de-Gurson,** which was built by Edward I of England, interesting as much for its site as for its history. **St-Martin-de-Gurson** and **Montpeyroux** (south of Villefranche) both have Romanesque churches worth discovering.

Further east, around the old stronghold of **Villamblard**, with its huge fortress, there is another clump of villages worth touring. **St-Jean-d'Estissac** has a fifteenth-century castle and **St-Hilaire-d'Estissac** was a Romanesque church. At **Issac** in the valley of the Crempse, the château of **Mont-Réal** gave its name to the Canadian city.

Finally, if you are satiated with architecture, by getting hold of an atlas and with a little careful navigation, you should be able to find the spot (south-west of **Montpon-Ménestérol**) where the Greenwich Meridian cuts latitude 45, placing you exactly half way between the North Pole and the Equator on the stroke of Greenwich Mean Time.

Périgueux

Périgueux is a wonderful town, but since it is a lot bigger and more traffic-plagued than anywhere else in the region, it can be quite exhausting, especially in baking hot weather. To get the best out of it, make a day of it and take things slowly.

The Romans built their city of Vesunna on the banks of the Isle, and an important place it was too, with a massive temple and a large amphitheatre. Throughout the barbarian invasions and the Dark Ages, Vesunna, or Vésone as it became called, lay huddled behind its much-repaired Roman wall. But with the founding of the cathedral of St-Front on the hillside above the river to the east, a second town began to grow, Le Puy-St-Front. For many years there was rivalry between the two, culminating in pitched battles on what is now the Place Francheville. Eventually, Louis IX forced the two cities into unison at the end of the thirteenth century, and the result is the Périgueux we have today.

It is very easy to be deluded into thinking that the medieval streets around the cathedral, with their crooked houses and small squares must be the oldest part of the city, and that down the hill there is nothing more interesting than the railway. At first glance this seems to be the case. But a little exploration reveals more.

The Roman city

Down the hill from the cathedral towards the railway line is the Quartier de la Cité – look for the unmistakable domed church of St-Etienne-de-la-Cité. Head down the Rue Romaine, cross the railway, and in front of you is a round brick tower, the **Tour de Vésone**, looking like a half-demolished factory. This 20-metre-high structure is in fact what remains of a huge temple that was built at the edge of the Roman forum. It once had a marble-clad peristyle and numerous extensions, and by walking around the tower in the public garden surrounding it you can see the layout of the Roman building clearly enough.

Behind the tower, the remnants of a villa, the **Villa de Pompeïus**, are exposed to view.

A walk north-west by the railway brings you to the **Porte Normande**, where the remains of the defensive wall can easily be seen; the wall is said to have been built hurriedly in the third century as a defence against the barbarian invasions. Stones and columns from Roman buildings were used, and you can still pick out odd colonnades and capitals stuck into the defence-works.

East of here, a wide circular garden marks the site of the Roman amphitheatre, which must have been an imposing structure. Nothing remains of it now, for it was turned into a castle by the renegade counts of Périgord (they sided with the English in the Hundred Years' War) and demolished in the late fourteenth century. Most of the stones ended up being used in the houses around the cathedral.

St-Etienne-de-la-Cité, an eleventh-century domed church, was built on the site of the Roman temple of Mars. It was much damaged over the centuries and only two of its original four domes now remain. It is a fascinating piece of early Périgord architecture, the two domes (built 50 years apart) are quite different in their techniques. In its way the church is a more interesting building than the heavily restored cathedral up the hill.

The medieval city

The closely packed streets of houses on the hill above the Isle first grew up around the chapel that was built over the tomb of Saint Front. The cathedral, which in 1173 replaced the chapel and a later church, makes a good starting-point for exploration. The **Cathédrale St-Front** is a bizarre building from the outside, with curious mini bell-towers (*clochetons*) like minarets rising from every extremity. These, and much more, are the result of a nineteenth-century restoration so comprehensive that the cathedral could be described as rebuilt. An impressive building, with its domes and tower, seems to belong more to a Byzantine waterfront than to rural France.

The interior was thoroughly pillaged during the Wars of Religion, when the tomb of Saint Front was destroyed, so few of the features are original. But it is worth stepping inside to admire the dimensions of the great domes and the comparative delicacy of the pillars.

The streets around the cathedral have been subjected to a programme of cleaning, restoration and pedestrianisation, which have made them ideal for a walk. Which route you take is irrelevant, for the Renaissance (and earlier) frontages are scattered throughout. However, you should aim to visit the Place St-Louis, the Place de l'Hôtel de Ville, where there is a house flanked by a fifteenth-century tower, and the Rue des Farges, which has a good atmospheric feeling to it and more old houses. The only other sight in Périgueux worth your time is the **Musée du Périgord** (open Apr–Aug, daily exc Tue 10–12, 2–7; Sept–Mar, daily exc Tue 10–12, 2–5). This has one of the best archaeological collections in the area and is especially strong on Roman remains from the old city. Unfortunately the layout is old-fashioned (nothing but glass cases).

Périgueux is the best shopping centre in the region. Its markets (Wednesdays and Saturdays) in the cathedral square and the streets all around are especially famed during the Winter for truffles, *foie gras* and poultry products, but are enticing enough at other times of year. Numerous shops sell local specialities, including *foie gras*, walnut oil and endless conserved poultry products. There are plenty of small eating places, Vietnamese and Italian are among them if you are satiated with poultry.

Around Périgueux

Above Périgueux the river Auvézère comes winding down from Corrèze to join the Isle. The country around the junction of these two rivers is sparse and wooded, but as you progress east it becomes gentler and more open. On the whole this is a less productive area for finding pretty villages and good touring routes than on the country roads further south. However, there are still things worth finding, and the easy terrain and the views from the shallow ridges make it good cycling country, as is the countryside between Périgueux and the Dronne valley.

Sorges

Sorges is the home of the **Eco-Musée de la Truffe** (open all year, daily exc Mon 10–12, 2–5). Everything you ever wanted to know about the truffle is here. Locals apparently complain that the museum gives away too much information and that they are losing numbers of the precious 'black pearl' to well-informed tourists. Whatever the strengths of this argument, the museum's trail through typical truffle-growing country is made fascinating by the lack of any obvious signs of where the fungus may be growing; a column of dancing gnats may be a give-away sign and you'll finally understand why a trained pig or dog is necessary.

So haphazard are the habits of this fungus (which favours the roots of some trees but not of others) that any attempt to cultivate it seems to be a matter of luck more than skill. Still, this museum will give you the necessary knowledge if you wish to try for yourself.

Château de l'Herm

(Open July–Sept, daily 10–7.)
This real treat of a ruined castle is 23 kilometres south-east of Périgueux, hidden in trees at the top of a hill and surrounded by an overgrown ditch, which is all that remains of a six-metre-deep moat. It was rebuilt in the early sixteenth century on its twelfth-century foundations. The castle was the scene of a series of mysterious and bloody deaths, involving forced marriages, stranglings, wicked stepmothers, betrayal, lawsuits and revenge. Now the ruin is a hollow shell, although the splendid fireplaces give clues to the function and the importance of every room.

Hautefort

Close to the border of the Dordogne and Corrèze *départements*, this is a palace rather than a castle (tel 53 50 51 23 open 2 Apr–15 Oct, daily exc Sun a.m. 10–12, 2–6; 15 Oct–19 Nov, daily 2–6) for the eleventh-century fortress was totally rebuilt between 1630 and 1670, also making it a good deal more modern than most of the others in the region. In consequence, its style belongs to one of the expansive periods of French architecture, with wings flanking a central building and symmetrically placed pavilions to round off the effect. You cannot imagine Hautefort's most famous overlord, the troubadour-warrior Bertrand de Born, inhabiting such a prissy place. He preferred fighting, mixing himself up in the quarrels involving Henry Shortcoat and Richard Lionheart and enduring several sieges of his castle. He expired in an abbey in 1214. Dante consigned him firmly to hell in the *Inferno* for 'sowing discord'. A later inhabitant (during the years 1616–19) was Marie d'Hautefort, who, as maid of honour to Marie de' Medici, incited King Louis XIII to fall in love with her – but by all accounts he never succumbed to the numerous temptations she offered him, including dropping letters to him between her breasts and requesting him to retrieve them.

These personalities are, truth to tell, rather more interesting than the castle itself, full of fine furniture and porcelain though it is. The formal gardens and the setting on a high ridge overlooking miles of peaceful hayfields are among the most pleasurable parts of the visit. Also look for the beautiful construction of the turret roof, whose wooden beams survived a bad fire in 1968.

Small sights in the Auvézère valley

West of Hautefort in the Auvézère valley, **Tourtoirac** has a large and imposing Romanesque abbey church, complete with dome and twin bell-towers. **St-Raphael** to the north has a good setting on a rocky outcrop and the ruins of a Romanesque priory, where, with careful inspection of the pillars, you can make out a series of carvings of men pulling at their beards. **Ste-Eulalie d'Ans**, west of Tourtoirac, is a pretty village with an ancient mill on the river. Upstream of Tourtoirac, beyond **Cherveix-Cubas**, the Auvézère has cut itself a gorge, which is gently spectacular. North of Tourtoirac, the château at **Excideuil** has ancient towers from the twelfth century, linked by a fifteenth-century building.

Jumilhac-le-Grand

Where the Isle dwindles to a stream on the edge of the Limousin plateau, this huge château (open mid-Mar–July and mid-Sept–mid-Nov Sun 2–6; July–mid-Sept, daily 10–12, 2–6) hangs above its narrow gorge. It was built in 1597 in Gothic style, although it is rather primitive for the period. Massive towers, spiky windows and conical roofs, all built of a curious rosy stone, form a roofscape which Gustave Doré, the illustrator, called the most romantic in France. For all this, it is a haphazard, sprawling building, with seventeenth-century wings tacked on. The interior is less riveting than the exterior, but there is a grand staircase, fine furniture and portraits.

THE DRONNE VALLEY

The Dronne is the most English of Périgord's rivers, an effect of the overhanging willows, the placid water-meadows and the still stretches where, in May, ducklings scutter across the surface behind their mothers and in October, leaves collect in gentle eddies. Gone are the great cliffs and frowning castles of the Dordogne; this is a village-scale river, and a village-scale landscape surrounds it.

The valley has few great sights to match those further south, but the small towns of Bourdeilles and Brantôme have all you could wish for by way of atmosphere, while the usual sprinkling of castles, churches and villages provide goals for walks or bicycle rides – this is excellent cycling territory.

The area is very popular with cottage-renting self-caterers, and good if you want to bury yourself for a quiet fortnight.

Forêt de la Double

This large area of scrub woodland is still in some ways feeling the effects of the Hundred Years' War, for that conflict turned it into a refuge for renegade soldiers, robber chieftains and wolves; it was never repopulated. Its natural forest cover disappeared soon afterwards to be used as charcoal or for ship-building, and the Double became a marshy area of no use to anyone, infested by the malarial mosquito and dubbed the 'kingdom of fevers'. It remained in this state until the second half of the nineteenth century, when drainage and afforestation gradually turned it into habitable countryside.

The only definite goal you need when exploring the Double forest is **St-Privat** at its northern edge, where there is a Romanesque fortified church of massive bulk, looking much like a giant turtle, and a small museum of life in the Double and in the Dronne valleys.

Ribérac

Ribérac's chief curiosity is one of those indescribably ugly neo-Byzantine churches, which were favoured by some early-twentieth-century architects. A rather better attraction, however, is its market (Wednesdays and Fridays). This is probably the best in the region, extending over a large car park, with stalls selling everything from live chicks to beautifully turned walnut salad bowls.

The town also seems to have been adopted as a base for a large community of expatriates (mostly British) who have found the cottage of their dreams nearby. Eat (or stay) at the unassuming Hôtel de France (see Where to Stay), and you will see them out in force.

There are a few sights in the immediate area, notably the fortified church at **Allemans** to the north and the château of **La Rigale** on the river to the east, the latter composed of the peculiar combination of a Roman tower (left over from a second-century temple) and an eighteenth-century mansion.

At **Tocane-St-Apre** you can embark on an excellent bicycle tour, riding parallel to the north bank of the river as far as Bourdeilles and returning on the south bank.

Alternatively, strike out for **St-Aquilin**, eight kilometres to the south, in search of the prehistoric dolmen, the tumulus, the Château de Belet and the caverns carved as dwelling-places or refuges (known as *cluzeaux*), all of which can be found in or around the village.

Bourdeilles

This riverside village is surprisingly untouristy, given the beauty of its setting. The Dronne curves around a cliff and splits in two to form a boat-shaped island. A hump-backed Gothic bridge with embrasures over the arches spans the river; there is a castle – part medieval, part Renaissance – built against the cliff, a cluster of steeply raked houses, a café or two and a well placed hotel. Everything is perfectly proportioned.

The **château** (open Feb–Apr, daily exc Tue 2–5; Apr–June, daily exc Tue 10–12, 2–6; July–early Sept daily 10–7; Sept–mid-Oct, daily 10–12, 2–6; mid-Oct–end Dec, daily exc Tue 2–5) is worth visiting largely for the views from its terrace and from the old octagonal keep. You can wander on your own, if you are prepared to indulge in a little persuasion, but guided tours are the norm. You certainly need to go on one if you wish to see the excellent collection of furniture in the Renaissance section, and the *salon doré* with its seventeenth-century painted ceiling. The Renaissance château was the creation of Jacquette de Montbrun, who planned to receive Catherine de Medici there. But Catherine never turned up and Jacquette died before the work was completed.

The most famous person to be born in Bourdeilles was Pierre de Bourdeille, known as 'Brantôme' after the abbey (see below), whose benefice he was granted in 1558. He was not cut out to be an abbot however, preferring the life of traveller and soldier. He was one of the party that came to Scotland with Mary Queen of Scots in 1561, voyaged to Italy, fought against the Protestants and set about organising an expedition to Peru. A fall from a horse cut short his active life and sent him back to his abbey, where he devoted his life to writing.

It is for his writing that he is best known. His *Vie des hommes illustres et des grands capitaines* is a straightforward Renaissance-style account of worthy men, but his *Les dames galantes* is a different matter, a compilation of gossip, scandal, filthy stories and dirty jokes, padded out with worthier passages–hardly the stuff to flow from the pen of an abbot; but then, for Brantôme, 'lechery was a branch of gastronomy'. You can buy copies of his work in the town of Brantôme but will have to wade your way through some fairly impenetrable antique French as a penalty.

Brantôme

Snuggled into a meander of the Dronne, Brantôme, the 'Venice of Périgord', is the biggest town on the Upper Dronne, but actually little more than the size of a respectable village. On one side of the river are the golden buildings of the abbey around which the town grew up. These are built in front of a cliff the colour of banana ice-cream, which is riddled with caves, quarries, sanctuaries and holes. On the opposite bank, neatly ringed by the clear river, the town is a small net of narrow streets, with – now and again – an open space by the water where cafés and bars have sprung up to cater to the tourists.

The only disadvantage of Brantôme is that it is not quite large enough to absorb all its visitors in comfort. But there are few better places in which to idle away an hour or two watching the ducks or reading under the shade of a café parasol.

The **abbey** (tel in advance 53 05 80 63) is the chief sight. The church stands four-square before the caverns that are dug deep into the rock behind. Part Romanesque, part Gothic, it has a bell-tower thought to be the oldest in France – perhaps dating from the time of the Visigoths – which certainly has the patina, and the slightly drunken look of extreme age.

Most of the original abbey was under ground. The remaining buildings are mostly eighteenth century and contain prehistoric fragments, strange paintings and some lovely carpentry. Behind these buildings, beneath the overhang of the cliff, there are stranger wonders. The spring from which the monks drew their water wells out from under ground; and the caves bear witness to an under ground life. One has sculpted walls, with *The Triumph of Death* and *The Last Judgement* possibly dating from the fifteenth century. Dance performances during the Brantôme classical dance festival take place in this strange setting.

Villars

There are two things to see close to this village: the **Château de Puyguilhem** (open Feb–end Mar, daily exc Mon 2–5;

Apr–end June, daily exc Mon 10–12, 2–6; July and Aug, daily 10–7; Sept–Oct, daily 10–12, 2–6; Nov–Dec, daily exc Mon 2–5) and the **Grottes de Villars** (open 9 Apr–mid-June, daily 12-6; 15–30 June, daily 10–12, 2–6; July and Aug, daily 10–6; Sept–mid-Sept, daily 10–12; mid-Sept–end Oct, daily 2–6). The former is a very beautiful Renaissance château at the end of a long avenue of shady trees. It was ruined for many years, so none of the original furnishings have survived, but the stonework has, and if you like huge fireplaces, coffered ceilings and idiosyncratic carvings, then the guided tour will be worthwhile. If not, wander the grounds and enjoy the exterior of the building with its high, elaborately carved windows and round towers, for the tour itself is fairly dull.

The caves draw more people. In comparison with the splendours of the Dordogne valley, Villars may be disappointing in terms of its prehistoric art, for most of the paintings and engravings are rather blotchy and many have been covered with a film of calcite. The rock formations, with feasts of stalactites

BASTIDES

A *bastide*, although the word is similar to *bastille* ('fortress'), is most simply defined as a planned settlement. In the Aquitaine basin, the *bastide* was the new town of the Middle Ages; they were founded by the local feudal overlord, or king, or bishop for the purpose of concentrating a scattered rural population into an area where the people could be controlled, taxed, indoctrinated against heresy, or act as an outpost in territory that might be disputed. All of these motives were current in the golden age of the *bastides* between the twelfth and fourteenth centuries, when the crusade against the Cathar heresy, the rivalry between the kings of France and the counts of Toulouse, and above all the dispute between England and France (which culminated in the Hundred Years' War) threw the region into political turmoil. However, it was none the less a time of gradually growing prosperity.

The *bastide* went some way towards replacing the huddle of huts in the shelter of the feudal castle, which had been the previous pattern of rural settlement. Parcels of land were measured out – in this sense the settlements were truly planned – and the *bastide* endowed with tax privileges or the holding of fairs in an effort to attract new settlers. Monks, nobles or other privileged people were likely to be frowned

turning ceilings into a Gothic frenzy, are much more likely to fascinate. The cave is one of the biggest in France, with over ten kilometres of passageways, but only a fraction is open to visitors.

Nontron

By the time you reach Nontron you are almost out of characteristic Périgord scenery and into much more open countryside, more heavily farmed and a good deal less scenic. It is a compact little place with a few medieval houses and an airy situation above the little river Bandiat. Neither its castle nor its old church have survived, however. (During one siege, the former was assaulted by a herd of goats with flaming torches strapped to them – an ingenious device to terrify the defenders.) Instead, Nontron has a **Doll Museum** (open early Feb–mid-Oct, daily exc Tue 10–12, 2–6; July and Aug, daily

upon – the *bastide* was to be a source of revenue after all, while the local overlords also had to make sure that all their serfs did not rush to enjoy the freedoms offered by the new towns. At the centre of the *bastide*, the square was the place for commerce – street traders elsewhere were forbidden. As the *bastide* developed, the overlord's bailiff was replaced by a self-governing council, and the *bastide* became in many respects the equivalent of the British borough.

Visitors to the *bastides* that sprinkle the south-west will be struck by the difference between those that have prospered and grown into towns and those that have scarcely expanded beyond their original boundaries. The position of a *bastide* was crucial to its success. Montauban is hardly recognisable as a *bastide* any longer, whereas Sauveterre-de-Rouergue might have been founded yesterday. Not only trade but war and plague put the *bastides* to the test; it is hardly surprising that many remain little more than villages.

The arcades around the main square, which are such a common sight, were not planned. The square was public space, but canny householders on the edge of it increased the size of their properties by building out and over it. Similarly, the walls or fortified gatehouses, which are such an attractive feature today, often had to be put in place at a relatively late stage in the *bastide's* history when warfare threatened.

10–7; mid-Oct–mid-Nov, daily exc Tue 2–5), where a fine collection is assembled in settings suited to their period.

WHERE TO STAY, EAT AND CAMP

There are two sections: establishments that we recommend and establishments that are worth considering but which we think do not merit a wholehearted recommendation. Both are marked on the map at the start of the chapter.

Key: ✦ = 0–250FF, ✦✦ = 251–450FF, ✦✦✦ = over 451FF; prices are per room without breakfast, which costs around 40–65FF extra. Some hotels insist on half-board during high season. Unless we say otherwise all have rooms with bath or shower and accept the major credit cards.

Recommended hotels

BEYNAC-ET-CAZENAC

Le Bonnet	✦-✦✦
24220 Dordogne	*Tel: 53 29 50 01; Fax: 53 29 83 74*

On a bend in the river Dordogne, at the foot of the medieval *bastide* town of Beynac, Le Bonnet's position is marred only by the busy main road that squeezes between the river and the gorge walls. Inside the hotel, there's no real disturbance from traffic noise, and the first-floor terrace makes a popular spot for lunch. The Bonnet family run a friendly household and the atmosphere in the rustic restaurant is informal and chatty. Bedrooms are old-fashioned and some have suspect plumbing, but if a clean, good-value room is what you're looking for Le Bonnet is a good bet.

Mid-Apr–mid-Oct; 21 rooms

BOURDEILLES

Hostellerie Les Griffons	✦✦
Le Pont	
Brantôme	
24310 Dordogne	*Tel: 53 03 75 61; Fax: 53 04 64 45*

The location, on the willow-lined bank of the river Dronne under the battlements of Bourdeilles' castle, is hard to beat. To make the most out of the river, the restaurant extends itself on to a small terrace which catches the sunset beautifully. Most of the bedrooms also face the water, with windows opening on to the village's hump-backed stone bridge, though there is little traffic to disturb sleep. Inside, the décor is plush rustic: tapestry-covered chairs, animal skins and a grand ornamental staircase. Bedrooms have huge carved chalk fireplaces and beamed ceilings.

End Apr–end Sept; 10 rooms

BRANTOME

Le Châtenet ◆◆◆
24310 Dordogne   Tel: 53 05 81 08; Fax: 53 05 85 52

Two kilometres south-west of Brantôme on a quiet lane off the D78, Le Châtenet is a characterful old farmhouse. On one side of the courtyard, sweeping steps lead up to a seventeenth-century verandah and the main entrance through which you reach eight large comfortable bedrooms; some are on a grand scale, with a mixture of old-fashioned furniture and antiques. Across the courtyard a converted stable block houses a rustic sitting room with plenty of books and games. For sunny days there's a pool, better for plunging than swimming in, and a full-size tennis court. Le Châtenet has no restaurant but there are plenty nearby.

All year; 8 rooms; outdoor heated swimming-pool, tennis

LE BUGUE

L'Auberge du Noyer ◆◆-◆◆◆
Le Reclaud de Bouny Bas
24260 Dordogne   Tel: 53 07 11 73; Fax: 53 54 57 44

It took five years for English couple Jenny and Paul Dyers to make a hotel out of their eighteenth-century farmhouse in peaceful green countryside five kilometres west of Le Bugue. Beautifully renovated, l'Auberge du Noyer has good-sized rustic bedrooms with beams and exposed-stone walls or pretty flowery wallpaper, and bathrooms are well equipped. Paul prides himself on a simple menu which changes daily and is made up of fresh local produce. All in all, a tranquil base for exploring the region.

End Mar–early Nov; 10 rooms; outdoor swimming-pool

CARSAC-AILLAC

Le Relais de Touron ◆◆
Le Touron
24200 Dordogne   Tel: 53 28 16 70

The main attraction of this hotel is its large and lovely garden, which has a good-size swimming-pool as well as lawns and shady trees and a little river flowing through. Most bedrooms (simple but comfortable) are in a modern annexe and overlook the garden and swimming-pool, as does the restaurant terrace. The food is local, homely and tasty. Le Touron stands on its own, half a kilometre outside the village of Carsac on the D704 road to Sarlat.

Apr–mid-Nov; 12 rooms; outdoor swimming-pool; tennis

CHAMPAGNAC-DE-BELAIR

Moulin du Roc　　　　　　　　　　　　　　◆◆-◆◆◆
24530 Dordogne　　　　　　　*Tel: 53 54 80 36; Fax: 53 54 21 31*

The old walnut mill on the Dronne was converted in the late 1960s; you can still see the ancient grinding stone and the press incorporated into the plush (there is no other word for it) décor of the sitting-room – low-beamed ceiling, flowery chairs, carved oak doors, chests and columns, flowers, elaborate table lamps. The same baroque effect is achieved throughout the rest of the hotel, including the bedrooms, where several of the beds are canopied and four-postered. To complete the idyllic picture, a bower stands by the river and a narrow curved wooden bridge crosses to more tree-shaded gardens and a secluded swimming-pool. Gourmet menus are excellent, though not cheap, and breakfast is a cut above average.

Mid-Feb–mid-Nov, mid-Dec–mid-Jan; restaurant closed Tue and Wed lunch; 14 rooms; indoor heated swimming-pool; tennis

DOMME

L'Esplanade　　　　　　　　　　　　　　　◆◆-◆◆◆
24250 Dordogne　　　　　　　*Tel: 53 28 31 41; Fax: 53 28 49 92*

The Esplanade is at the top of the *bastide* town of Domme, with a brilliant view of the river gorge. People flock here for the sunset as much as the food. The large restaurant is the focus of the hotel – a beautiful room with beams, potted plants and bright sunny yellow tablecloths, where a team of professional staff serve regional dishes, including *cèpes* in various guises and their famous fillet of lamb in brioche. The bedrooms appear rather plain after the public rooms, but are well-kept and have good bathrooms. Latecomers find themselves rather cut off in the annexe down the road, so it's worth booking ahead and asking for a room overlooking the river.

Mid-Feb–mid-Nov, closed Mon in low season ; 25 rooms

LES EYZIES-DE-TAYAC

Les Glycines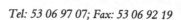
Route de Périgueux
24620 Dordogne   *Tel: 53 06 97 07; Fax: 53 06 92 19*

Les Glycines' friendly, informal atmosphere combined with its high standard of service make it very good value. At the quiet western end of the tourist centre of Les Eyzies, this hoTel: makes a good base for visiting the caves of the Vézère valley; the beautiful gardens and pool area mean you could happily spend a restful day here too. Well-kept bedrooms, clean and comfortable rather than stylish, overlook either the road, the river or the garden, where you can have breakfast and lunch. The smart restaurant serves regional dishes using fresh produce from its own riverside plot.

End Apr–end Oct; restaurant closed Sat lunch; 25 rooms; outdoor swimming-pool

LALINDE

Hôtel le Château
1 Rue de la Tour
24150 Dordogne   *Tel: 53 61 01 82; Fax: 53 24 74 60*

If lingering for a day or two in the western Dordogne, near Bergerac, you could do worse than base yourself at the little castle right on the banks of the river in Lalinde, complete with winding staircase and witch-hat turrets. It's part of the Logis chain, family-run and very easy-going and friendly, with good regional cooking and newly smartened up bedrooms – all tastefully decorated in pastels and matching drapery, and good showers or bathrooms; one bedroom, number seven, is positively palatial. For hot days there's a terrace above the river and even a small swimming-pool at the back.

Early Feb–end Dec; 7 rooms; outdoor swimming-pool

LA ROQUE-GAGEAC

La Plume d'Oie   ♦♦
24250 Dordogne   *Tel: 53 29 57 05; Fax: 53 31 04 81*

This *auberge* fronts the riverside road below the sheer rocks in the pretty though touristy village of La Roque Gageac. The instant impression is one of space, neatness and light, with much use of tiles, stone and light-coloured wood. The main attraction here is the food: local ingredients are presented in a *nouvelle cuisine* style. Even the breakfast is mouth-wateringly displayed and includes an artistically arranged fruit bowl. The creator of all these gastronomic delights is English (Marc-

Pierre Walker); his Dutch wife, Hiddy, performs her front-of-house duties with friendliness and gusto.

Mar–end Jan; closed Mon and Tue midday exc. July and Aug closes Sat and Mon midday; 4 rooms

ST-SAUD-LACOUSSIERE

Hostellerie St-Jacques   ✦✦-✦✦✦
24470 Dordogne   *Tel: 53 56 97 21; Fax: 53 56 91 33*

In the centre of a small village in the northern part of Périgord, Hostellerie St-Jacques is an old ivy-covered coaching inn run by the friendly Babayou family. Recently refurbished in parts, the hotel has a mixture of atmospheres – the sitting-room, with its grandfather clock and books, has an old-fashioned rustic feel, while the sunny restaurant, with its yellow tablecloths and windows opening on to the garden, is more cheerful. Bedrooms are well-equipped and comfortable, with simple furnishings and generally lots of space. Those overlooking the pretty garden and swimming-pool area are the most peaceful and the best value.

Apr–end Sept; 15 rooms; outdoor heated swimming-pool; tennis

VEZAC

Manoir de Rochecourbe   ✦✦
24200 Dordogne   *Tel: 53 29 50 79*

As a bed-and-breakfast base from which to explore the Dordogne, Manoir de Rochecourbe is hard to beat. It scores bonus points for location and romantic appeal: it is seven kilometres from Sarlat, creeper-clad with sixteenth-century turrets. The hospitality of the Roger family is an extra advantage. The six bedrooms are named after wild flowers and are individually decorated with comfortable solid furniture; the bathrooms are modern and of a good size. The sitting-room, with its heavy antiques, huge stone fireplace and beamed ceiling has a baronial feel, while the breakfast room is warm and pretty, with deep orange walls and fresh flowers on every table. Madame Rogers breakfasts are a cut above elsewhere too.

Mid-June to early Oct; 6 rooms

Worth considering

LES EYZIES-DE-TAYAC

Le Centenaire
Rocher de le Penne
24620 Dordogne   *Tel: 53 06 97 18; Fax: 53 06 92 41*

Famous for its food which is expensive and somewhat overrated, this hotel is comfortable if rather bland.

Early Apr–early Nov; restaurant closed Tue lunch; 24 rooms; heated outdoor swimming-pool; sauna; gym

LIMEUIL

Au Bon Accueil
Le Bourg
24510 Dordogne   *Tel: 53 63 30 97*

Inexpensive, rather shabby rooms in lovely *bastide* village. Pretty terrace restaurant.

MARNAC

La Grande Marque
St-Cyprien
24220 Dordogne   *Tel: 53 31 61 63; Fax: 53 28 39 55)*

Old farmhouse in wonderful hilltop position, informally run by artists.

RIBERAC

Hotel de France
Rue Marc Dufraisse
24600 Dordogne   *(Tel: 53 90 00 61; Fax: 53 91 06 05*

Traditional former posthouse with attractive garden restaurant. Family-run with enthusiasm. Particularly good hotel for staying in on the eve (Thursday) of market day, but book ahead.

Campsites

Key: ✦ = 0–60FF, ✦✦ = 61–100FF, ✦✦✦ = over 101FF. Prices are for two adults, tent and car; children are half-price or less. All campsites listed have lavatories and washing facilities.

BELVES

Les Hauts de Ratebout	✦✦✦
24170 Dordogne	*Tel: 53 29 02 10; Fax: 53 29 08 28*

Immaculate site with good facilities for children.

May–end Sept; reservation advisable peak season; shop, rest/café; swimming-pool; tennis

BELVES

Les Nauves	✦✦
24170 Dordogne	*Tel: 53 29 12 64*

Small site in very quiet rural spot. Horse-riding from site.

May–end Sept; reservation advisable peak season; shop; rest/café; swimming-pool

BIRON

Etang du Moulinal	✦✦-✦✦✦
24540 Dordogne	*Tel: 53 40 84 60; Fax: 53 40 81 49*

Restful views with informal pitches at a neighbourly distance clustered on the bank of a small, still lake. Good value and a good family atmosphere with plenty of organised activities.

Apr–mid-Sept; reservation advisable peak season; rest/café; supermarket; swimming-pool; tennis

CALVIAC-CARLUX

Les Chênes Verts	✦✦
Sarlat	
24370 Dordogne	*Tel: 53 59 21 07*

Medium-sized site with relatively private pitches and extremely friendly owners. Lots going on in high season.

May–end Sept; reservation advisable peak season; shop; rest/café; swimming-pool; tennis

CARSAC-AILLAC

Le Rocher de la Cave ◆
Sarlat
24200 Dordogne *Tel: 53 28 14 26, low season 53 28 12 57*

Small, inexpensive, low-key site in superb location on the river. Bar and canoes are the focal points.

June–end Sept; reservation advisable peak season; shop; rest/café (July and Aug only)

CENAC

Le Pech de Caumont ◆◆
Domme
24250 Dordogne Tel: 53 28 21 63, low season 53 28 30 67; Fax: 53 29 99 73

Nothing special except the panoramic view of the citadel of Domme. Plain with basic facilities; good for a stopover.

Apr–end Sept; reservation advisable peak season; rest/café; swimming-pool

GROLEJAC

Les Granges ◆◆
Domme
24250 Dordogne *Tel: 53 28 11 15; Fax: 53 28 57 13*

Friendly site with leafy, biggish pitches. Busy and lively.

May–end Sept; reservation advisable peak season; shop; rest/café; swimming pool

MONPAZIER

Le Moulin de David ◆-◆◆
Gaugeac
24540 Dordogne *Tel: 53 22 65 25*

Thoughtfully laid-out site with stream running through. Popular with British and Dutch. Lots of activities.

May–mid-Sept; reservation advisable peak season; shop; rest/café; half-court tennis; swimming pool

ROUFFIGNAC

Cantegrel ◆◆-◆◆◆
24580 Dordogne *Tel: 53 05 48 30; Fax: 53 05 40 67*

Low-key, remote, mid-size site with good views.

Apr–mid-Oct; reservation advisable peak season; shop; swimming-pool

SARLAT

Le Moulin du Roch ✦✦✦
Route des Eyzies
24200 Dordogne　　　　　　*Tel: 53 59 20 27; Fax: 53 29 44 65*

Steep and heavily wooded seclusion. Not cheap.

Apr–end Sept, reservation advisable peak season; shop; rest/café; swimming-pool; tennis

SARLAT

Les Périères ✦✦✦
24200 Dordogne　　　　　　*Tel: 53 59 05 84; Fax: 53 28 57 51*

Rather sedate, old-fashioned high-grade site

Easter–end Sept; reservation advisable peak season; shop; bar snacks; swimming-pool; tennis

ST-CYBRANET

Bel Ombrage ✦✦
24250 Dordogne　　　　　　*Tel: 53 28 34 14*

Quietish pretty site on river banks. Dominated by British. Better suited perhaps to active adults than to children.

June–mid-Sept; reservation advisable peak season; swimming-pool

ST-CYBRANET

Le Céou ✦✦
24250 Dordogne　　　　　　*Tel: 53 28 32 12*

Sedate and old-fashioned enclave popular with British

May–end Sept; reservation advisable peak season; shop; rest/café; swimming-pool

ST-GENIES

La Bouquerie ✦✦-✦✦✦
24590 Dordogne　　　　　　*Tel: 53 28 98 22*

Leafy site near Sarlat with good-sized pitches. Lots of activities; good for young children.

Mid-May–mid-Sept; reservation advisable peak season; shop; rest/café; swimming-pool

ST LEON-SUR-VEZERE

Le Paradis ♦♦♦
Montignac
24290 Dordogne   *Tel: 53 50 72 64; Fax: 53 50 75 90*

Very busy, lively and well-organised. Excellent for children.

Apr–end Oct, reservation advisable peak season; shop; rest/café; swimming-pool; tennis

STE-NATHALENE

Les Grottes de Roffy ♦♦♦
Sarlat
24200 Dordogne   *Tel: 53 59 15 61*

Green location close to Sarlat, with a cheerful holiday camp atmosphere. Good for children.

Early Apr–end Sept; reservation advisable peak season; shop; rest/café; swimming-pool; tennis

STE-NATHALENE

La Palombière ♦♦-♦♦♦
Sarlat
24200 Dordogne   *Tel: 53 59 42 34; Fax: 53 28 45 40*

Good value and spacious, with fun for all the family.

May–mid-Sept; reservation advisable peak season; shop; rest/café; swimming-pool; tennis

TREMOLAT

Bassin Nautique ♦♦-♦♦♦
24510 Dordogne   *Tel: 53 22 81 18; Fax: 53 09 51 41*

Riverside site, excellent for families.

May to end Sept; reservation advisable peak season; tennis; swimming-pool, bar snacks

VITRAC

Le Soleil Plage ◆◆

Sarlat
24200 Dordogne   *Tel: 53 28 33 33; Fax: 53 29 36 87*

Split site – pitches on the river banks are the best. Small beach. Good facilities but rather crowded.

End May–end Sept; restaurant from end May; reservation advisable peak season; shop; rest/café; swimming pool; tennis

THE LOT

The river Lot is often described as being like the Dordogne in miniature, a sort of poor relation perhaps. It is true that for much of its central stretch between Figeac and Cahors it, like the Dordogne, has cut its way through bands of limestone, creating the same colourful effects of striped grey- and apricot-coloured cliffs against green fields and blue skies. But in other respects it is a very different river. Its valley is narrower and more tortuous; it is also less free-flowing than the Dordogne, with long calm stretches interrupted by sudden weirs or rapids. Above Figeac it becomes a mountain river, rushing through a narrow valley between wooded hills (see the Aubrac, Tarn Gorges and Western Cévennes chapter). Below Cahors it starts to wind in great sinuous curves, and it is here that the grapes of the Cahors *appellation* are grown. Further downstream again, past Puy l'Evêque, the Lot becomes a river of the flatlands, draining slowly towards the Garonne past the old *bastide* town of Villeneuve-sur-Lot. This part of the river is ignored by most visitors, probably with justice, for the scenery becomes dull by comparison with what is to be found higher up in the limestone country.

The river Lot is the central feature of what, before the French Revolution, was the province of Quercy, an irregular chunk of land enveloping the Dordogne valley in the north-east and reaching down to the river Garonne in the south-west. Haut Quercy is the country of the limestone plateaux – the *causses* de Gramat, de Martel and de Limogne – while Bas Quercy, or Quercy Blanc, is the area of chalky hills above the Garonne basin. The boundaries of today's Lot and Lot-et-Garonne *départements* are not much different, and you will discover that people and guidebooks use the names Quercy and Périgord (for the Dordogne *département*) just as often as the newer ones.

Quercy is above all limestone country. The *causses* here are called *petits* to distinguish them from the Grands Causses around the Tarn Gorges, but there is nothing small about their extent. Barren, almost deserted landscapes of scrub oak and crumbling stone walls where people once farmed, the *causses* have a hypnotic attraction. This is provoked by the sense of loneliness that infects them, in marked contrast to the well-populated valleys below, with their roads and their fertile riverside fields. The contrast is sudden: climb up out of the Dordogne or Lot valleys and you leave human habitation behind. The blue butterflies that gather around the merest dribble of water, and the buzzards that wheel above the woods are the only signs of life. A good way of seeing the *causse* is to go pony-trekking (on sections of the *Grandes Randonnées* open to horses). There are numerous equestrian centres: ask for the leaflet *Tourisme équestre dans le Lot* from the Cahors tourist office (tel 65 35 09 56).

There are a number of extremely good reasons for spending time in the Lot valley, and even for preferring it to the Dordogne. There is less traffic and fewer tourists and the river itself feels much more like a river of the south: the overhanging houses in the towns, the red tiles and the blinding sun belong more to the Mediterranean. The towns of Figeac and Cahors, often unjustly ignored by visitors who succumb easily to the more obvious charms of Sarlat and the Dordogne villages, are full of atmosphere and history, and are both worth spending time in.

THE DORDOGNE FROM SOUILLAC TO BRETENOUX

This is one of the most beautiful stretches of the river, running from the border between Périgord and Quercy to the point where the Dordogne curves north towards the distant hills of

Good bases

● **Martel** This medieval town stands on the *causse* north of the Dordogne and is full of magnificent houses. Although busy, it is not as crowded as the river valley, and the surrounding countryside is attractive. It makes a good spot from which to tour the Upper Dordogne.

● **Gourdon** A market town set in fertile countryside to the west of the Causse de Gramat. The surrounding villages are ideal for touring or for self-catering holidays. It is well-placed for exploring the Dordogne.

● **Cajarc** The obvious base for touring the valley of the Lot, this large village is well-organised for tourism but manages to feel relaxed and friendly. For isolation, search for accommodation on the *causses* to the north or south. For more animation, stay in the river valley.

● **Puy L'Evêque** A good spot from which to range over the Cahors vineyards and the hidden countryside to the north. The town is medieval and full of character.

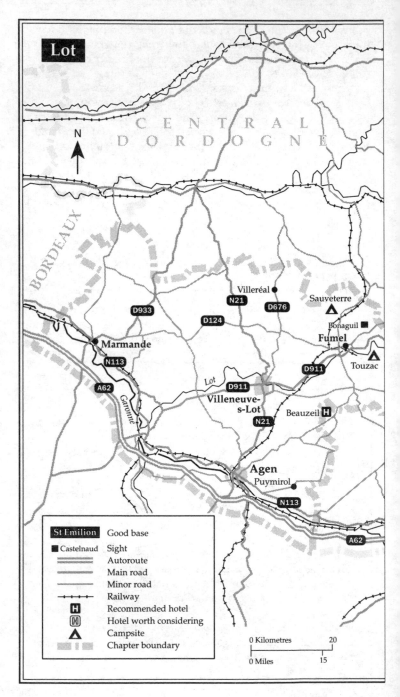

Lot

CENTRAL DORDOGNE

N

BORDEAUX

Villeréal
N21
D676
D933
D124
Marmande
N113
A62
Lot
D911
Garonne
Villeneuve-s-Lot
N21
Sauveterre
Bonaguil
Fumel
Touzac
D911
Beauzeil H
Agen
Puymirol
N113
A62

St Emilion	Good base
Castelnaud ■	Sight
	Autoroute
	Main road
	Minor road
	Railway
H	Recommended hotel
H	Hotel worth considering
▲	Campsite
	Chapter boundary

0 Kilometres   20
0 Miles   15

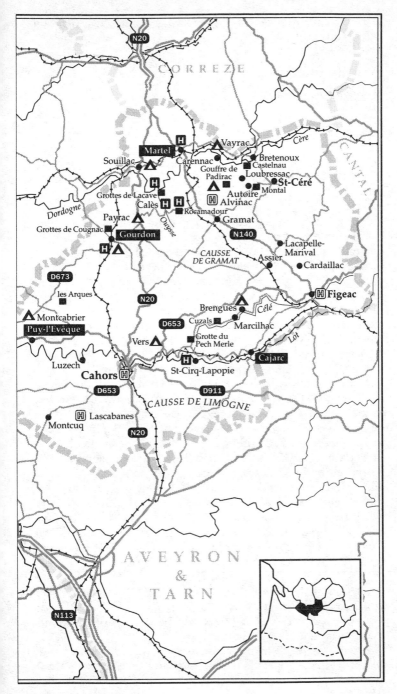

CORREZE

N20

Cère

CANTAL

H Martel
Souillac
Carennac
Vayrac
Bretenoux
Castelnau
Gouffre de
Padirac
Loubressac
St-Céré
Montal
Autoire
H Alvinac

Grottes de Lacave
Calès
H
Rocamadour
Dordogne
Ouysse
Payrac
Gramat
Grottes de Cougnac
Gourdon
N140
H
CAUSSE
DE GRAMAT
Lacapelle-
Marival
Assier
Cardaillac

D673
les Arques
N20
Brengues
Cuzals
Célé
H Figeac
Marcilhac
D653
Montcabrier
Puy-l'Evêque
Vers
Grotte du
Pech Merle
Lot
Cajarc
Luzech
H
St-Cirq-Lapopie
Cahors H
D653
D911
CAUSSE DE LIMOGNE
Montcuq
H Lascabanes
N20

AVEYRON
&
TARN

N113

Corrèze. Take your time and spend a day among the castles and villages on the banks.

Souillac and around

Souillac

Souillac is a medium-sized country town, right on the border between Périgord and Quercy. It is plagued by the main N20 road that runs right through it. This blight stops it from becoming over-visited by tourists; and away from the main street, with its roaring lorries and lines of cafés and pizza parlours, it reveals itself as a dignified place, with a good deal to look at.

The most interesting building is without doubt the abbey church of **Ste-Marie**, one of the best domed churches in Quercy. Three domes rise above the nave and transept, with a further half-dome over the chancel. The church was built in around 1145 (the fashion for domes being a direct result of the crusades – in which Quercy families played a large part) but was much restored in the seventeenth century. One of the more remarkable achievements of this restoration was to turn the original west door inside out, so that the magnificent carved tympanum now lies on the interior side – rather spoiling its impact, perhaps, but preserving it from the weather.

Unfortunately, it was not preserved from mutilation during the Wars of Religion, but enough remains to show that this was another Romanesque masterpiece by the same school of carving that wrought Beaulieu and Moissac. The legend of Theophilus forms the centrepiece: he was an all-too-human monk who forged a pact with the devil in order to become abbot. Then repenting, he implored the Virgin to save him and she seized the contract from the devil, leaving him outwitted, as usual.

Columns of intertwined animals writhe on the pilasters which support the tympanum, inflicting the usual cruelties on each other and on the occasional human who intrudes. The statue of Isaiah, to the right of the door, is a wonderful piece of work, full of life and expression. After this masterpiece, the rest of the carvings in the church can seem ordinary, but there are some fine sculpted capitals to the pillars nevertheless. The abbey church is close to the old quarter of Souillac, small in comparison to the rest of the town, but well-garnished with open squares and narrow lanes.

Around the back of the cathedral you will find the **Musée de l'Automate** (open Jan-Mar, Nov and Dec, daily 2–4 exc

Mon and Tue 2–4; Apr, May and Oct, daily exc Mon 10–12, 3–6; June and Sept, daily 10–12, 3–6, July and Aug daily 10–7). This is a splendid, modern, computer-operated museum with a very comprehensive collection of working models of all kinds, largely historically arranged. Among the many groups of figures that come to life (a shop-window-sized cameo of the Paris métro, for example), there are some very strange creations indeed. A favourite turn-of-the-century joke seems to have been to place a life-size automaton among your dinner guests, or to put a pram with an 'automatic' baby in it for people to coo over. The most modern automaton is a disturbingly alive industrial robot, which, in a setting of a medieval alchemist's parlour, solemnly opens a box and makes a neat stack of bricks before putting them all back again. It is a fascinating place, bound to appeal to children, and worth making a special visit to Souillac to see.

Martel

This small but very beautiful medieval town was once capital of the vastly powerful viscounts of Turenne and a considerably more populous and important place than it is now. No trace remains of the courtiers, the *justiciers* and the dignitaries who inhabited the town right up until the eighteenth century except for the magnificent houses they left behind. Today, off-season Martel is sleepy and seems half-forgotten in the middle of the sparsely populated *causse* surrounding it. However, the town comes to life rapidly in summer; it is a favourite stopping-off point for tourists, who do the circuit of the buildings and then retire to one of the numerous cafés. It seldom becomes desperately overcrowded, however, and makes a very good half day's expedition.

The heart of the town is the Place des Consuls, with its eighteenth-century covered market (it looks much older at first glance, but is too ostentatious to be medieval). On the eastern side, is the wonderful **Hôtel de la Raymondie** (open July and Aug, Mon-Fri 10-12, 3-6), which used to be the local château of the Turenne viscounts. The building dates from the thirteenth century and contains numerous vaulted chambers as well as a small museum of Roman finds. In another of the houses on the square, the **Hôtel Fabri**, Henry Shortcoat (son of Henry II of England) died in agony on a bed of ashes weighed down by a huge wooden cross in penitence for rebelling against his father and pillaging the shrine at

Rocamadour. Martel was where he made his confession and died.

Hardly a street in Martel is without at least one grand mansion, many of them dating from the seventeenth and eighteenth centuries. But the other building especially worth seeing is the fortified Gothic church of **St-Maur**. More stronghold than church, it was built during the thirteenth and fourteenth centuries when the town was in constant danger from the English (it was never taken by them). The doorway has a Romanesque tympanum (the carving is not up to the standard of that at Souillac). Inside, the long dark nave is illuminated by some fine Renaissance stained glass.

Grottes de Lacave

(Open mid-Mar–Oct, daily 9–12, 2–6, 6.30 mid-July to mid-Aug.)

This is probably the second most-visited unpainted cave in the Dordogne valley after the Gouffre de Padirac, and the queues can build up to horrendous proportions (a fact noted by the proprietors of the café opposite the entrance, which sells some of the most expensive soft drinks in France). The cave is only really worth visiting if you don't have to queue for too long.

An electric train trundles you into the depths, where, from a rocky chamber, the guided tour branches off through two separate systems of tunnels and concretions. Lacave is not an overwhelming cave, but it is very rich in strangely shaped columns and other effects caused by the millennia-long seepage of calcium-laden water. Sections of it have been much improved by ultra-violet light, which shows up the stalactites in a ghostly white. It has the curious effect of endowing each 'living' one with a glowing star at its tip – the effect is quite magical as long as it is not eclipsed by the day-glo colour of your neighbour's white shirt. Another fairy-like effect is achieved by lighting a small pool in such a way that the reflected stalactites of the ceiling appear powerfully like the minarets and spires of some Arabian city seen from across a distant plain.

In the face of this high-technology brilliance, the traditional jokes of the cave, such as the simulacrum of a human face sunk under the calcite and lovingly dubbed the 'dead tourist', fall a little flat.

A short way west of the cave, the **Château de Belcastel** dominates the junction of the Ouysse and the Dordogne from the top of a tall precipice. This is one of the most photogenic castles in the Dordogne valley. A fraction further west, the Château de la Treyne is now an extremely smart hotel, and its setting, again high above the river, is almost as good as that of Belcastel.

Just upstream of Lacave, **Meyronne** and **St-Sozy** are both pretty places, the latter with a lovely, naive *pietà* in its church. If pushed for time, however, **Creysse** is better than either, with an unusual double-apsed Romanesque church. **Gluges**, upstream again, has a semi-troglodytic church and a nearby viewpoint high above a curve of the Dordogne, while **Montvalent** and **Floirac** are made attractive because of their positions on top of or under the typically sheer cliffs, which rise on both banks of the river at this point.

Carennac to Bretenoux

Carennac

The village swarms in high season, not surprisingly, since it is not only built of a peculiarly luminous creamy stone, but also has its own small château and Romanesque church, the latter with yet another carved tympanum from the Moissac school. This one has Christ in Glory surrounded by Apostles, bears and peacocks. Inside the church there are carved capitals with lions, dragons and eagles, and also a superbly realistic and emotional carved Deposition from the fifteenth century. The cloisters of the old priory to which the church belonged have been heavily restored, and much of them is Gothic rather than Romanesque. But they make a peaceful, shady spot if the crowds are too great elsewhere.

Loubressac and Autoire

Heavily prettified by huge tubs of flowers and definitely over-populated by throngs of visitors in the summer, Loubressac has one of the best viewpoints in the upper reaches of the Dordogne. From the esplanade you can gaze northwards over the bumpy region of country known as the Limargue with the château of Castelnau in the foreground, the towers of St-Céré and the distant ruins of Turenne beyond. The glistening silver of the Dordogne runs through the landscape – on a clear day the views are well worth stopping for.

Other than the views, Loubressac is a harmonious place of small lanes and ancient houses. It briefly entered modern history as the spot selected for an enormous parachute drop to the *maquis* of the Lot in 1944. There's a memorial to this event in the town.

Autoire, tucked away just around the corner but hidden at the bottom of a steep valley topped by a cirque of cliffs, is altogether different. It is a tiny, narrow village with none of the souvenir shops or superficial glamour of Loubressac, but simply a collection of typical Quercy houses, spiky with turrets and pigeon lofts, many of them half-crumbled into the landscape. It is a beautiful place to walk round for ten minutes, which is all the time it takes. Be warned – there is nowhere much to park.

After the village, continue up the road to the top of the cirque. Here, just before it emerges on to the *causse*, a parking place allows you to stop and gaze back down the valley or scramble around the top of the precipice in the hope of catching a glimpse of the waterfall plunging over it. The voices of people walking up the stream from below echo around the cliffs. It is a suddenly wild place in an otherwise lush landscape. The nearby **Grottes de Presque** (open Mar-Nov, daily 9–12, 2–6, 7 in July and Aug) are not up to Lacave in beauty or interest but are much less visited and would make a good substitute if the former cave is crowded. Their speciality is thin 'candles' of calcite, which stretch from floor to ceiling.

Château du Montal

(Open Easter-Nov, daily exc Sat 9.30–12, 2.30–6.)
One of the most beautiful and fascinating castles in the Dordogne valley, and one of the very few where the interior is as good as, if not better than, the exterior. From the outside, as you approach, it has the look of a feudal stronghold, with its round towers poking above the treetops. But this is actually a Renaissance château, so delicate in conception and so finely executed that it seems to belong to the glories of the Loire rather than to a humble corner of Quercy.

This is also a romantic place. The château was built (or rather remodelled) in 1523 by Jeanne de Balzac d'Entraygues, and it is her face that you see looking down at you in the inner courtyard. Busts of herself and her family are positioned here in niches between the beautiful mullioned windows and under the long carved frieze of stone that runs between the first and second storeys. The legend goes that Jeanne built this paradise in stone as a surprise for her eldest son on his homecoming from the Italian wars. He never came back, and so Jeanne had the knight bearing a scroll with the words *plus d'espoir* ('No more hope') carved by the window from which she used to watch for his return.

While the exterior of the Renaissance wings is wonderful enough, the real marvel of Montal is the staircase, which you reach on entry. However, tantalisingly, you are not allowed to examine it before being taken through the lower rooms. This staircase is built of Carennac stone and carved on the underside with a riot of grotesques, birds and shells. Its proportions are so perfect and the intricacies of the carving so intriguing that it is a huge temptation to sit on the steps and gaze.

Montal was saved – and this is the second romantic tale – by an oil millionaire, a Monsieur Fenaille, in 1908. For many years it had passed from family to family, until, at the end of the nineteenth century, its magnificent stonework, its carvings and its massive fireplaces were cut out and sold off to museums and collectors world-wide. The only reason that the staircase was saved was that it could not be dismantled. Fenaille spent his life and fortune tracking down and re-acquiring everything he could and restoring the stonework to its original position. In order to get the final pieces he had to hand the château over to the State, so that the Louvre could 'lend' the missing pieces that it owned.

There are other things to see in the château apart from the stonework, including some fine glass, furniture and tapestries. But it is the stone, and especially the staircase, that inspire. For such a perfect place, Montal is curiously little known. It is just off the beaten track of the Dordogne valley, but it is most certainly worth visiting.

St-Céré

The charm of this small town is rather eclipsed by its position on a busy road and by the fact that its old centre is overshadowed by the surrounding modern development. However, once you are away from the main road there are streets of ancient houses to wander through, a museum of vintage cars and a gory legend to go with the town's foundation. Spérie, daughter of Cérénus, an eighth-century duke of Aquitaine, had been promised in marriage to a local lord by her brother. Having dedicated herself to God, however, Spérie fled from her wedding and was pursued by her angry brother, who proceeded to decapitate her. Miraculously, her body rose and carried her severed head to a nearby well to wash it. First her tomb, then a chapel, then a town – such are St-Céré's supposed origins.

Just outside the town on a conical hill, two medieval towers are almost all that remains of the château that once crowned it. Rising high above the scenery, the towers are visible from miles around, making a most effective landmark for the town. Once you have found your way to the suburb of St-Laurent-des-Tours and then to the steep road that leads to the towers, you may wonder if they are worth the journey. But they are, for not only is the view wonderful, but the towers were once the home of Jean Lurçat, the Cubist artist who single-handedly revived the French tapestry industry. Here you can see his **home** and his **workshop** (open mid-July-Sept, daily 9.30-12, 2.30-6.30). If the scale and colour of the work catches your attention, there is a permanent Lurçat exhibition in St-Céré (open all year, daily exc Tue in low season 9–12, 2–7, Sun 11–12, 2–7).

Château du Castelnau-Bretenoux

(Open 1 Apr–30 June and Sept, daily exc Tue, 9.30–12, 2–6.15; in low season 11.30–6.30.)
This angry, red fortress on a rock above the tiny village of Prudhomat looks all that a medieval fastness should be, if that is, one ignores the seventeenth-century additions. Its size and its seeming arrogance in the way it squats above the surrounding country, are not illusions: it is the second largest fortification in southern France, and the Castelnau family, who were its overlords throughout the Middle Ages, styled themselves 'the second barons of Christendom'. They recognised their feudal lord only in the count of Toulouse, and to say that they were offended when he offered the overlordship of the castle to neighbouring Turenne would be too mild a way of describing their violent armed reaction. Eventually, King Louis VIII was called in to pacify both sides. He judged that Castelnau did indeed owe Turenne feudal duty, and this should be paid annually in the form of a single egg. For years the egg was carried from one castle to the other in a ceremonial procession.

However, Castelnau is rather disappointing inside. Although you get a good idea of its triangular shape, of the thickness of the walls and of the massiveness of the fortifications, in 1851 fire damaged much of the interior, and the more modern buildings are still in some state of decay. There is a grand, square keep, plenty of rather hideous furniture and a whole sequence of passageways, but they do not compensate for the fact that the castle is better from the outside; and visiting the interior is worthwhile only if you have the time and the interest.

EASTERN LOT

St-Céré is on the edge of the limestone country. East of here you are into the granites and schists of Auvergne, and the countryside becomes higher. The villages lose the warmth of the white stone and become dour grey places – at least so they seem by contrast. This part of the Lot *département*, the Ségala, is really an out-thrust of the kind of landscape you find all over Cantal, and mass tourism stops dead at its edge.

It has to be said that there is not a great deal to be seen here, but the area can make a welcome relief from heat and crowds. The valley of the Cère is inaccessible to cars, so the most obvious circuit runs through **Souceyrac** and **Latronquière**. The latter is an old Templar stronghold but there is little remaining today. Bessonies to the east, at the very edge of the Lot *département*, is where Marshall Ney was arrested after Waterloo in 1815, but again there is little to show for it.

By far the best village in the area is **Cardaillac,** close to the N140 Gramat-Figeac road. Seat of another powerful family, this village on a cliff seems to consist of little but towers and fortifications. A well-signposted circuit leads you through the houses and walls.

A little north-west, **Lacapelle-Marival** is less a village than a clump of houses surrounding a huge château, a cross between a town hall (which it now is) and something from a horror film. The Cardaillac family, who established the château, left little room for anything else.

THE CAUSSE DE GRAMAT

The great sheet of limestone separating the Dordogne from the Lot valley is for the most part high, semi-deserted countryside, with not a lot to detain the visitor in a rush. However, because it is the setting for the shrine of Rocamadour, France's second most-visited sight (after Mont-St-Michel in Normandy), the eastern part of the *causse* is one of the tourist centres of the area, with many secondary attractions having sprung up around Rocamadour itself. The equally famous, if rather less enchanting, Gouffre de Padirac is also in this area. At its western end, around the town of Gourdon, the limestone gives way to a fertile country of reddish earth and small hills. This is a quiet area of châteaux and churches, many of which have lovely fifteenth-century frescoes.

Gourdon and around

Gourdon, built all over the summit of a conical hill, looks wonderful as you come towards it on the D704 from Sarlat. In medieval times it was one of the most important towns of the area, with a population reckoned at 5,000 (much the same as today's); now, its only claim to fame is as the market town for the surrounding area. An excellent market town it is too, and in summer, whether it is market day or not, the parking spaces are full of foreign cars, most of them British, as families stock up for the holiday ahead.

Gourdon rather disjointedly combines its two roles, one as a busy, commercial town and the other as an ancient, picturesque tourist attraction. The medieval part occupies the top of the hill and is bounded by the circular road running along the line of the old city walls. Most of the workaday shops are on this road, while higher up the hill you are more likely to find antique and craft shops and cafés.

Steep streets run up the hill. The Rue Majou has the best combination of overhanging corbelled houses and good shop windows to gaze in, while the Rue Zig-Zag is aptly named. At the summit you come across a tiny cobbled square, most of it occupied by the grey bulk of the fourteenth-century **Eglise St-Pierre**. Much larger inside than you might have been led to expect, this Gothic church has overtones of the region's fortified churches. Massive buttresses support the high vault of the nave and chancel. The history of local families is traced on the walls, in one instance by a dark band decorated by numerous coats of arms.

Behind the church, steps lead up towards the summit of the hill, once crowned by a powerful castle. This was demolished in the seventeenth century, and all that remains now are a few fragments. Paths wind among stony outcrops, the haunt of lovers, boys in search of adventure and tourists who have made the climb to admire the view (which takes in miles of countryside, with the red blotches of distant villages showing up among the trees).

Just to the north of the town, the twin caverns of the **Grottes de Cougnac** (open Easter–early Nov, daily 9–12,

2–5.30; July and Aug daily 9.30–6) are comparatively ignored. This is rather surprising when you consider that one of them has some very beautiful rock formations, and the other some fine prehistoric art. This latter is particularly noteworthy for the rare depiction of human figures, two of them pierced by spears; there are also a giant deer and many other animals. Off-season, you may have to wait for some time for enough people to gather to make up a tour group, but during the peak season this scarcity of visitors is a real advantage.

The Northern Bouriane

A short circuit of the country immediately around Gourdon takes you through a sequence of villages – as varied in their attractions (all of them small) as any in the Dordogne. Start by the river Bléou beneath Gourdon with the thirteenth-century Notre-Dame des Neiges, then go to **Le Vigan** to see the glass and the Romanesque capitals in the once-prosperous abbey church, which was pillaged by the English in the Hundred Years' War. Due north, **Lamothe-Fénelon** is the tiny village where Nancy Cunard once lived. **Masclat** has a beautiful château, **Fajoles** a church doorway with finely carved but weathered pillars, and **Milhac** another powerful-looking castle and a cluster of pretty houses.

Rocamadour

Rocamadour is the second sight of France after the great abbey of St-Michel in Normandy. However, whereas St-Michel is worth enduring any discomfort to visit, Rocamadour, frankly, is not. The setting has to be seen, but this can be done from a distance, and then you can turn your back on the crowds, the souvenirs and the over-restored buildings and go somewhere more peaceful.

However, if you can plan a visit to avoid the worst of the crowds and the heat – perhaps by rising early to get here before 9am (when there may even still be some parking space near the village) – then come, for the shrine of Rocamadour carries an extraordinary patina of the past. As you mount the stairs that lead up the impossible precipice, you are treading in the foot-steps of kings and of saints, of Henry II and Thomas à Becket, of seven French kings, and of Saint Dominic, Saint Benedict and Saint Antony of Padua.

It all started with Saint Amadour, a hermit who lived and died in a cliffside cave. He was identified with the Zacchaeus of the New Testament who climbed the tree to see Christ, and when his mummified body was discovered in 1166, Rocamadour rapidly became a place of mass pilgrimage.

The setting is quite extraordinary, even in a land of superlatives, and it is well worth seeking out the best viewpoint, which is on the little D32 road south of Rocamadour. An old saying – 'houses on top of the river, churches above the houses, cliffs above the churches and a castle above the cliffs' – is an exact enough description, but does not mention that the bulky yellow and orange precipice overhangs the village below to such an extent that all the buildings seems to cling to the rock face in defiance of gravity.

This was a large site in medieval times and the ancient gateways remain, as do the closely clumped houses along the main street. From this street, a stair cut into the rock face leads, in a flight of 144 steps, towards the religious complex above. The devout make the climb on their knees. Built around the niche cut into the cliff where the body of Saint Amadour was discovered, a series of semi-troglodytic chapels, a basilica and a so-called bishop's palace form the heart of the holy ground. A further stairway, set up with the stations of the cross, winds vertically upwards again, leading to the château on top of the precipice (fourteenth century in origin but heavily restored) and to the ramparts from which you can gaze straight down on the village beneath.

It need not be as exhausting as this. At the nearby village of L'Hospitalet, which indeed started as a hospice for pilgrims, and in front of the château, there is space for hundreds of cars, and a two-stage lift will carry you without fuss (though at a cost) down to the churches and the village.

Early risers will be limited in what they can see, because you can only see around all the chapels by guided tour. But the most fascinating is always open – **La Chapelle Miraculeuse Notre-Dame**. This tiny place, half-cave, half-building, illuminated only by candles and blackened by their smoke contains the much revered Black Madonna – a tiny statuette almost impossible to see from the rear of the chapel, crudely cut and dating perhaps from the twelfth century. The chapel is festooned with votive offerings – fetters left by prisoners who redeemed their crimes by pilgrimage, plaques of all kinds, and several model ships to remind you that many of the Madonna's miracles were wrought at sea. A tiny bell – dating possibly from the eighth century – is reputed to ring whenever a miracle is performed, however far away. Altogether this is a strange and numinous place, infected by generations-worth of human faith.

The much larger **Basilica St-Sauveur** is ordinary by comparison. It is twelfth century but, like many of the other buildings, heavily and rather too romantically restored in the nineteenth century. In the cliff face, the niche where the body of Saint Amadour was found is visible, as is the hilt of a sword, apparently thrust into the rock face. Legend has it that Roland, nephew of Charlemagne, stopped here on his way to Spain to offer his famous sword, Durendal. The sword was stolen by Henry Shortcoat, when he pillaged Rocamadour (see Martel, above) and this, at best, is a late-medieval replacement.

The guided tour takes you around the Chapel of St-Michel, unremarkable except for the superb thirteenth-century frescoes inside (even earlier ones are visible on the outside) and the Chapel of St-Amadour, which has modern frescoes. But the crowds can be so great and the chapels are so tiny, that the experience of visiting may not be worth the wait.

Down in the village there are overpriced souvenirs in every shop, throngs of tourists and nowhere to rest your feet. The town hall has an exhibition of Lurçat tapestries.

Sights around Rocamadour

Not surprisingly, commercialism has followed the pilgrims to Rocamadour and there are a number of nearby attractions that have nothing to do with the shrine itself. Most popular of these is the Monkey Forest (*Forêt des Singes*), but it is barely worth coming all the way to the Lot just to look at monkeys. More exciting and less common are the birds of prey to be seen at the **Rocher des Aigles** (open Apr-Oct daily 10-12, 2-6; demonstrations three to five times daily). Falcons, eagles and vultures are flown from and return to their trainer's wrist – and even if you miss one of the demonstrations, these magnificent birds in their large aviaries are an impressive sight.

A further bizarre sight is worth a mention. This is the **Féerie du Rail** (demonstrations three to eleven times daily depending on season), which is simply a huge model railway layout, run by an impressively large bank of computers. However, not content with his trains, the creator has made *everything* work, and the layout becomes a hive of activity as hot-air balloons rise and descend, a bridal procession pours out of a church, skaters skate and footballers race up and down their pitch. In case you miss anything, video screens, tacked to the moving platform on which you stand, give close-ups of what is going on, while in a further fervent attempt to illuminate the workings, the owner's wife rushes up and down with a torch to pick out points of extra interest. It is modeldom run riot, a lot of fun and great for kids.

The **Grotte des Merveilles** (open Apr–Oct, daily 10–12, 2–6; July and Aug daily 9–7) is a stone's throw from the village of L'Hospitalet. This small cave has fairly good rock formations and a smidgeon of prehistoric art, including a galloping bull and the negative of a human hand. But it is not a patch on most other caves in the area.

For peace and quiet after Rocamadour, look no further than the **Ouysse valley**. This hidden mysterious river runs from west of Rocamadour to join the Dordogne by Lacave. Surging from unknown depths out of the Gouffre du Cabouy, the river runs clear and limpid through a rocky valley that is as arid as the riverside is lush. The section of the GR6 which follows the Ouysse, makes one of the most attractive walks in this area, although the tourist train, which now chugs over part of it in season is inclined to ruin the rural solitude. Landscape aside, the only sight down here is the **Moulin de Cougnaguet**, a fourteenth-century fortified mill set back under a rock face. It is in working order, and there are demonstrations in season, but it is the building, brooding behind its thick walls on its own, the rock and the slow sliding of the river that give the place its appeal.

Gouffre de Padirac

(Open Apr-June and Sept, daily 9–12, 2–6; early July 8.30–12, 2–6.30; mid- and end-July, 8.30–6.30; Aug daily 8–7.)
This is the biggest and grandest cave in the region. It is also over-commercialised and over-visited, its guides so eager for tips and its surroundings so grotty, that today's visitor finds it hard to believe old-timers who speak of the joys of being punted up the underground river with only the echoes for company.

Still, it is massive and it is difficult to ignore. What looks like the shaft of a huge mine opens in the barren ground of the *causse*. Standing by the edge you can watch the tiny figures of visitors making their way down flights of caged-in stairs, exactly like a scene of damned souls descending into hell. Joining them (there are lifts too) brings a curious sensation of trepidation as the circle of the sky grows smaller and the darkness beneath looms closer. At the bottom of this enormous shaft a short corridor leads to a landing-stage, where you embark and are poled along an underground river, populated by blind cave-shrimps, to a lake where the roof, covered in strange crystalline formations, rises high over your head. Beyond, the journey on foot passes further enticing rock formations and an isolated little green lake before returning you the way you came.

If there were fewer people, and the set-up was less brash, this would be one of the most splendid caves around. If only. . . if only.

THE CELE VALLEY

The Célé is a tributary of the Lot, rising high in the Auvergne mountains, passing into limestone country at Figeac and then running almost parallel with the larger river until their junction a short distance upstream of Cahors. Like both the Lot and the Dordogne, it runs beneath spectacular apricot-coloured cliffs and encloses tiny, half-crumbling, red-roofed villages in its meanders. However, everything here, roads, villages and scenery, is on a smaller scale than by the two larger rivers, and in our opinion, the more charming for it. There are few tourists and fewer tour coaches; even in the height of summer there is peace in plenty to be found here.

Figeac

Figeac is probably the most interesting town in the whole region, but many of those who travel around it may be put off by its greyish, shut-in look, which seems a far cry from the golden villages of the Dordogne. Certainly, it is not a town that lays its charms open to the passer-by, yet a few hours spent here reveals a range of architecture that you would be hard put to find anywhere else in the area.

The history of Figeac is one of waves of prosperity interrupted by periods of neglect. This explains why its best buildings, from the thirteenth, fourteenth and fifteenth centuries have survived later building fashions. The town sprang up around an abbey, founded on the banks of the Célé in AD 838 and for a long time the abbey rivalled Conques in importance. By the thirteenth century Figeac had seven quarters, seven gates and seven consuls to govern it. The Hundred Years' War and the Wars of Religion did their usual damage, and Figeac suffered again in 1944 when 540 of its people were arrested by

Nazis and deported to Germany; the town narrowly escaped being bombarded by artillery.

In Place Vival stands Figeac's best building, once part of the Royal Mint, and now the tourist office. This thirteenth-century house shows many of the features that you will see elsewhere in the old streets of the town – the neatly ornamented pairs of windows, the elaborate façades and above all the *soleilho*, an open, roofed-over space at the top of the building, used variously for storage, weaving or catching the sun. There is a **museum** (open Apr-June, Sept-Oct daily 10–12, 2.30–6; July and Aug, daily 10–12.30, 2.30–7; Nov–Mar, daily exc Sun 11–12, 2.30–5.30) of fragments collected from demolished buildings. There is also an excellent bookshop – Le Livre en Fête – nearby, which has a particularly good selection of regional histories and guides.

Thereafter, to see the best of the architecture, wander through the old town, taking in Rue Gambetta and Place Carnot, and also the steep Rue Delzhens, which winds uphill to the much-restored church of Notre-Dame du Puy.

On your peregrinations you will find a small, restored square covered in what looks like grey marble covered with scratchings. This is an enlarged reproduction of the Rosetta Stone, set up in memory of J F Champollion, Figeac's most famous son. It was he who deciphered the Rosetta Stone (which has parallel text in two sorts of ancient Egyptian writing and in Greek), enabling scholars to start reading hieroglyphics. There is a museum in the house of his birth (open Nov-Feb, daily exc Mon 2–6; Mar–June and Sept–Oct, daily exc Mon 10–12, 2.30–6.30; July and Aug daily 10–12, 2.30–6.30), which, as well as examples of his own work, has a comprehensive and fascinating collection of artefacts from ancient Egypt.

Close to the Célé, the abbey church is all that remains of the original monastery. Parts of it date from the eleventh century, but most of it was hacked about and rebuilt in later years, so it is not the most interesting of local churches.

Figeac's hotels are rather bland, but you will have a warm welcome and good food at the Hostellerie de l'Europe (see Where to Stay) – often called Chez Marinette after its restaurant. It is on the left bank of the river.

The Célé from Figeac to Marcilhac

Swing north-west out of Figeac to visit **Assier**, birthplace of Galiot de Genouillac, who was armourer to François I of

France. His only intrusion into English history is the fact that he arranged the Cloth of Gold meeting between François and Henry VIII. But he was renowned in France and this village is a memorial to his (mild) megalomania. First comes his château, built in imitation of those on the Loire. Next there is the church, surrounded by a most inappropriate frieze decorated with cannon, gunpowder casks and many other accoutrements of war. Finally there is his *pigeonnier*, capable of holding 2,300 birds and one of the most elaborate pigeon lofts to be found in the south-west.

Drop down into the Célé valley by the D113, which brings you above the red roofs and fortified clump of houses of the village of **Corn** and turn downstream. At **Espagnac**, a tiny and lovely village of crumbling farmhouses, the church is surmounted by a beautiful and very curious belfry, propped over the roof like a half-timbered garret.

Two further typical villages, crushed against rock faces, are **Brengues** and **St-Sulpice** before you arrive at **Marcilhac**. This last is only slightly larger than the others, squashed into a bend of the river, but at its centre lie the remains of what was once a rich and powerful abbey. It has almost crumbled away, but there are signs of restoration. There's a fortified bell-tower from the fourteenth century which has a very rare and much-weathered pre-Romanesque doorway with a carved tympanum. Much of the abbey church is ruined and covered in moss, the remainder was rebuilt in Flamboyant style and is now the parish church. Marcilhac once held Rocamadour as one of its fiefs, but lost out to the enterprising abbey at Tulle, which moved in when Rocamadour began to grow famous.

The old church is surrounded by a close cluster of red-roofed, tottering houses, many dating from the sixteenth century or earlier. It is a charming spot for a short walk.

On the hill behind (the road down from it showing Marcilhac at its best) the **Grotte de Bellevue** (open Easter, July and Aug daily 10–12, 2–6; Sept and Oct weekends only) has no paintings but fairly good rock formations, including racks of the millimetre-thin stalactites called 'macaroni'.

Marcilhac to Cabrerets

Further downstream, high on the barren *causse* above the river, you will find the **Musée de Cuzals** (open Apr, May and Oct, daily exc Sat 2–6; June, 9.30–6.30; July and Aug daily exc Sat 10–7; Sept daily exc Sat 10–6). This folk museum is both subversive and fascinating. Alas, there is no English labelling, so you will have to puzzle through the French to understand the full, glorious irony of the place.

In the grounds of a nineteenth-century burned-out château of considerable ugliness, all kinds of artefacts and buildings from Quercynois folk-life have been assembled. The museum does not differ in this from many other similar folk museums; its originality lies in the fact that it does not seek to conserve or to restore things, but to present them as part of the rubbish that human beings accumulate, rubbish that is lost, broken, patched up and eventually decays.

At the entrance, two exhibits exemplify this approach and poke fun at archaeologists. One presents a twenty-first century 'dig' with improbable futuristic explanations for the junk uncovered, which ranges from a battered Deux-Chevaux to various plastic cast-offs. The second is a dilapidated farm cart, which an earnest notice assures you is photographed several times each day to trace the process of entropy.

Further into the museum you find ranks of ancient tractors, refreshingly unsentimental explanations of Quercynois pigeon lofts, and a *grenier*. The notice explains that the *grenier* is the attic in which the Quercy farmers put all the junk they do not know what to do with, so the museum has done the same. In the middle of an indescribable confusion of nets, old boots, barrels and pieces of ironwork, a conservationist's workshop has been set up, where a Scrooge-like antiquarian can be seen peering at a tiny piece of metal, carefully brushing its surface, while all around, heaps of dusty junk, books and paper threaten to over-whelm him.

One of the best parts of the museum is a small (equally dusty) shed where examples of 'running repairs' have been laid out. These range from tiny car engines shoved into tractors to home-made bodywork for vans, boots patched with metal, metal tools patched with wood, tools turned to saucepans and saucepans to tools. It is the kind of collection no other museum would bother to make, and it is riveting.

There's a pleasant café in what remains of the château. There is some serious activity too – notably the making of bread in wood-fired ovens and a magnificent steam traction engine (built in England) which hisses into life now and again, especially on Sundays.

The only disadvantage of the place is that it can be intolera-bly hot in mid-August. Otherwise, it is one of the best muse-ums in France.

Grotte du Pech-Merle

(Open mid Apr–Oct, daily 9.30–12, 1.30–5.30; rest of year by appointment; tel 65 31 27 05.)

Behind the village of Cabrerets, in a dry valley surrounded by scrub and super-heated rock, you will find this first-class cave. In our estimation only Font-de-Gaume and Lascaux surpass it for prehistoric art.

It is also not as desperately overcrowded as the more famous caves. Seven hundred visitors per day are permitted, allowing twenty-eight groups per day in July and August, the peak months. So there is a good chance of getting a place within an hour or two even if you just turn up.

The wall-paintings are concentrated in two caverns. There are 68 animals, 28 human figures and over 500 enigmatic signs or symbols. The most impressive are the animals – a whole parade of hairy mammoths and horses marches along one wall. In another place, beautiful dappled horses are moulded against a bulging stone. The best estimate is that these drawings were done roughly 22,000 years ago.

Another rarely seen (by ordinary tourists) · sight is the imprints of human footsteps in the soft clay, those of a woman and an adolescent, who must have penetrated the darkness of the cave 15 or more millennia before Christ.

This is a good guided tour, with everything lucidly and clearly explained. A modern and well-stocked museum attached to the cave has a section given over to preparing you for the visit to the cave itself.

Below the cave, **Cabrerets** is little more than a stopping-place for visitors to Pech-Merle. The château, however, built on its rock high over the entry to the Célé's last gorge before it joins the Lot, is threatening and full of impact.

THE LOT FROM FIGEAC TO CAHORS

This is the most popular section of the Lot valley, and indeed the river is at its most spectacular and most like the Dordogne here. Small roads run along both banks, often fringed by high cliffs riddled with caves and holes, some of which may have been troglodyte dwellings, others places of refuge in time of war or plague.

On the south side of the river, the Causse de Limogne is even more desolate than the Causse de Gramat, although much more thickly wooded. Such life as it has centres around the tiny market town of Limogne-en-Quercy, little more than a cross-roads, a café and a garage in the middle of the scrub oak and bare limestone. Driving over this *causse* is a great pleasure, not least because it remains so unvisited. Wandering over the network of small roads linking Limogne to Caylus (see Aveyron and Tarn chapter) and then on south to St-Antonin-Noble-Val is by far the prettiest route from the Lot to the Aveyron. The occasional spire or tower rising above the low bulges of the hills provide the only landmarks, and villages such as Beauregard or Saillac, half-deserted and blown on by dry, hot winds, have the appeal of haphazard treasures found on the road.

The attractions of the Lot valley itself are much the same as the Dordogne. There is one exceptionally good-looking village, St-Cirq-Lapopie, and several that are only marginally less pleasing. Camping, kayaking and lazing by the water's edge are the pastimes in which most visitors indulge.

Cajarc and around

Cajarc is an old town, once one of the most important in Quercy, although there is little left to mark its past. It was also once a considerable riverine port, but since the river traffic on the Lot went into oblivion, Cajarc has become the tourist centre for this section of the river.

The town is buckled into a large and relatively flat curve of the river and looks (and mostly is) a modern place of villas and supermarkets, camp-sites and swimming-pools. However, it manages to feel like just another large village, with its cafés, shady trees around the square and its red plastic chairs.

Françoise Sagan, author of that beloved school text *Bonjour Tristesse* was born here, and indeed, that novel is set in and around Cajarc. However, it is Georges Pompidou, a later resident, who has possibly done more to bring the tourists in his wake. For many years the French president had a home here, and is now remembered at **La Maison des Arts Georges Pompidou** (open Apr–end Oct, daily exc Tue 2–6; June–Aug daily 10–12, 3–7) which puts on a series of exhibitions of contemporary art, usually very good ones.

Hanging over the river valley on the opposite bank, the partially ruined Renaissance château of Salvagnac does much to lend some antiquity to the scenery. Follow the D146 a little way beyond it and strike out into the fields to find the **Gouffre de Lantouy**. This green pool among shady trees – a typical resurgence of water which has fallen high up on the *causse* – is far deeper than it looks. Barely discernible ruins beside it are the remains of an old nunnery, to which a sinister legend is attached: one of the novices, the daughter of a local lord, was offered as a sacrifice to Satan by the Mother Superior. God, in consequence, destroyed the nunnery with a thunderbolt, and the copper bells of the chapel tumbled into the *gouffre*. It is the copper that colours the water green. On the eve of the feast of Saint John (24 June), come here and you might hear the sound of the bells' muffled ringing in the gloomy depths. Despite this gruesome tale, the *gouffre* is a pleasing place on a hot day.

The cirque of cliffs on the next bend of the river upstream from Cajarc is the **Saut de la Mounine**. The legend in this case concerns a lady who, pursued by an unwelcome suitor, dressed a monkey in her clothes and threw it from the clifftop, causing the unfortunate man to believe she had committed suicide rather than yield to him.

Downstream from Cajarc, two very pretty villages, one clinging to the cliffs, the other more open and with a photo-genic château (which you can also visit, in season), are **Calvignac** and **Cénevières**.

St-Cirq-Lapopie

This is the village above all others on the Lot that draws superlatives from everyone who sees it. André Breton, watching it lit by fireworks, described it as '*une rose impossible dans la nuit*', and Pierre Daura, a surrealist artist, and his friend hit upon the beautiful image of *les toitures qui semblent voler comme des papillons* ('roofs appearing to fly like butterflies'). From the north bank of the Lot (a difficult place at which to stop to admire it) the cottages and houses look as though they have been allowed to tumble down the sloping side of a cliff, almost as if they have been emptied from a box of toys.

As usual with these magical riverside villages, it is the combination of vertical cliff, blue-green river and the red, lichen-speckled tiles of houses poised one above the other, which creates such a striking impression of complete harmony. The proportions and reflections, the vertical and horizontal perspectives, and the felicitous combination of chimneys, rock pinnacles, gardens and trees are such as to draw artists in dozens and indeed the village was for many years the haunt of surrealists and water-colourists.

However, the village has never been of great importance in history. For most of the medieval period three families ruled from three separate castles, all built beside each other on the edge of the clifftop above the village. Sometimes they took different sides in religious and civil quarrels; sometimes they were allies. The English apparently scaled the frightful cliff to take the fortresses during the Hundred Years' War. The castles were eventually demolished, and the village was left in peace with a reputation for wood-turning.

Today, of course, its life-blood is tourism, and to say that its beauty remains entirely unspoilt would not be true. It has been cleaned up and its streets are populated with craft shops, cafés (of the kind where they throw you out at lunchtime if all you want is a coffee) and tubs of flowers everywhere. But this is a very superficial despoliation, and for the most part the place feels lived in and not all that grand.

Be warned: to walk up from the bottom to the top of the village is an exhausting task in the heat. Yet this is the best way to appreciate its charm. Parking is not allowed inside the village itself and it may be wiser in the long run to park some distance away and walk rather than dither about on the very narrow road.

Apart from one or two carved doorways or windows and a pleasant but not stunning church, there is not actually much sightseeing to be done in the village. But then sightseeing is not the point of the place. For the best views you must climb past the town hall to the very peak of the cliff where the castles once stood. From here you can gaze vertically downwards to the river, or sideways to take in the whole fall of the village, with its layers of roofs and its yellow-white stone.

Cahors

At first glance Cahors is big and noisy and far removed from the peaceful villages of the countryside. But these are not reasons to flee it; stay long enough to get a flavour of the place. For Cahors is a peculiarly pleasing town, almost Italian in the way that life is lived on its streets, full of young people in no hurry to be anywhere else, with an old town full of secret corners and new brash squares that smell of self-confidence. It is not, however, a tourist town in any conventional sense, and lacks anything special by way of hotels or restaurants, so it may be as well to be on your way before dark.

A great oxbow of the river Lot encloses the town on three sides, and this constant watery presence adds an indefinable quality to the place. You are never far from the sound of the weirs and know that you can never wander far without ending up on the river bank staring across to the steep, tree-covered banks on the far side.

A Roman city to start with, Cahors became extremely prosperous during the thirteenth century when the Lombard bankers set up here, in great numbers, lending money to popes and to kings. Even the Templars, who were also here, seem to have become seduced by this lucrative habit.

The major sight in Cahors is the **Pont Valentré**. This is an early fourteenth-century fortified bridge, with three tall towers, complete with machicolations for dropping boiling oil, rising above its arches. It is a structure of grace and harmony, particularly when reflected in the still water beneath, and restoration has not spoilt it. Extraordinarily, it remains open to cars, so walking along it can be hazardous. This is most certainly worth doing, however, for walking is the best way to appreciate the strength of the bridge and how difficult it would have been to force a passage over it. Indeed, there is no evidence that anyone ever did.

Much the best way of reaching the Pont Valentré is from the centre of town, even though this takes you past all the detritus around the railway station. Roads on the far bank are narrow and there are few places to park.

Cahors' other great sight is the **Cathédrale St-Etienne**, the first of Quercy's magnificent domed churches. It was started at the end of the eleventh century on the remains of a sixth-century church. Behind the towered and fortified façade of the west front, two huge domes roof the nave. The interior of one of these was found to have been painted with frescoes showing the stoning of Saint Stephen. It is hard to make out the details.

The choir and the chancel belong to the Gothic period and are full of colour from stained glass and paintings, in marked contrast to the austere purity of the nave.

Above the north door is carved a magnificent Romanesque tympanum, showing the Ascension. Unfortunately, this doorway gives straight on to the street and there is little room to contemplate the carving in peace. Traffic has done little to preserve the purity of the stone either. Perhaps here it is less the carving than the majesty of the whole composition that is most striking. Christ, enfolded in a kind of cloud, stands in the centre surrounded by angels, with the Apostles and Mary beneath, sheltered in little archways, gazing up in a mixture of stupefaction and admiration.

A little way south of the cathedral is Cahors' third great attraction, its covered **market**. One of the best in Quercy for wine and cheese, it is mouth-watering at any time of year. In the square it inhabits are shops selling Cahors wine – very much the place to pick up a bottle or two if you do not plan to go vineyard-visiting.

Cahors is split into two irregular halves by the Boulevard Gambetta, which used to carry all the north–south traffic, but is now a great deal more peaceful since the bypass was opened to the west of town. This is the street that also splits the old town from the newer parts, for medieval Cahors never expanded beyond the south-eastern portion of the peninsula. The boulevard is lined with cafés (none of them very peaceful) and town-centre shops of all kinds. On the western side of this boulevard, the Place A Briand is a modern esplanade of concrete, glass and fountains, where couples wander of an evening and where the tourist office dispenses maps of the Cahors wine region and advice about what to see in town.

To reach the old quarters, head eastwards from the tourist office and then amble vaguely south-east through a network of narrow streets flanked by tall houses on each side. All along the way there are details to observe – carved doorways, tiny grotesques etched on a wooden corbel, well-moulded windows. It is impossible to put a date to many of the houses, but some are sixteenth-century and some may well be earlier. In such streets you will find restaurants of the kind that display only a steamy window and a hand-scrawled menu to the outside world and small shops full of junk, toys and books. You can happily spend an hour or so here, coming out on to the river bank now and again and having to plunge back in.

Only the fearfully keen need make the journey to the northern end of the old town to see the remains of the ramparts that defended the neck of the peninsula. One ancient tower remains; otherwise there are just a few bits of wall.

If you want to stay in Cahors, the best hotel with any degree of comfort is the Chartreuse (see Where to Stay), which is across the river at the end of the Boulevard Gambetta and to the right – within easy walking distance of the centre. Eat at the **Auberge du Vieux Cahors** on the south-eastern edge of the old quarter (144 Rue Ste-Urcisse; tel 65 35 06 05). The food is fine and the atmosphere friendly.

Cahors is the starting-point for expeditions along the old single-line railway track which runs beside the river. Quercyrail runs three different tours, which may include a river-trip and meal as well. Details and reservations from the Cahors tourist office (see Practical Information).

THE LOT WEST OF CAHORS

The Cahors vineyards

Cahors marks the end of the country of vertical cliffs beside the river. West of the city the country on each side of the river is composed of rubbly hills, topped by a thin coating of scrub, which drop in stages down to the river valley. This is the region where the grapes to make the thick red Cahors wine are grown – so dark that it is often known as *'vin noir'*.

The Cahors vineyards were devastated by phylloxera in 1868 and have taken a long long time to recover. Indeed, they were abandoned until after the Second World War, when it was decided to replant with the traditional Auxerrois grape. The wine received its Appellation d'Origine Contrôlée, largely, it is said at the insistence of President Pompidou, and there are still those who consider it overrated.

If you enjoy exploring vineyards, these are particularly rewarding ones to discover, partly because they are small enough to get to know quite quickly, and partly because of the views you get as you swing through small villages on the way up to the stony heights or down to the river banks.

Vines are grown on both sides of the river between Cahors and Puy-l'Evêque. The Cahors tourist office has a complete list of properties, owners, telephone numbers and opening times, and most growers are only too happy to welcome you. The star places are probably the Château de Mercuès (a lovely building and a luxury hotel as well as a wine-producer) and the Rigal establishment down at Parnac on the edge of the river, where Château St-Didier-Parnac and Prieuré de Cenac are both well worth sampling. For more 'rustic' growths, try the area just south of Cahors around Trespoux-Rassiels or the village of Prayssac not far from Puy l'Evêque.

Cahors wine is the better for keeping. Take the vineyard-owner's advice about which of his vintages to try; some years are a lot thinner than others.

Cahors to Villeneuve-sur-Lot

Since it lacks the drama of the scenery further east, this stretch of river does not attract many, but it is a popular area for *gîte* holidays. This is not surprising when you consider that many of the villages are as attractive as those further up river, and that both Puy l'Evêque and Villeneuve make good centres for stocking up on supplies.

North of the river, heavily wooded country conceals small villages and some little-visited sights. Southwards, you soon arrive in the rather different landscape of Quercy Blanc, where there are fewer trees, distinct ridges of low hills, and a hot, dusty, chalky feel to the air.

Luzech is, like a miniature Cahors, almost entirely enfolded by a bend of the Lot. Like so many other small towns in Quercy, it was once of far greater importance than it is today, being fought over during the Albigensian Crusade and also the Hundred Years' War. All that remains of its château is a great square keep, which rises above the houses of the old quarter. However, the medieval gateways and the gaggle of ancient houses are quite sufficient to give the place an air of historical authenticity, to add to the natural beauty of the site. This is a good spot for short walks – the energetic can climb to the summit of the hills overlooking the town (one of which is among the four Quercynois candidates for Uxellodunum, site of the last Gaulish resistance to Julius Caesar); others can rest content with simply making a circuit of the peninsula, with the little chapel of Notre-Dame-de-l'Isle as a goal.

Downstream, **Albas** on the south bank is made attractive by its steep site rather than by anything ancient, while **Castelfranc** is a severely symmetrical *bastide*, with a fine fortified church in the centre. It also has a tiny chapel on its outskirts, to mark the miraculous halt of the plague just outside the town walls in 1507.

Prayssac is a busy wine centre, and would be prettier if it had not been ruined by Simon de Montfort in the thirteenth century (during the Albigensian Crusade when it was destroyed). A 'prehistoric circuit' of the *causse* starts here, taking you to nearby dolmens and a megalith or two.

Puy-l'Evêque is certainly the most beautiful and interesting place on this section of the river. Its houses climb up the riverside cliff almost as neatly as do those at St-Cirq-Lapopie, with nice gradations of size and class leading to the château and the church at the summit.

Its name dates from the Albigensian Crusade – it was a Cathar town – when it was taken by the Bishop of Cahors and thus became an episcopal city.

Again, it is mostly the site that makes the place worth exploring, though the ruined keep of the bishop's castle can still be seen, and the fortified fourteenth-century church is gloomily enticing. From the Place de la Truffière, underneath the castle, there are superb views of the river valley, and if you follow the streets down to the river you will come across many old houses. The best view of the town itself is from the south bank on the far side of the suspension bridge.

The next village downstream, **Duravel**, is tiny and nondescript, but once had a priory that was a major satellite of Moissac, and was a pilgrimage centre in its own right. Estimations of its medieval population rise as far as 5,000, in contrast to today's 900 souls. The sight people come for is the pre-Romanesque crypt beneath the church, a tiny, square cell with heavily decorated columns.

The Lot becomes distinctly ordinary from here on. **Penne d'Agenais** is worth a glance, but most of the town was destroyed in the Wars of Religion, and Richard Lionheart's fortifications have to be imagined. There are a few old houses left, and it's a lively enough place, with some good restoration – just a little bare of atmosphere.

Villeneuve-sur-Lot was founded in 1253 as a kind of centre to the circle of smaller *bastides* all around. It's the biggest place between Cahors and Agen, and is largely built of brick or reddish stone – gone is the golden-white touch of the Upper Lot. It's a thriving place, with a vividly metropolitan feel to it and plenty of modern and restored buildings. Apart from the ancient bridge (thirteenth century) and two pompous-looking city gates, there is not much of historical interest here. But glance at the Eglise Ste-Cathérine, an ugly church built in 1937 on the site of a previously demolished one, to see how far Quercy ecclesiastical building style has degenerated since medieval times.

If Villeneuve is just too modern, try **Pujols**, a kilometre to the south. This hilltop medieval town remains intact inside its ramparts, and the view down over Villeneuve shows the original layout of the sprawling *bastide* at its best. Pujols, because of its closeness to its neighbour, is something of a tourist trap on summer weekends but most agreeable at other times. The tiny church of Ste-Foy-la-Jeune is given over to art exhibitions, the paintings contrasting nicely with the remains of the fifteenth-century frescoes.

NORTH OF THE LOT

Very quiet countryside, ideal for a morning's aimless touring, borders the Lot on its northern bank. There is nothing much to see – just villages and trees, but some of the villages are worth visiting. At **Catus**, about 13 kilometres north-west of Cahors, a splendid Romanesque chapter house abuts the Gothic church. There's a good atmosphere of slow decay about it, with only minimal signs of restoration. The beautiful carved pillars do not look any the worse for being unvisited and unloved.

Lherm, due west on the D172, is exactly the kind of village that you come to the Dordogne basin to find, but all too often don't. Lost among the rocky dry valleys that surround it, Lherm consists of a small dusty square more like a village green, about half a dozen Quercynois turreted farmsteads and cottages, a church, a fortified mansion-house, and two ageless sculpted stones. There is also a rickety bar from which to contemplate it all.

Deeper in the forest, at **Les Arques**, there is a wonderful museum (open mid-June–mid-Sept and school holidays, daily 11–7; otherwise Sat and Sun pm only) to the Russian-born sculptor Zadkine (see Caylus). Les Arques was where he holed up in the 1920s and where he created, in bronze and wood, sculptures that vary from the flowing lines of the Italian baroque to the stilted agonies of Cubism. His *pietà*, in the crypt of the local church, which also contains several other pieces, is worth the journey.

To the south-west, on the far side of the D673 road, is the **Château de Bonaguil** (open Feb–May and Sept, four tours daily; June–Aug, 10–6, tours hourly, in English twice a day; Oct–Nov, three tours Sun only). Touring this huge fortress may be too exhausting for those whose interest in military architecture is a only fleeting one. The guides are earnest and dedicated, tours are long, and you need a good deal of enthusiasm to stay the course. But what a magnificent place this is – well worth visiting if only to stare at the looming grey towers and massive curtain walls.

The castle was built between 1480 and 1520, just at the time when artillery and firearms were becoming a serious menace to traditional defensive techniques, and also, oddly enough, just when the Hundred Years' War was safely over and no real danger threatened Bérenger de Roquefeuil, its builder.

He seems to have built it out of a personal need to be absolutely safe from everybody – 'from my own lousy tenants, from the English, should they ever return, and from even the most powerful soldiers of the king of France'. He was not a fool; he knew about artillery and built accordingly. It is here that the fascination for the military historian lies, for already, in the plan of the castle, there are the beginnings of the star-shaped fortress with clear fields of fire that was to become the Europe-wide defence against artillery until the eighteenth century.

So not only are the traditional ingredients of massive towers, high walls and a separate barbican all there, but also carefully positioned loopholes for harquebuses, a network of vaulted passageways to rush troops from one threatened area to another and a series of *cannoniers* – carefully sited chambers which allowed flanking fire.

All this you learn about, and much more, as you follow the guide through a labyrinth of walls and passages. At the centre of the construction, the traditional keep, still immensely strong, seems positioned to act more as a fire-control centre in a modern warship.

The castle, hardly surprisingly, was never attacked, coming through the Wars of Religion without scathe. It was the jealousies of the Revolution that ruined it – for such an arrogant symbol of power could hardly be allowed to remain intact. But even revolutionary fervour made little impression, and the castle still seems as if the bold Bérenger could take up arms again tomorrow and defend himself against all comers.

BAS QUERCY AND THE AGENAIS

South or west of the unpleasantly industrial town of Fumel, few visitors penetrate, largely because the scenery is gentle and less spectacular than that which is to be found along the river valleys. This is much more fertile countryside, largely given over to fruit (strawberries and apples, plums and apricots). If you want to travel between Bergerac or Cahors and the Garonne valley, this is a pleasing stretch of country to pass through. Particular towns and villages to make for include the following.

● **Villeréal** This is one of the stops on the circuit of *bastides* centred on Monpazier, about 35 kilometres south of the Dordogne valley. It is nothing like as pretty or as well-preserved as Monpazier, but it still has some of the arcades left on the central square, as well as an unusual two-storey market and a massive fortified church.

● **Montcuq** In hilly country south-west of Cahors, this village was once a Cathar stronghold and, like so many others, was besieged and taken by Simon de Montfort. Only the keep of its castle remains, poking squarely up from the ridge on which it is built, with the oldest part of the village beneath. Climbing here, past half-timbered houses and ancient alleyways, allows you a wonderful view of the surrounding countryside. Modern Montcuq sprawls around the bottom of the hill, with attractive shady parts down by the river.

To the east and west, the valleys of the Lendou and the Séoune make good rural through-routes to the Garonne, with sprinklings of small sleepy villages.

● **Puymirol** This old village, high on a ridge above the Garonne close to Agen, is a curious place to find one of the best restaurants in the south-west. The L'Aubergade on Rue Royale (tel 53 95 31 46), is a lovely ancient house, opening on to a tiny terrace where tables are laid out under huge parasols. The food is superb too – try the peppers stuffed with haddock or sample the famous hamburger of hot *foie gras* and *cèpes*. Weekday lunch is the time to aim for – when you'll find both a spare table and the best-value menu.

The village itself is a pleasant place to wander around. There is not much to see, but away from the main street, lanes lead past colourful gardens to views of scrubby hillsides and hot, deserted fields.

● **Agen** Big, bustling and superficially rather ugly, Agen is none the less worth visiting for the sake of its excellent **museum** (open all year round, daily exc Tue 11–5). This is housed in four old buildings more or less in the town centre and easily reached on foot. One of the buildings used to be the town prison, and it is rather disconcerting to wander around the prehistory collection with the old rings to which prisoners were fettered on the wall behind the exhibits.

The best piece in the museum is the statue known as the Vénus du Mas, a graceful work, probably of Greek origin, dug up among the remains of a Roman villa not far away. There are excellent paintings too, including several by Goya and a Tiepolo. The collection of Impressionists and pre-Impressionists is very strong with an excellent Courbet and several northern landscapes by Boudin.

Agen is the centre for the production of the best-reputed French prunes. You can find these in tins all over the region, but they may be available cheaper in the town. There's a **museum** (open all year, Mon–Sat 8–11, 2–6, Sun 3–6) and shop celebrating the Agenais plum and prune in the village of **Granges-sur-Lot** north-west of Agen, about 12 kilometres upstream of the junction between the Lot and the Garonne.

PIGEONNIER AND CASELLE

The pigeon lofts of Quercy are one of the features that make the farms and houses so appealing. Virtually every farm you see has some kind of a pigeon loft, for until the days of chemical fertilisers the manure produced by pigeons was of vital importance on the dry *causse*, while the birds themselves were a valuable source of meat. Although few pigeons are kept today, you will notice that even the new villas springing up on the outskirts of the towns are inclined to have a small built-in tower imitating the *pigeonnier*.

Quercy pigeon lofts come in all shapes and sizes. Some are detached, some built in to the farmhouses. Their common characteristic is their steeply sloping roofs, which often give them the aspect of a defensive tower or turret, and which add strongly to the impression of moving through a medieval landscape. Detached pigeon lofts were usually built on the very edge of a farmer's land in the hope that the birds would feed on his neighbour's crops rather than his own. This practice, and also the complicated rules in medieval times about who was and who was not allowed to keep pigeons, led to long legal wrangles.

Caselles or *cabanes* are the small stone huts you see occasionally on the edge of fields on the *causses*, built in the shape of a beehive and looking like a house for gnomes. They were used as stores or shelters, and were one way in which the farmers could use the innumerable stones that had to be cleared from the *causse* fields before any tilling could take place. It is well worth looking closely at one or two, because the building technique used for them, involving a very gentle corbelling of the roof and a gradually decreasing size of stone, must have involved a great deal of skill for what is in essence a very simple purpose.

WHERE TO STAY, EAT AND CAMP

There are two sections: establishments that we recommend and establishments that are worth considering but which we think do not merit a wholehearted recommendation. Both are marked on the map at the start of the chapter. Unless we say otherwise, all have rooms with bath or shower and accept the major credit cards.

Key: ✦ = 0-250FF, ✦✦ = 251-450FF, ✦✦✦ = over 451FF; prices are per room without breakfast, which costs around 40-65FF. Some hotels may insist on half-board during high season.

Recommended hotels

CALES

Le Pagès	✦-✦✦
Route de Payrac	
46350 Lot	*Tel: 65 37 95 87; Fax: 65 37 91 57*

Le Pagès makes a comfortable good-value overnight stop in a quiet village of mellow stone buildings convenient for exploring the eastern Dordogne. Until recently the hotel was a no-frills, family-run business, but since refurbishment has become rather more luxurious while retaining its friendly atmosphere and inexpensive menus in the café-style restaurant. Rooms in a new block are large and characterful with spotless, well-equipped bathrooms; some rooms overlook the large wild garden.

Open all year exc. two wks mid-Oct; 20 rooms; closed Tue in low season; outdoor swimming-pool

GLUGES

Hôtel Les Falaises	✦-✦✦
Martel	
46600 Lot	*Tel: 65 37 33 59; Fax: 65 37 34 19*

Backed by sheer limestone cliffs on the banks of the river, Gluges is a tiny medieval village some distance from the tourist bustle of western Dordogne but within striking distance of main routes heading north. On the edge of the village, Les Falaises is in a quiet spot and has a pretty vine-covered terrace. Service in the conservatory-style restaurant can be slow but the food worth waiting for – regional dishes include trout, which was particularly good when we visited. Bedrooms are clean, simple and well decorated, though those on the second floor have very thin walls. Larger rooms are better value.

Early Mar–end Nov; 14 rooms

GOURDON

Hostellerie de la Bouriane
Place du Foirail
46300 Lot   Tel: 65 41 16 37; Fax: 65 41 04 92

Staying at la Bouriane will not put you in Gourdon's medieval centre, but you'll be just a short walk away down the hill in a quiet leafy suburb. A spruce white façade and a courteous greeting welcome guests. Attentive service extends to the bright, air-conditioned restaurant, where flowers and crisp pink cloths decorate the tables against the backdrop of a huge stone fireplace. Food is good value and beautifully presented, although it can be a little bland. There's also a summery residents' lounge and a sunken front patio shaded by chestnut trees. Bedrooms are very well maintained, with gleaming white bathrooms, though the décor is rather plain and unimaginative.

Mar–mid-Jan; restaurant closed Mon exc. pm in high season; 20 rooms

LACAVE

Le Pont de l'Ouysse
46220 Lot   Tel: 65 37 87 04; Fax: 65 32 77 47

At the end of a quiet road overlooking the Ouysse, a tributary of the river Dordogne, this hotel has a popular leafy terrace restaurant, a landscaped swimming-pool area and access to a small beach on the river. Combined with pretty rooms, friendly professional service and good food, the hotel scores highly on all fronts. The restaurant has a particularly good reputation, and includes eel and crayfish for variety in addition to the usual regional specialities like *foie gras*. Though still not cheap, the smaller rooms are good value for money.

Mar–end Dec; restaurant closed Mon lunch and Mon pm in low season; 13 rooms; heated outdoor swimming-pool

ROCAMADOUR

Les Vieilles Tours ◆-◆◆
46500 Lot   Tel: 65 33 68 01; Fax: 65 33 68 59

In open countryside on a hill with vast views of the Alzou and Ouysse valleys, Les Vieilles Tours is a peaceful alternative to staying among the tourist frenzy of Rocamadour, four kilometres to the east. Dating from the thirteenth century, the hotel is a motley collection of former barns and outhouses with good-value rooms, which vary in size and luxury, most leaning towards simplicity. Mealtimes are flexible – an encouraging sign of hospitality – and include late breakfasts around the pool, from where the views are best. Booking ahead is advisable.

Apr–early Nov; 18 rooms; outdoor swimming-pool

ST BEAUZEIL

Château de l'Hoste ◆◆
82150 Tarn-et-Garonne *Tel: 63 95 25 61; Fax: 63 95 25 50*

Miles from anywhere, on the borders of Quercy 42 kilometres north-east of Agen, this white eighteenth-century manor-house stands at the end of an avenue of shady trees. It is a genial hotel, with large rooms scattered along its various wings. There is a sunny courtyard, a small swimming pool, tables on the terrace (the food is very pleasant) and a small, plush bar. It makes an excellent place in which to tuck yourself away for a night or two.

Mid-Mar–mid-Feb; closed Sun pm and Mon Oct–end Apr; 32 rooms; outdoor swimming-pool

ST-CIRQ-LAPOPIE

Hôtel de la Pélissaria ◆◆-◆◆◆
46330 Lot *Tel: 65 31 25 14; Fax: 65 30 25 52*

The main attraction of this hotel is the location near the centre of St-Cirq-Lapopie, which clings dramatically to a cliff above the river Lot. The hotel is built into a steep slope so that many of the well-equipped rustic rooms have their own terrace with parasol and loungers, from which there's an uninterrupted view of the gardens and the gorge. The hotel has only ten rooms and a small restaurant, so you'll need to feel sociable. You are required to order dinner an hour in advance: home-made fresh pasta dishes, smoked trout, delicious lamb with strongly flavoured *cèpes*, and local cheeses make up a typical meal, and the male voice in the background music is a recording of your host.

Apr–mid-Nov; 10 rooms, restaurant closed Thur and Fri; small heated outdoor swimming-pool

Worth considering

ALVIGNAC

Hôtel du Château
46500 Lot *Tel: 65 33 60 14; Fax: 65 33 69 28*

A large, simple hotel close to Rocamadour, liable to have rooms free even in high season. Family atmosphere.

Apr–mid-Oct; 36 rooms

CAHORS

La Chartreuse
St-Georges
46000 Lot   *Tel: 65 35 17 37; Fax: 65 22 30 03*

Bland package-style hotel within walking distance of centre. Riverside setting improves it.

Mid-Jan–end Dec; 51 rooms

FIGEAC

Hostellerie de L'Europe
51 Allées Victor Hugo
46100 Lot   *Tel: 65 34 10 16; Fax: 65 50 04 57*

Big and old-fashioned place, but very friendly and with good food.

All year; restaurant closed mid-Jan–mid-Feb; 30 rooms; outdoor swimming-pool

MONTCUQ

La Petite Auberge
Domaine de St-Géry
Lascabanes
46800 Lot   *Tel: 65 31 82 51; Fax: 65 22 92 89*

A tiny cottage-hotel in isolated country, run in good guest-house style. You'll need to speak some French. It is booked solid in summer.

Early Mar–early Jan; closed Mon and Tue in low season; 5 rooms; outdoor swimming-pool

Recommended campsites

Key: ✦ = 0–60FF, ✦✦ = 61–100FF, ✦✦✦ = over 101FF. Prices are for two adults, tent and car; children are half-price or less. All campsites listed have lavatories and washing facilities.

BRENGUES

Le Moulin Vieux
Assier
46320 Lot   *Tel: 65 40 00 41; Fax: 65 40 05 65*

A comfortable modern site in a scenic river gorge with all basic facilities to make a relaxed stay.

May–mid-Sept; reservation poss; rest/café; shop; indoor & outdoor swimming-pool; tennis

GOURDON

Municipal Ecoute s'il Pleut ✦-✦✦
46300 Lot   *Tel: 65 41 09 88, low season 65 41 06 19*

Set in a densely wooded retreat so lots of peace and quiet and ideal for a self-catering holiday. No shop or bar but every amenity in the local town. Gates are shut at 10pm prompt. Levelled pitches on hard ground.

June–end Sept; reservation poss; food shop; swimming-pool; no credit cards accepted

MONTCABRIER

Moulin de Laborde ✦✦
46700 Lot   *Tel: 65 24 62 06*

A small, quiet, exposed site with basic facilities and few activities, making it restful. Lack of shade may deter some.

Mid–May–mid–Sep; reservation poss; food shop; rest/café; swimming-pool; no credit cards accepted

PADIRAC

Les Chênes ✦✦
46500 Lot   *Tel: 66 33 65 54, low season 79 08 21 68; Fax: 65 33 71 55*

A good base in an area heavily frequented by tourists. Reasonable shade on spread-out terraces and exceptional washing facilities.

Mid Apr–mid–Sept; reservation poss; shop; rest/café; swimming-pool

PAYRAC

Les Pins ✦✦✦
46350 Lot   *Tel: 65 37 96 32; Fax: 65 37 91 08*

Set on a hill with neighbourly shady pitches at the top end and more spacious around the open lawn at the bottom. Excellent facilities for children.

Apr–end Sept; reservation poss; supermarket; rest/café; swimming-pool; tennis; volleyball

SAUVETERRE

Moulin de Périé ♦♦♦
Fumel
47500 Lot-et-Garonne   *Tel: 53 40 67 26; Fax: 53 40 62 46*

Efficiently run and welcoming family site in a secluded but lovely setting with the latest sanitation facilities.

Early Apr–end Sept; reservation poss; shop; rest/café; swimming-pools

SOUILLAC

Domaine de la Paille Basse ♦♦♦
46200 Dordogne   *Tel: 65 37 85 48; Fax: 65 37 09 58*

Bustling designer site with wooded, rustic charm. Stony ground and tents not as spread out as you might expect. Lots of amenities especially for teenagers who like a bit of night life.

Mid-May–mid-Sept; reservation poss; min stay one wk; supermarket; rest/café; swimming-pool; tennis

TOUZAC

Le Ch'Timi ♦♦
Puy l'Evêque
46700 Lot   *Tel: 65 36 52 36*

A small British enclave on a moderately busy road with a cheery, homely atmosphere. Reasonably sized pitches with most shade on road side of site.

Mid-May–end Sept; reservation possible; shop; rest/café; swimming-pool; tennis; no credit cards accepted

VAYRAC

Les Granges ♦♦
46110 Lot   *Tel: 65 32 46 58; Fax: 65 32 57 94*

Reasonable rates, open spaces and most of the standard amenities are the attractions of this well-situated site close to the Dordogne river.

Mid-May–mid-Sept; reservation poss; min stay one wk; supermarket; rest/café; swimming-pool

VERS

La Chêneraie
Cahors
46090 Lot   Tel: 65 31 40 29; Fax: 65 31 41 70

This small compact site makes a good base from which to visit the Cahors area. Lively entertainment.

Mid-Apr–mid-Sept; reservation poss; bar; tennis; no credit cards accepted

CORREZE

Corrèze is a Cinderella of a *département*, ignored and unloved by most foreign visitors, and by the French themselves. Here is none of the fertility of Périgord, none of the sunny heat of the Midi and little even of the mountain scenery associated with better-known parts of the Massif Central. The area of Corrèze which does extend into the lowlands around Brive and Turenne is lumped in with the Dordogne in most people's minds and, if the name means anything at all, it is merely short-hand for that section of the Dordogne basin where comfort and good scenery run out, and where most guidebooks come to an abrupt halt.

Popular wisdom is not altogether wrong. Much of the *département* is high, rough country, heavily forested, mist-clad and wet. The whole of the north-east corner is part of the Millevaches plateau, once one of the poorest parts of France (the name does not refer to herds of grazing cows, but to the thousand of springs which make this plateau one of the great watersheds of the country). The south-east side is corrugated by steep valleys running towards the Dordogne, which passes through the hills in a continuous wooded gorge. The river, constrained by a series of huge dams, has become a sequence of deep lakes, pretty enough in parts, but hardly on a par with the open rippling shallows below Argentat. Only to the west in the basin of the Vézère and to the south around Brive is there any abundance either of beautiful scenery or historic sights. Small wonder then that most of Corrèze is left to its traditional indus-

Good bases

● **Argentat** Where the Dordogne emerges from its gorges, this small town is set in a bowl among the hills. Off the tourist trail and frequented mainly by canoeists and campers, it is an attractive place with a pleasant riverfront. Stay in one of the town's simple hotels, or look for a gîte in the hills directly to the north.

● **Bort-les-Orgues** Avoid the town itself, which lies in a trench beneath a huge dam. The country on all sides is rocky, with secret valleys and small villages. Look for accommodation on the high ground to the west for preference.

● **Meymac** This unspoilt, old market town has some interesting shops and there are good walks nearby.

tries of forestry, furniture making, arms manufacture and small-scale upland farming, and that the tourists who come are mostly hardy Dutch families who enjoy camping by the many lakes and walking along the woodland paths.

And yet, to write off the whole region apart from the area south of Brive as devoid of pleasure for holidaymakers would be misleading. There are places here worth travelling to: tiny outbreaks of beauty, all the more fascinating for being unsung; villages which no one has heard of, as appealing in their way as those lower down the Dordogne, and châteaux or museums all the better for being almost deserted. In fact, if the crowds or the heat in the Dordogne valley become oppressive, or if you have become bored with caves, queues and guides, then spend a day or two wandering the byways of Corrèze. There are those who find the region curiously addictive. It is unspoilt and green, its people gruff and independent.

BRIVE TO BEAULIEU

This is the most visited part of Corrèze, for it abuts directly on to one of the more attractive parts of the Dordogne valley and contains the three popular sights of Turenne, Collonges-la-Rouge and Beaulieu-sur-Dordogne. Brive-la-Gaillarde is the railhead for the Upper Dordogne area, and if you come by rail (the overnight motorail from Boulogne is currently the most convenient method of getting car and family painlessly, if expensively, into the area), it is here that you will be searching for breakfast. The land around Brive was once part of the fief of Turenne – in the Middle Ages the most powerful feudal *domaine* in the region. It is fertile country, surrounded by low hills on three sides, with knobbly outcrops crowned by ruined castles.

Brive-la-Gaillarde

The long lines of hypermarkets and do-it-yourself warehouses extending eastward towards Tulle testify to Brive's importance as a regional centre. It is a gritty sort of town, scoured by heavy traffic on its outskirts and beset by sweeping one-way systems further in. The town centre is attractive enough, however, with the Rue du Dr Massénat, lined by cafés and shops, running down from the Eglise St-Martin. Other, older streets surround the church in concentric circles, and there are some Renaissance

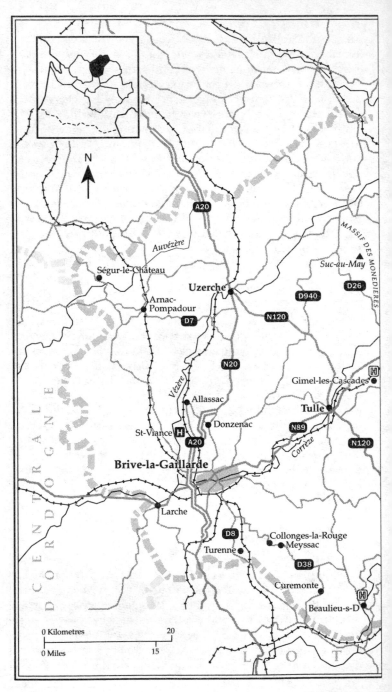

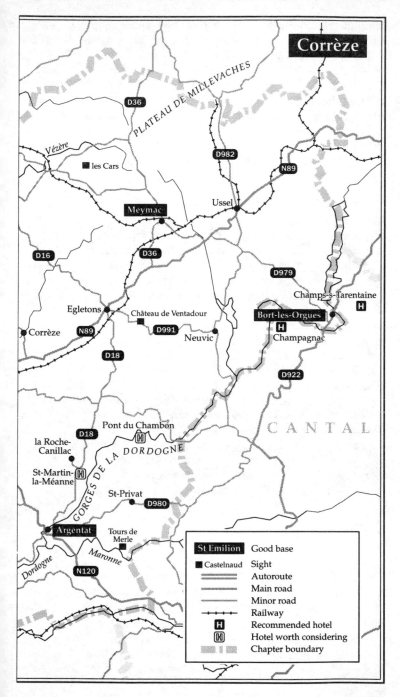

Corrèze

PLATEAU DE MILLEVACHES

D36

Vézère

les Cars

D982

N89

Meymac

Ussel

D16

D36

D979

Champs-s-Tarentaine   H

Egletons

Château de Ventadour

Bort-les-Orgues

Corrèze   N89

D991

Neuvic

H

Champagnac

D18

D922

D18

Pont du Chambon   H

la Roche-
Canillac

GORGES DE LA DORDOGNE

St-Martin-
la-Méanne   H

St-Privat

D980

Argentat

Tours de
Merle

Dordogne   Maronne

N120

CANTAL

St Emilion	Good base
■ Castelnaud	Sight
≈≈≈≈	Autoroute
——	Main road
——	Minor road
+—+—+	Railway
H	Recommended hotel
H	Hotel worth considering
▓ ▓ ▓	Chapter boundary

windows and towers to look at. Brive's best building, the Hôtel de Labenche, is a solid piece of Renaissance architecture, and shelters a particularly good local **museum** (open daily, April–Oct, 10–6.30; Nov–Mar 1.30–6; closed Tue). To pass some time, there is a pleasant park with a good children's play area on the banks of the Corrèze. If you enjoy reading French, ask for the novelists of the Brive school (Peyramaure, Michelet, Tillinac, Signol and Bordes) in local bookshops. Their works are mostly set locally, draw on the rapidly vanishing traditional way of life for inspiration, and are often unashamedly nostalgic and romantic.

Turenne

This small village of houses huddled beneath the ruins of an imposing castle on a rocky spire conforms exactly to everyone's picture of a medieval settlement. You can just about manoeuvre a car through the narrow lanes and up to the esplanade beneath the curtain walls, but it is worth the walk, for the turrets and doorways are better seen at close quarters. Most of the village dates from the fifteenth century – the oldest part of the castle, the Tour de César, is from the eleventh.

Tiny though the place is, the Viscounty of Turenne once held sway over 1,200 villages throughout Limousin, Quercy and Périgord. The lords of Turenne, emerging into the fifteenth century as the 'de la Tour d'Auvergne' family, retained a virtually independent power until the mid-eighteenth century. Louis XIV's greatest general, known as 'le Grand Turenne' was the most famous.

You can visit the castle (open April–Oct 9–11.45, 2–6.45), although since most of it was demolished on the orders of Louis XV, there is not a great deal to see. But the view from the top of César's tower is stunning and merits the climb.

Collonges-la-Rouge

This is one of the most famous villages in the Dordogne basin, and often has more tourists than inhabitants wandering its lanes. Coaches park in columns beside the D38 and disgorge their loads. For preference, come in the evening when visitors are fewer and when the sinking sun colours the red sandstone of which the whole village is built with an extra daub of crimson.

The colour of the place is extraordinary enough, but what makes Collonges so special is that much of the village consists of large houses – mansions, some of them – which seem to strive to outdo each other in intricacy. It is not so much the ornamentation, but the multitude of towers and turrets, corbelled out at every possible angle from the walls and poking up above the slates with tiny conical caps and even tinier windows. No sooner have you admired every corner of one such house than another, even more splendid, draws your eye. Unified by their colour and style, the houses form a kind of fantasy of the architecture of the Dordogne valley.

The reason for Collonge's splendour is simple enough. This is where the administrators of the Turenne estate lived, and doubtless the rivalry among the governors, the agents and factors of the Viscount's court was more than enough to spark this competitive splendour of building. Most of the houses date from the sixteenth century; the church on the other hand, itself graced with defensive turrets and towers from the same period, is Romanesque at its core and has a magnificently carved (if weathered) tympanum showing the Ascension. The white chalky stone of the carving contrasts oddly with the reds and purples of the rest of the building.

If Collonges is too crowded, try **Meyssac**, a couple of kilometres to the east. It is also built of red sandstone and has some splendid houses, though they cannot match the grandeur of Collonges. **Curemonte**, a little further south-east, is another beautiful medieval village.

Beaulieu-sur-Dordogne

On the edge of a shingly sweep of the Dordogne, just where it emerges from the outlying slopes of the Massif Central, Beaulieu was once the seat of a rich and important abbey. Now, if you travel on the main road south from Tulle (D940) it looks an ordinary enough village, but by prowling down towards the river you come to streets of fine houses leading towards the **Eglise Saint-Pierre**, the chief glory of the village. The south doorway has excellently preserved Romanesque carving which depicts a vision of the Last Judgement and is considered the finest in the region. It dates from 1125. The theme, as usual, has provided the sculptors with freedom to exercise the medieval delight in the ghoulish; the damned are eaten, speared, burned and poisoned with equal abandon. At the base of the scene, the dead rise from their graves, while in the centre, the figure of Christ, both sorrowful and severe, sits in judgement.

Beyond the church the Dordogne ripples past grassy banks and you can explore round the back of the village at the river's edge without too much difficulty.

Le Turenne (Tel 55 91 10 16) is an excellent spot for lunch, with a restaurant where well-flavoured food is served in style. The rooms in this ancient abbey building are well worth considering for an overnight stay.

Above Beaulieu, the D12 towards Argentat makes a scenic drive. The river here is the province of kayakers and campers; gone are the riverside villages and the fields of tobacco.

NORTH AND WEST OF BRIVE

This is an attractive stretch of country, almost completely ignored by tourists. It borders Périgord to the west, but not many visitors coming east from Périgueux penetrate beyond the château at Hautefort. For most British visitors, this part of the country is only seen from the main N20 road north, and Uzerche, a town worth an hour or two of anyone's time, is probably most remembered as an appalling traffic bottleneck which turns the homeward drive into a nightmare. Incidentally, the Uzerche bypass is unlikely to be completed before 1996 – if you have to drive north on a July or August Saturday, make sure you are through the town before 9 am or use an alternative route.

A day spent in the Vézère valley west of Brive, away from the main road, will not be wasted. There are a number of fascinating villages – without a great deal to see by way of sights perhaps – but ideal for a gentle tour.

The Vézère valley to Uzerche

Heading west from Brive under the motorway you come to water-meadow country where the river Corrèze joins the Vézère. Further west, the land rises into a muddle of low hills which culminate in the **Puy d'Yssandon**. There's nothing much up there apart from fruit trees, narrow lanes, a couple of viewpoints and small trout streams, but it is a good area for a roadside picnic and a more pleasant route west than the main N89 in the valley.

Another spot in which to while away some time is the **Lac du Causse** to the south of the traffic-plagued village of Larche. The D19, which winds along the south shore of the lake, passes under a ruined fortress and overlooks the roofs of the tiny village of Chasteaux. On the northern side of the lake there is a large water-sports complex, with three long slides bumping down the hillside. A good place to cool off hot children or to unpack the sailboard.

Failing these diversions, head north to **Donzenac** and **Allassac,** both well-placed medieval villages, both with interesting churches, small market squares and an air of fortified watchfulness left over from times past, which contrasts with the modernity of the Brive basin below. **Objat** makes another good spot for ten minutes' wander, but if you are bent on relaxation, persist to the best village of the lot, **Ségur-le-Château,** built in a loop of the Auvézère north-west of Arnac-Pompadour.

Ségur is tiny, but ideal. For a start it has a great swathe of shaded grass along the banks of the river where you can either picnic or sit at one of the outlying tables of the local *auberge*. The river cuts the village in two – with old and splendid houses on either side of the narrow bridge (they owe their splendour to the fact that lawyers built them – Ségur was once seat of the regional judiciary). A ruined castle crowns a rocky hill above the river, and a short walk takes you to a hidden well carved deep in the rock – said to have been used by Richard the Lionheart. If you are seduced by the place, there is a *chambres d'hôtes* (very pretty) in the old Tour St-Laurent (tel 55 73 54 17).

Arnac-Pompadour

If the name sounds familiar it is on account of Louis XV, who acquired the château to present to his favourite mistress – Madame de Pompadour. Today, Pompadour (the Arnac part is usually neglected) is famous as a horse-racing and breeding centre, with one of France's national studs based in the old (actually rebuilt to look old) château. It is a curious experience to sit in one of the local cafés and to find yourself surrounded by the Parisian horsey set. Pompadour specialises in Anglo-Arabian stallions. If you are interested in horses, there are countless events in summer – from steeplechasing, carriage-driving, shows and trials to days of *'équitation pour tous'* (riding for everyone). Telephone the tourist office (55 98 55 47) for details.

Uzerche

A loop of the Vézère, which here cuts deeply through the hills of the Limousin plateau, is the setting for this town, named 'Uzerche the Virgin' because it was never taken by storm or siege throughout its history. It is a place full of turrets and towers, which spring up from the many ostentatiously large houses. It is a good town to stroll through – though fairly steep – for as well as the architecture to admire, there are intriguing glimpses of the river far below to be caught through narrow side lanes. If you have the energy you can pick your way down to the banks and wander around the bottom of the town. The only sight in Uzerche worth making a special effort to see is the Romanesque church which crowns the hilltop, its belfry the characteristic Limousin pattern of square tower topped by octagonal final storey. Inside, the church is rather gloomy (it was heavily fortified), but there are some good carved capitals to the pillars and curious narrow aisles, scarcely wide enough for two abreast. A bench outside is placed to give you the best view of the roofs, the river and the heavy lorries below.

TULLE AND SOUTH-EAST CORREZE

For the most part, this is hidden country. You will not see much of it if you travel along the main valley road (N120) from Tulle to Argentat, which is what most people do. Take an extra hour or two to travel through the lanes on the hilltops to the east; the rewards are a number of picturesque villages above the Dordogne, the fairly spectacular gorges which the river has cut through the hills, and finally a theatrical ruined castle by the Maronne in the forested district of Xaintrie.

Tulle

Tulle is a thin snake of a town, so jammed into the steep declivity of the river Corrèze that there is little room for expansion on either side. It is easy to think you have arrived at the town centre when in fact it lies a further kilometre ahead. Tulle is the nearest Corrèze comes to an industrial town – arms manufacture is a traditional business here and is still going strong. Few visitors would choose to stay for long (and Brive has better shops), but Tulle merits a browse all the same.

The most historic part of the town is round the cathedral – itself a sombre building in a mixture of Gothic and Romanesque with a fine cloister attached. The old quarter to the north has narrow lanes and overhanging houses and is by far the most interesting part of the town in which to wander. Just round the corner from the cathedral at 2 Quai Edmond-Perrier, you will find the **Musée Départemental de la Résistance et de la**

Déportation (open Mon–Fri 9–12, 2–6; closed Sat, Sun). Corrèze, heavily forested and isolated, was an ideal area for active resistance during the Nazi occupation, and the region's towns suffered heavily from the inevitable reprisals. Tulle suffered the worst of these – it is a story repeated on a smaller scale throughout the region, but nowhere with quite such horror this side of Oradour-sur Glane (near Limoges), where the inhabitants of an entire village were burnt or shot.

On 8 June 1944, two days after the Normandy landings, the local resistance decided to liberate Tulle. After a fierce battle they succeeded in forcing the surrender of all but a small portion of the German garrison. Their triumph was short-lived, however, for the very next day, elements of the notorious SS division 'Das Reich' reoccupied the town. The *maquis* hastily pulled out – very few of the victims subsequently condemned by the SS had been involved in the fighting. Ninety-nine men were hanged on the lampposts which lined the river banks, their bodies were thrown on the town's rubbish dump, now a memorial park on the western edge of the town. A further 101 inhabitants died in camps in Germany. The museum has graphic records, not just of the Tulle massacre, but of other acts, noble and ignoble which took place 50 years ago in what today is a near-forgotten backwater of France.

There is perhaps a certain irony that the museum housing examples of Tulle-manufactured weapons – **Collection de la Manufacture d'armes de Tulle** (open Jun–Aug, 2–6, closed Sat, Sun) should be rather better laid out and better patronised. Here, three centuries of ever more efficient weapons from flintlock muskets to semi-automatic machine-pistols are exhibited in glass cases like so much family silver. The collection is on the western edge of town in the Souillac district.

Back roads to Argentat

South and east of Tulle the land is gently corrugated, full of small streams rushing towards the Dordogne or the Corrèze and sprinkled with upland villages, most of them rather dour, but some with considerable appeal. **Gimel-les-Cascades** is one of the best, even if it does become fractionally overpopulated on sunny weekends. As the name suggests, the waterfalls are the draw: the river Montane plunges down a fault in the rock, making a frothy picture on several levels. Unfortunately, you have to pay to scramble down alongside them, one of the less attractive features of such privately-owned beauty spots, but it is worthwhile if you want a stiff walk. Otherwise reasonably good views are to be had from the road bridge. Apart from the waterfalls, there are other diversions in Gimel: a ruined castle, a venerable church and a wayside *auberge*. The *auberge*, l'Hostellerie de la Vallée (see Where to Stay) is entirely adequate for a night or two's stay, but don't expect any luxuries in the rooms or on the menu.

Moving southwards, **La Roche-Canillac**, is a rather weird place, built on the edge of a steep declivity, and consequently imposingly situated. A large and prosperous square is fringed by tiny alleys where hens bathe in the dust and the houses have sagged at the joints; a medieval fortress-tower sticks up from the centre of the village. There are a number of good walks round here – through rocky woodland to various viewpoints or tumble-down barns.

St Martin-la-Méanne is an upland village, belonging to Auvergne in the style of its houses, built of basalt with roofs of split schist or *lauze*. There's a comfortable inn here, Les Voyageurs (Tel 55 29 11 53), seemingly purpose-built for escaping the crowds. You'll find yourself in the company of anglers and French pensioners on holiday. The dining room is big and bright and the fare is solid in best Auvergne fashion.

St Martin is on the northern edge of the Dordogne valley, and progress further southwards means dropping down into the gorge by one of the few and steep roads. The lakes behind the three enormous dams in the depths of the gorge are too sunless and narrow, and, it must be said, too full of mud and driftwood to be ideal pleasure spots, but from above they are pretty enough. Apart from fishing (get the leaflet *Je pêche en Corrèze* for details), the only activity on the lakes are boat trips in a restored (or reconstructed) *gabare*. The history of these boats is worth a short digression.

Before being taken over by canoeists and dammed for electricity, the Dordogne, shallow and unpredictable though it is, had a species of river trade. Boats were constructed among the forests of Auvergne, loaded with timber and navigated down the river to Bergerac or Bordeaux where the wood was used for wine barrels. The *gabare* itself was broken up at the end of the voyage and put to the same use. With the coming of rail transport, the river trade declined, and the building of the dams put an end to it. The village where most of the boats were launched now lies drowned beneath the Lac du Chastang. During the season when the river was too low to be navigable, the boatbuilders found employment throughout Auvergne constructing roofs for barns and houses. If you can steal a glance inside an old barn somewhere in the region you will see the roof timbers put together exactly like the inverted keel of a boat, held in place by wooden pegs rather than nails.

The Dordogne reaches a brief open space among the hills at **Argentat**, a pleasant enough town without a great deal to see apart from the old houses which line the quays by the river banks. Argentat is outside the main tourist routes and remains quietly French. There are enough shops for half an hour's stroll, and several cafés with good views of the river.

Tours de Merle

The area of Corrèze south-east of the Dordogne is Xaintrie, a high country of thick forests – conifers for the most part and not attractive. **St Privat** is about the only village here worth getting out of the car for – a pleasing cluster of Auvergnat houses, some rather old and splendid, set in a quiet green space among the trees. Down in the gorge of the river Maronne (a beautiful river where it is not dammed), the Tours de Merle rise on a rocky promontory above the water. From a distance this old fortress looks like a town of ruined mini-skyscrapers, for the various families who were overlords of the fortress all seem to have built separate defensive keeps, and often allowed their relatives to build one too. It is not easy to discover whether the owners of the Tours de Merle in the thirteenth and fourteenth centuries were useful subjects of their liege-lord or merely robber-barons. Accounts differ, but certainly the place was a thorn in the flesh of the English, who eventually besieged and took it during the Hundred Years' War. Today the ruins are dramatic enough for most tastes – well-preserved grey towers rise from various points within a walled enclosure. Guided tours are exhaustive and exhausting and you may be as well off sitting by the river contemplating the ruins above. The fortress now makes money (and a lot of it judging by the entrance fees) by medieval entertainments on summer afternoons and *son et lumière* shows at night. The former is fine if you have a yen for jugglers and fire-eaters, and the latter is made more spectacular by the setting than by the actual entertainment.

NORTH-EAST OF TULLE

You can pass time in two ways in this country: tour gently through it on a hot clear day when the views will be good and the coolness welcome or camp beside one of the small lakes and go fishing in the trout streams or walking on the heathery hills. This is the wildest part of Corrèze – not that it is a deserted wilderness. It is simply undeveloped, undramatic and underpopulated.

The N89 road, running north-east through Egletons and Ussel towards Clermont-Ferrand allows a fast traverse from one point to another before branching out on the small country roads. A swing north of the road and an exploration south of it will serve to convey the flavour of the country. The small town of Meymac is the place for lunch or shopping.

North of the N89

Between the valleys of the Vézère and the Corrèze lies the Massif de Monédières, a group of heather- and forest-clad hills which culminate in the rounded lump of the Suc-au-May, the highest point in the area. Climb up from Tulle through the town of Corrèze with its fortified gatehouse, and circle round the hills on the D121, D32 and D128, diverting up to the top for the magnificent view south. The hills here are thick with *myrtilles* (bilberries) and equally thick with notices dissuading you from picking them. In local towns, especially Meymac, you can buy jam, bottled bilberries and especially fine *tartes aux myrtilles* in season (mid-August). The Monédières massif has numerous short walks laid out through the trees (Chaumeil is the starting point for several of them).

Plateau de Millevaches

High, lonely country this, consisting of clumps of trees interspersed with clumps of heather or boggy-looking grassland. Unfortunately, the horizon is seldom clear enough to gain any sense of space. Once you have seen one part, you have seen the lot. The single sight worth making for (and it forms a good goal) is the Roman ruins at **Cars**, east of Bugeat. Here, in the middle of a desolate countryside, the remains of a temple constructed out of giant granite blocks lie tumbled on the ground. The scale of the building and the workmanship are both extraordinary. About two hundred yards away the remains of a further building – some kind of house or lodging – have been uncovered. There is plenty of speculation about what this place may have been. The likeliest explanation is that it was a shrine which attracted large numbers of pilgrims into an otherwise little-inhabited area.

Meymac

This small hill town is the most attractive centre in the area. There is not much of it – really just a single street which runs downhill to a square and a fountain. But there are rustic stone houses, a distinguished-looking church and several shops selling local products. Among the honey and the bilberries, keep an eye open for local crafts. You are likely to find some good value woodwork and knitwear.

South of the N89

The steep, rocky country running down to the Dordogne valley continues right up to the border of Corrèze and Puy-de-Dôme. It is more interesting scenery than the Plateau de Millevaches, for every river valley is a little different. The most attractive road to explore is the D991 which runs from the tedious (and war-damaged) town of Egletons. Underneath the fragmentary ruins of the once-powerful Château de Ventadour the road is dug into the side of a red rock gorge. To explore the ruins (a somewhat hazardous do-it-yourself operation) you need to find the road across the gorge and follow the signs. The D991 ends at Neuvic – a popular base for watersports and camping on the lake formed by the dam on the river Triouzoune. If you travel south again from here to the edge of the Dordogne gorge, you can drive along the old road known as the *Route des Ajustants* (D168) which fringes this very steep section. It is a lonely route and the scenery is splendid.

Bort-les-Orgues

This fairly substantial town lies within reach of both the Monts Dore and the Cantal mountains and is surprisingly popular with holidaymakers, surprising because it is at the bottom of a deep trench and in the shadow of one of the largest dams on the upper Dordogne. It does not itself make an attractive base, but the country on both sides of the valley, studded with knobbly volcanic outcrops, does. Look for accommodation outside the immediate valley of the Dordogne or the Sumène and you will not be disappointed with your surroundings.

On the west bank of the Dordogne is the outcrop of columnar basalt from which the town takes its name, although the resemblance to organ pipes is not that great. A steep road takes you to the top of the rock face, where benches have been laid out in a row, exactly as if in a public park, to allow you to get the best of the view. This is worth the short journey: the Monts Dore and the Cantal volcano line the horizon, while Bort-les-Orgues and its dam lie, in miniature, a long way below.

The huge lake created by Bort's dam has much improved the setting of the **Château de Val**, a medieval towered fortress now almost surrounded by water. As usual it is more interesting for its photogenic exterior than for anything of interest inside, although there are often art exhibitions. The museum of radio and telegraphy on the D922 just before the turn-off to the château is really only for enthusiasts who can recognise merit in the jumble of valves and knobs.

Boat trips run from just above the dam at Bort, taking you for lengthy excursions up the lake. The views of the Château de Val from this form of transport are the best you will get.

WHERE TO STAY AND EAT

There are two sections: establishments that we recommend and establishments that are worth considering but which we think do not merit a wholehearted recommendation. Both are marked on the map at the start of the chapter.

Key: ✦ = 0-250FF, ✦✦ = 251-450FF, ✦✦✦ = over 451FF; prices are per room without breakfast, which costs around 40-65FF extra. Some hotels insist on half-board during high season. Unless we say otherwise all have rooms with bath or shower and accept the major credit cards.

Recommended hotels

BORT-LES-ORGUES

Château de Lavendès   ✦✦-✦✦✦
Champagnac
15350 Cantal   *Tel: 71 69 62 79; Fax: 71 69 65 33*

See full description in Cantal chapter.

End Mar–mid-Nov; closed Sun pm & Mon; 8 rooms; outdoor pool

Auberge du Vieux Chêne   ✦✦
34 route des Lacs
Champs-sur-Tarentaine
15270 Cantal   *Tel: 71 78 71 64; Fax: 71 78 70 88*

See full description in Cantal chapter.

Mid-Mar–mid-Nov; closed Sun pm & Mon; 15 rooms

SAINT-VIANCE

Auberge des Prés de la Vézère   ✦✦
19240 Corrèze   *Tel: 55 85 00 50*

You can't actually see the river from the windows, but the Vézère is
close enough for a short walk to take you to it. The hotel stands on the
edge of a small village north-west of Brive, with trees providing shade
for the array of tables gathered in front of the building. A row of
arched French windows open out from the dining-room, bedrooms
line the two storeys above. It is a comfortable, well-run place, fractionally anonymous perhaps, but helpful enough. The bedrooms are
mostly large, light and fresh. Food, served out on the terrace in
summer, is highly competent.

May–mid-Oct, closed Mon, 11 rooms

Worth considering

BEAULIEU-SUR-DORDOGNE

Le Turenne   ✦✦
1 Boulevard St Rodolphe de Turenne
Place de la Poste
19120 Corrèze   *Tel: 55 91 10 16*

An ancient abbey building with an excellent restaurant and large, interesting bedrooms.

GIMEL-LES-CASCADES

Hostellerie de la Valleé   ✦
19800 Corrèze   *Tel: 55 21 40 60*

Fairly basic accommodation in a pretty village. Adequate for a night or
two.

161

ST-MARTIN-LA-MEANNE

Hotel des Voyageurs ✦
19320 Corrèze   *Tel: 55 29 11 53*

Traditional and comfortable village inn with a good local atmosphere and reasonable, hearty food.

ST-MERD-DE-LAPLEAU

Au Rendez-Vous des Pêcheurs ✦
Pont du Chambon
19320 Corrèze   *Tel: 55 27 88 39*

Right down on the very edge of the Dordogne at the bottom of its gorge, this isolated hotel is a popular Corrèze hideaway.

CANTAL

The *département* of Cantal forms a rough circle round the Monts du Cantal, the southernmost of the three volcanic mountain massifs of Auvergne. This rugged mass was once a single giant volcano, over 3,000 metres high, whose lava flows extended 70 kilometres around its flanks. The last Ice Age decapitated it and eroded it to such an extent that the tallest peak is now less than 2,000 metres, but the base of the mountain, with valleys radiating from it in all directions, survives.

The volcano's ruins form a spectacular collection of rocky tops, alpine pasturelands and deep-cut valleys. Too low for respectable skiing, but too high and wet for the climate to be much sought after, and about as far from the sea as you can get, the Cantal mountains are comparatively unfrequented by French holidaymakers, and tourist facilities are not abundant. This makes them all the more to be relished if you enjoy mountain country, for they remain unspoilt. The high, verdant pastures, where the hairy, brown Salers breed of cattle graze, turn into a carpet of flowers in early summer, and you can walk for hours along the ridges without seeing another human being. The woods offer abundant bilberries (*myrtilles*), which locals gather with a special rake and turn into tarts or jam, while the steep and wooded gorges, up and down which you ceaselessly climb as you travel, come into their own in autumn when the beeches and oaks turn to burnished copper.

A scattering of market towns lies on the fringes of the mountain, and tiny villages built of solid black basalt cling to the sides of valleys. Roofs are of the heavy split sandstone called *lauze*, and where the timbers have sagged under the weight, the farmhouses take on a drunken look, leaning together for security. Life here revolves around the age-old rituals of haymaking and summer pasturing. The fragrant Cantal cheeses are sometimes still fabricated in the mountain huts called *burons*, and you can arrange to visit and watch.

Each flank of the old volcano has a different character. On the western side, from which the tributaries of the Dordogne flow, long valleys penetrate into the heart of the mountains, each with its own small river and its distinct scenery. To the north, flat uplands carved by gorges separate the Cantal mountains from the Monts Dore. On the eastern side of the mountains, the high rolling plateau known as the Cézallier has striking views, over bare expanses of grassland, while to the south, the tangled gorges of the river Truyère and its tributaries are wild, virtually uninhabited and linked together only by steep twisting roads.

Because of the area's remoteness, you need to be fairly self-sufficient. Aurillac is the only town of any size, and the valley of the Cère which runs north-east from it is the only spot which has seen any development, thanks to small-scale skiing on the Plomb du Cantal. Elsewhere, a number of campsites are to be found by the more attractive river banks, while among the simple village inns there are a few which have been upgraded into friendly family hotels. The GR400 and GR4 long-distance paths (*Grandes Randonnées*) wind among the mountains, designed to take in the best of the scenery at the expense of many a steep climb in and out of valleys.

Cantal works very hard to keep its visitors happy in summer. Throughout July and August every tiny *commune* worth its salt lays on some kind of festival. Dog shows, barbecues, firework displays, sales of junk and folk festivals are the most common. Most of them are great fun precisely because they are small-scale and friendly.

Good bases

● **Aurillac**

There is not a great deal to see in this genial, workaday town, but it is the best starting point for exploration of the Cantal valleys. Look for accommodation in the Cère or Jordanne valleys.

● **Salers**

An ancient hilltop town with its original ramparts and imposing architecture. It is a popular tourist spot and becomes animated in summer. The countryside around is the most beautiful in Cantal.

● **Bort-les-Orgues**

(See Corrèze chapter for description). Useful for exploring the northern Cantal. Stay outside the town.

● **St-Flour**

This venerable place, set on the edge of an escarpment can be grim in bad weather, but it is the obvious staging post for the wilds of the Cézallier plateau. The Truyère valley to the south-east is the best area to look for out-of-town accommodation.

● **Chaudes-Aigues**

With the hottest spring in Europe, this tiny spa has been popular since Roman days. It is down in a dark dip, but is a lot less gloomy than most French spas. There is a range of accommodation in the centre of town, but not much outside.

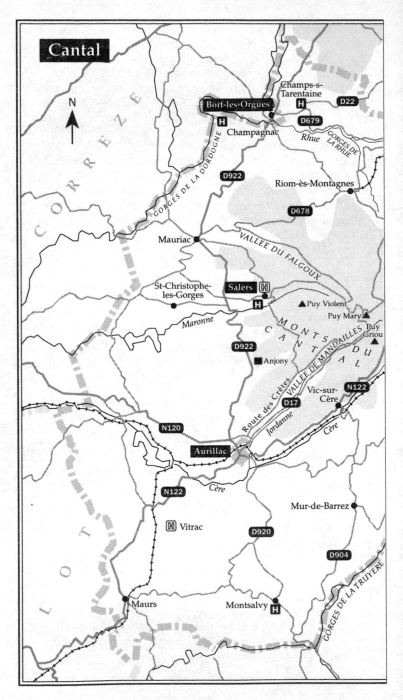

Cantal

N

Champs-s-Tarentaine
H
D22

Bort-les-Orgues
H
Champagnac
D679
Rhue
GORGES DE LA RHUE

CORREZE

GORGES DE LA DORDOGNE

D922

Riom-ès-Montagnes

D678

Mauriac

VALLÉE DU FALGOUX

St-Christophe-les-Gorges

Salers
H
H

Puy Violent
Puy Mary
Puy Griou

MONTS DU CANTAL

Maronne

D922

Anjony

Route des Crêtes

VALLÉE DE MANDAILLES

D17
Jordanne

Vic-sur-Cère
N122

N120

Cère

Aurillac

N122
Cère

Mur-de-Barrez

Vitrac
H

D920

D904

LOT

GORGES DE LA TRUYÈRE

Maurs

Montsalvy
H

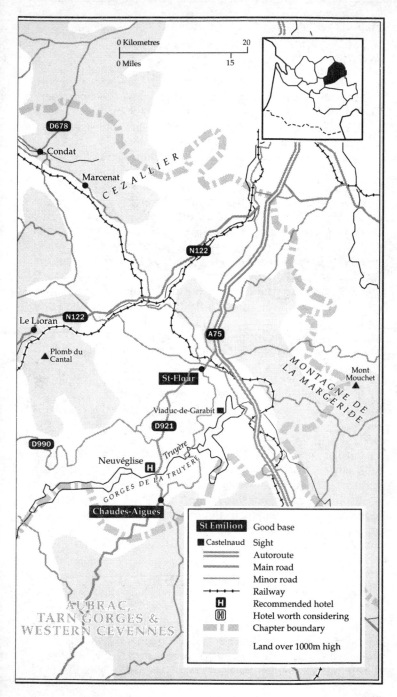

0 Kilometres 20
0 Miles 15

D678
Condat
Marcenat
C E Z A L L I E R
N122
Le Lioran N122
Plomb du
Cantal
St-Floar
Viaduc-de-Garabit
D921
D990
Truyère
Neuvéglise H
GORGES DE LA TRUYÈRE
Chaudes-Aigues
MONTAGNE DE
LA MARGERIDE
Mont
Mouchet
A75
AUBRAC,
TARN GORGES &
WESTERN CEVENNES

St Emilion	Good base
Castelnaud	Sight
	Autoroute
	Main road
	Minor road
	Railway
H	Recommended hotel
H	Hotel worth considering
	Chapter boundary
	Land over 1000m high

WEST CANTAL

Aurillac

Aurillac is a large, atmospheric town, capital of Cantal, but with a distinctive touch of warmer climes in its red-tiled houses and shaded squares. Its chief claim to fame is as the birthplace of the first French Pope in AD 999, the man who is supposed to have introduced Arabic numerals to the western world.

There is not a great deal left of the quaint or the historic in Aurillac. The tourist office in the Place du Palais-de-Justice is helpful and useful, but after a visit here and a walk through the pedestrianised streets, sightseers have only really got the choice of the Eglise St-Géraud (somewhat knocked about over the centuries), the art and archaeological collections in the town museum, or the more interesting **Maison des Volcans** (opens July 1995 after restoration; Tue–Sat 10 to 12, 2–6, Sun in July and Aug 2–6), where the history and the geology of the Cantal volcano is displayed in one wing of the mostly nineteenth-century château. A visit here makes an excellent starting point for exploration of the mountain; you will find specimens of the local rocks and will learn that the Cantal volcano is officially classified as dormant, not extinct (not that there is any likelihood of an eruption).

The best way to enjoy Aurillac is to relax and sample the local life in which city suits rub shoulders with weatherbeaten hill farmers. A climb up the steep back lanes to the château is rewarding for the views and the series of narrow stairs and stepped gardens.

Aurillac may not have much to see, but, with a wider range of shops than anywhere else nearby, numerous cafés, and a surprising number of Italian restaurants, it makes a good base for exploring the south-western part of Cantal. For preference, look for accommodation in the Jordanne or Cère valleys. The otherwise tedious suburb of Arpajon-sur-Cère to the south has a well-sited municipal campsite by the river.

Mountain routes around Aurillac

The Cère Valley

Pretty though it is, this is not the best of the valleys for a quiet day in the country on account of the main N122 road which runs through it. This is the only major east–west route through the mountains, which means that it is a road to avoid if at all possible, for heavy lorries turn its narrow upper stretches into a torment for other drivers, and the noise of them echoes from the mountains. A far more interesting way of exploring is to take one of the infrequent trains from Aurillac up to the head of the valley at Le Lioran, stopping off at Vic-sur-Cère if time-tables allow. There are excellent views of the mountains as the train growls slowly uphill, and it is altogether more enjoyable than sitting in a car.

Vic-sur-Cère, situated about halfway up the valley, is an animated place in summer, with a touch of health resort atmosphere to it. There is a large park, an ancient village centre with some surprisingly distinguished houses (lawyers built most of them) and a good sprinkling of hotels and small restaurants. Walks to the local waterfall or steeper expeditions to the crag known as the Rocher des Pendus in the hills above the village provide exercise and excellent views.

Through the tunnel at the head of the valley, **Le Lioran** and **Super-Lioran** compose Cantal's modest skiing resort. Out of season the latter is a little too grim and functional and the former too much down in the valley bottom to be pleasing to stay in, but Super-Lioran's year-round chairlift, linked directly to the railway station, provides a painless method of getting to the highest peak of the Cantal Volcano. The **Plomb du Cantal** is little more than a bulge on a high ridge, but the views south over the furrowed ridges dropping to the Truyère and north to the conical peaks of Puy Mary and Puy Griou are well worth seeing.

Vallée de Mandailles

The next valley north is altogether more rustic and possesses better mountain scenery than that of the Cère. The villages in its lower stretches are thick with the modern houses of commuters to Aurillac, but a little further up you are into typical Cantal scenery of green pasture, low barns built of black volcanic stone, and the small huddled villages of regions where the snow arrives early. The journey is made extra attractive by the changing perspectives of the **Puy Griou,** a scree-covered triangular peak which juts over the valley's head. This valley is also the most scenic route to the **Puy Mary** (see under Salers, below). Where it reaches the enclosing cirque at the head, the road dog-legs up a south-facing mountainside carpeted in flowers before disappearing abruptly round a shoulder to a whole new vista of mountains beyond.

Route des Crêtes

This is the mountain road (D35) from Aurillac to Salers. It winds along and between the west-facing ridges of the volcano over two high passes and makes an excellent half-day's drive or an energetic cycle ride. There is easy access to the GR400 at the Col de Legal if you want to walk at some stage. The woods along this route are a good place to search for bilberries (they usually ripen around the second or third week of August).

La Châtaignerie

The 'Land of the Chestnut' is a high granite plateau sloping gradually down to the south-west of Aurillac towards the valleys of the Lot and the Dordogne. The sweet chestnut trees which gave the district its name still exist in huge numbers by the roadside. In the past, chestnuts were the staple diet of a country where even rye grew with difficulty: ground into flour, the nuts were turned into bread. Modern farming techniques have brought a better standard of living to the countryside and most of the chestnut trees are now ornamental rather than useful. There is little to see in this countryside, but the driving can be attractive, especially where the land plunges down towards the Lot. For a casual drive, follow the Rance valley (D17), past Marcolès and its old château, down to Maurs.

Montsalvy, on the main D920 south of Aurillac, is a village worth pausing for – its imposing medieval gatehouse suggests a cramped historic centre. In fact, the village is fairly spacious and modern inside the old gates, but still an attractive place, especially if you can take time for lunch at the Auberge Fleurie (see Where to Stay).

Maurs on the south-western edge of Cantal, enjoys a micro-climate sufficiently divorced from the cold and damp of the mountains to enable the town to produce vines and abundant spring flowers and vegetables. It is known as the 'Nice of Cantal' – although the extent of this riviera among the hills is severely limited. Maurs still has the circular layout of a pre-Roman stronghold, but it grew around a tenth-century monastery, now long gone except for the fourteenth-century abbey church. This is well worth exploring in detail, for the massive choir stalls and the fifteenth-century wooden statues above them are intricate and beautiful. The chief work of art, however, is the peculiar bust of Saint-César, a wonderful enamelled carving of a tonsured monk with liquid cows' eyes and outsize elongated fingers raised in blessing. The expressiveness of the piece is such that it is difficult to believe that it dates from the thirteenth century.

Salers and the Maronne Valley

Salers, high on the north-western flank of the Cantal volcano, is a compact old town surrounded by ramparts from the Hundred Years' War and with squares of imposing sixteenth-century houses in its centre. It is the only town in the area with any appeal as a stopping point for coach tours, and so is apt to become overcrowded on hot summer days. The tourists actually help to animate what might otherwise be an austere place of black volcanic stone, bringing an air of festivity to the squares, the small fountain and the arched gateways. Most of the boutiques selling carved walking sticks, bottles of Gentiane eau-de-vie, and postcards of folk dancers are confined to a small street by the car park. The town's classier tourist shops concentrate heavily on food – tinned, bottled or packaged.

The town's situation is half its appeal, for it stands right on the edge of the Maronne valley and high above it. From the Esplanade de Barrouze you can gaze across to the shapely Puy Violent on the far side and listen to the cow bells echoing up from the valley.

The Grande Place is surrounded by turreted mansions and elaborate doorways. In the centre is the statue of Tyssandier-d'Escous, the man who preserved and improved the breed of the Salers cow, whose milk is used for the Cantal cheese. Elsewhere, tortuous streets lead to the heavily fortified Porte de la Martille and to the Eglise St-Matthieu (worth visiting to see the fifteenth-century Deposition, cut from stone and then painted). Two of the old houses are open during spring and summer (guided tours only). The more remarkable of them is the Ancien Bailliage, a Renaissance building garnished with turrets. Salers was the seat of the regional judiciary in the sixteenth century, a fact which explains the fine building.

The town makes an excellent base for travelling up and down the Maronne valley or from which to walk on the Puy Violent or the Puy Mary. The most civilised hotel in town has for many years been the Hotel des Remparts (see Where to Stay) and this makes a good place for a night's stop if you do not wish to indulge in the luxury of the Hostellerie de la Maronne in the valley beneath (see Where to Stay).

Expeditions from Salers

Château d'Anjony

Outside the village of Tournemire, about ten kilometres south of Salers, stands this fifteenth-century feudal castle, a menacing but shapely pile, with four great towers at each angle of a narrow keep. It only needs the braying of trumpets and the glint of armour on the ramparts to belong to a dreamland of Arthurian knights. Furthermore, the interior is well worth visiting (open mid-Feb–mid-Nov daily 2–6.30; July and Aug 11–6.30), chiefly for the sake of the lovely sixteenth-century frescoes which decorate the second-floor room.

The Maronne Valley

The Maronne is the most beautiful of Cantal's rivers – at least until it becomes penned behind the massive dam of the Barrage d'Enchanet. West of Salers you can follow its course through a succession of small villages before arriving at **St Christophe-les-Gorges**, which is by far the sunniest of them, with a central café and several rather grand farmhouses. A steep walk down from here takes you into the Maronne gorge to a tiny chapel (Notre-Dame-du-Château) built on a knobble of rock by the river. The spectacular railway which wound through the gorge has recently been closed, putting a stop to the last leisurely method of seeing this countryside.

East of Salers the Maronne is a small stream hidden in a peaceful open valley. By its junction with the Aspre, the village of **Fontanges** stands out from its neighbours in being built of mellow, sun-reflecting stone.The houses with their clumps of irises growing by the doorsteps might be in the Dordogne, so cheerful are their aspects.

Puy Violent

A tiny road climbs up from St-Paul-de-Salers on to the high *planèze* (pastureland) beneath the abrupt pyramid of this peak. The mountain is far less visited than the Puy Mary (see below), and is an ideal place to come in search of flowers or simply to be alone with the broad horizons. The grassy heights are dotted with ruined *burons*, where cowmen and cheesemakers used to live through the summer months. Today, most of the farmers go home for the night, and much of the milk goes off in tankers to the creameries of Aurillac. There are still scattered farms around Salers, however, where you can watch Cantal cheese being made.

Puy Mary

From Salers the D680 runs east along a high ridge then through thick woods to the Pas de Peyrol beneath the peak of Puy Mary. Roads from five different valleys converge close to this central point of the old volcano. Partly because of this, and partly because of the views, Puy Mary is one of the few local peaks to suffer from the uglier side of tourism in the shape of souvenir shops and an eroded path to the summit. However, as is usually the case in such places, you can escape quite easily by walking a few hundred yards away from the road. Each season covers the ground with a different array of flowers. Crocuses and narcissi when the snow melts, followed by mountain pansies, dianthus, turk's cap lilies and the tall yellow gentian whose roots go to make the local eau-de-vie.

It is worth avoiding this area during summer weekends if you can, for the roads are steep and narrow and every bus operator in the region seems to run an excursion to the peak, making the driving fractionally nerve-wracking.

Mauriac and around

Mauriac is one of the small market towns which mark the border between the volcanic lava and the wooded country to the west. It is marred by a sewage works at its northern end, but this should not put you off a quick visit to the centre where dour old houses cluster around a mossy square. The church here has a carved tympanum, much damaged during past outbreaks of religious vandalism, but still worth seeing. You can also visit the remains of the old monastery to which the church once belonged, reduced to a wall and a pillar or two.

The country to the west of Mauriac is furrowed by the steep gorges of various Dordogne tributaries, with several surprisingly grand farmhouses in the small villages in between. The sleepy **Brageac,** on the very edge of the Auze gorge is one of the best villages. It does not even run to a café or a shop, but has a tiny Romanesque church and a single street of low cottages. Close to Ally, the château of **La Vigne** (open Apr to Oct, 2 to 6) is another towered medieval relic, less interesting inside than Anjony, except for enthusiasts of model cars – there is a large collection.

NORTH AND EAST CANTAL

The plateau between the Monts du Cantal and the next massif north, the Monts Dore, is high and dotted with glacial leftovers – good for growing trees, but not much else. The valley of the Rhue forms almost the only practical route east from the Dordogne basin, and this is a slow route at the best of times, climbing through thick forests of beech. East of Condat the ground rises to over 1,000 metres and the trees give way to mile upon mile of high grassland, with conical hills thrusting up out of it. This is the Cézallier plateau, probably the loneliest part of the Massif Central, with barely a village worth the name before you come down to the Allier basin to the east.

This is not an area in which to base yourself unless you are either a keen fisherman or have the temperament for this kind of countryside. Still, a tour east from Bort-les-Orgues to St-Flour is a magnificent day's drive in fine summer weather, and you are unlikely to regret it.

East of Bort-les-Orgues

There are two routes well worth exploring. From Champs-sur-Tarentaine, the D22 takes you north-east towards Besse-en-Chandesse, the most pleasant way of getting from Cantal to the eastern side of the Monts Dore. The road runs through a high country of boulders, heathers and pines, with the small Lac Crégut half-lost among them. The D679 up the Rhue gorges does not have the same views, but runs through a tangle of trees and rivers to Condat. The only thing to see on the way is a giant beech tree (signposted from the road).

Condat, set in a bowl amongst the hills, is a spacious village on the edge of the treeline, used as a base by fishermen in pursuit of the small trout in the five river valleys which meet here. Beyond the village the road climbs over the valley's edge and the horizons suddenly widen as you emerge on to the Cézallier plateau.

The Cézallier, depending on the weather, is either a paradise of birds, flowers and views, or else a bleak and windswept wilderness. Hardly a tree breaks the sweep of the grassland, and such few houses as there are huddled in the sheltered nooks of small river valleys. On a clear summer's day, with the jagged tops of the Monts Dore rising in the blue distance to the north, and with kestrels hunting along the verges of the roads, it is a magic place. In many ways it is more like parts of Scotland than

France, ideal for walking (there is cross-country skiing in winter) and made for people who like wild, open country.

If you are making a round trip from the Dordogne valley, pick your way back from Condat via the tiny, strangely industrial town of **Riom-ès-Montagnes**, where there is an exhibition about the fabrication of eau-de-vie from the roots of the yellow mountain gentian, and a Romanesque church, both merit a glance.

If, on the other hand you are striking east or south, it is only a matter of picking a route through the Cézallier to suit your taste. Roads southwards have great views of the Cantal volcano to the west; roads east descend gradually from the high ground into one of the wooded gorges leading to the Allier valley. Life up here is unsophisticated: villages have a tumbledown, barricaded look to them, dogs chase the few passing cars, and there is nowhere much to stop. But the reason for traversing the Cézallier is not the local life, but the wildlife and the scenery. Birds of prey, skylarks and pipits abound, while the grassland is studded with the flowers of spring and summer, or the purple swathes of autumn crocuses.

At **Marcenat** there is an exhibition about lightning (mostly photographs) and a good waterfall a few kilometres north-east. The scenery as you cross the Cantal border on this road (D724) is excellent, with fine views both to north and south. Curious volcanic hillocks stud the land in all directions, except to the east, where the blue haze of the Allier valley with the Livradois mountains beyond it lies on the horizon.

St-Flour

This town makes a good finishing point for a tour of the Cézallier. It is set on a rocky bluff on the edge of the high pastures, its old houses grouped on a shelf above the River Ander. The weather makes a great difference to the feel of St Flour. On a hot sunny day the squares and cafés are delightful, but on a cold spring day, the black stone asserts itself and the town feels poised on the edge of the Arctic. The **Musée de la Haute Auvergne** (open Mon–Sat 10–12, 2–6, Sun in July and Aug) is worth visiting whatever the weather, for it holds a good collection of artefacts from the surrounding country. It is partly a folk museum – head-dresses, peasant furniture and scenes from rural life, partly a collection of religious art, including a lovely twelfth-century statue of St Peter and partly an archaeological collection, with bits of Roman bronzework and prehistoric arrow heads. It's a well laid out and friendly place to pass an hour. The **cathedral** is Gothic (the Romanesque version collapsed) and a bit grim, thanks to the black stone and to the fact that it served both as a prison as well as a church. West from it, narrow streets of solid houses recall the medieval layout of the town – it was a frontier post between the territories of the kings of England and of France, and suffered accordingly.

SOUTHERN CANTAL

The A75 motorway, extending its way slowly towards Montpellier, whips most tourist traffic through south Cantal on its way to the Tarn gorges and beyond. But a day spent in this region is worthwhile, for there is some very pretty country and one or two curiosities. The Cantal mountains are less in evidence here, for the land drops steeply to the River Truyère; on this southern side of the volcano the climate is a touch or two warmer, and the land more welcoming.

The Margeride

The Montagne de la Margeride is a long low range of forested hills separating the Truyère basin from the River Allier to the east. It is a forgotten country of small villages and fields, with fragrant woods of pine on the higher slopes. If many of the villages on the western slopes of the hills seem more modern than usual, this is because the Margeride was the scene of one of those tragic battles between the Resistance and the occupying Germans after the D-Day landings in 1944, and many houses were burnt in reprisal. The Resistance made their headquarters at **Mont Mouchet**, and driving there past monuments recording the death of one after another group of French freedom fighters is a sobering experience. At the end of the road, a modern **museum** (open May–end Oct, daily 9–12, mid-Sept to mid-Oct Sat, Sun only 10.30–12, 2–6; during week by reservation only. Tel 71 23 43 52) set up to remember the battle has gathered together relics from 1944. Among the usual collection of uniforms and weapons, a tiny card to be given to potential recruits stresses that, while a *maquisard* cannot expect any salary, he must bring at least three pairs of socks with him into the underground.

Tracking down the various components of the **Ecomusée de la Margeride** (open June–mid-Sept, daily 10–7) takes you from one quiet village to the next. There is a farm, a garden, a school and a 'domaine' (the last housing a permanent exhibition about the men who built the Viaduc du Garabit). Between them they evoke nineteenth-century life in this part of the world – and the fact that this is a split site museum turns visiting it into something of a map-reading challenge. On the way, aim to pass **Chaliers**, a village set into a rocky bend of the Truyère. It has a very fine setting between cliff and water and may warrant a photograph or a brief halt.

For the French, the main tourist attraction in this district is the **Viaduc de Garabit** which carries the railway south from St Flour over the Truyère. It was built by none other than Gustave Eiffel before he went on to construct his famous tower in Paris. The damming of the river has made his viaduct a little less dramatic, but there is no mistaking the author of the work when you see the single arch of girders which supports the railway. The single track railway bridge now looks inadequate faced with the concrete flyover which carries the multi-lane motorway further upstream, but it remains the more elegant design. A number of large hotels have been set up in the shadow of the viaduct and if you are in need of a bed, this is a good place to look. There are boat trips down the lake formed by the dam on the Truyère when you are bored with the viaduct, and you will get a glimpse of the Château d'Alleuze from them – an imposing feudal ruin on the north bank of the new lake.

Chaudes-Aigues

Chaudes-Aigues is a tiny spa town tucked into a steep valley on the south bank of the Truyère. Its chief claim to fame is that one of its springs, the Source du Par, is the hottest in Europe, pulsing out from the earth at 82°C. This is quite hot enough to flay pigs, which is what the spring was used for, and also to heat houses. Chaudes-Aigues also has a good claim to be the place where central heating by hot water was pioneered. The Romans probably started the practice, and for centuries the hot water was conducted from house to house in hollowed out pine logs. Some of these can be seen, together with the huge corkscrew-like drills used to make them, in the excellent **Musée Géothermal** (open May–mid-Sept 10.30–12, 2–6) which is built above the spring. As well as diagrams of the heating system of the village (a subject of endless lawsuits over water diversions, and the rights to the hottest flow) there are panels showing just how and where in the Earth's bowels the water reaches such a high temperature, and a display (illuminating if you are not a devotee) of the history of medical treatment using hot mineral water.

Away from the tourists plucking up the courage to test the heat of the water gushing from its spring, Chaudes-Aigues is a simple little place, with a distinguished church, a few streets of pre-nineteenth-century houses, a hotel or two and a swimming pool heated from the Source du Par. It is a good deal less gloomy than many French spa towns, and makes a fine base for a couple of days' stay.

Gorges de la Truyère

The Truyère spends more of its life behind dams than any other river in the region. Between the Viaduc de Garabit and Entraygues, where it joins the Lot, the river is just one long narrow lake at the bottom of steeply wooded gorges. It is possible to drive down, on either bank, but do not expect a speedy journey for the land is furrowed with tributary valleys and the roads wind faithfully up and down each of them. There are several

CHEESES OF THE VOLCANOES

With so much high mountain pasture available, the volcanic region of Auvergne produces three fine cheeses: Cantal, Saint Nectaire and the Bleu d'Auvergne. All three are available in Corrèze, Cantal and points south, though Saint Nectaire can be found as far away as Normandy.

Cantal is a large cylindrical cheese, 35 kilos or more in weight, needing the milk from around 40 cows. It is usually halved and then cut into triangular wedges before being sold. Good cheese merchants will sell it in three stages of maturity: *jeune, entre-deux* and *vieux*. It is worth sampling all three types, for the flavour is very different, ranging from something like a strongly cow-flavoured cottage cheese to something closer to mature Cheddar. Milk produced in the high summer pastures (and such milk only) is allowed to be made into 'Salers' (sometimes sold as Cantal-Salers). It is basically the same cheese, but has a herbier and more vigorous flavour.

The key to buying or eating **Saint Nectaire** is to insist on '*production fermier*'. Pasteurisation affects this cheese badly, turning some-

viewpoints, but otherwise not much worth stopping for. If you need a break from the gorge, the village of **Mur-de-Barrez**, with the ruins of its old château still visible, is a welcome sign of human habitation and a possible place for lunch.

WHERE TO STAY AND EAT

There are two sections: establishments that we recommend and establishments that are worth considering but which we think do not merit a wholehearted recommendation. Both are marked on the map at the start of the chapter.

Key: ✦ = 0-250FF, ✦✦ = 251-450FF, ✦✦✦ = over 451FF; prices are per room without breakfast, which costs around 40-65FF extra. Some hotels insist on half-board during high season. Unless we say otherwise, all have rooms with bath or shower and accept the major credit cards.

thing that ought to be deliciously varied in flavour into something resembling an undistinguished slice of processed cheese. A Saint Nectaire is a smallish, flat, round cheese, covered with a grey-green mould on the exterior and soft but neither creamy nor crumbly inside. The real home of this cheese is Besse-en-Chandesse in the shadow of the Monts Dore, but it is also made all over north and east Cantal.

Bleu d'Auvergne is rather less common than the two other cheeses, and it is rare to find one made in a farmhouse instead of in the big creameries. It is 'seeded' with the mould which turns it blue (sometimes the same species of penicillin that is used for Roquefort) at an early stage in production, then pricked to allow the veins of blue to develop in the interior of the cheese.

It should not be too difficult to see Cantal or Saint Nectaire being made in farmhouse dairies or even in mountain *burons*. The area between Salers and Mauriac has several small farms making Cantal where you can watch and buy, and it is worth asking in the tourist office in Salers or Vic-sur-Cère to see whether visiting a *buron* is possible.

Recommended hotels

BORT-LES-ORGUES

Château de Lavendès ✦✦-✦✦✦
Champagnac
15350 Corrèze   Tel: 71 69 62 79; Fax: 71 69 65 33

This is rather a smart hotel high up in pleasantly broken country to the west of Bort, just inside Cantal. It is much too isolated to have been turned into a luxurious haven for big spenders – the smartness is due more to the fine proportions of the seventeenth-century house and to the good taste with which it has been furnished. The owners are friendly and proud of their building and their food; bedrooms are large and there are fairly extensive grounds in which to doze away hot afternoons. This is a good place to pass a relaxing day or two.

End Mar–mid-Nov; closed Sun pm & Mon; 8 rooms; outdoor pool

Auberge du Vieux Chêne ✦✦
34 route des Lacs
Champs-sur-Tarentaine
15270 Corrèze   Tel: 71 78 71 64; Fax: 71 78 70 88

East of Bort, in a kind of hanging valley between rocky, tree-clad slopes, Champs-sur-Tarentaine is a substantial village. The *auberge* is on the edge of it – a low cottagey building with a green lawn to the front. It is a small hotel, likely to be full in high season if you do not book in advance, and popular as much for its rustic atmosphere as anything else. Bedrooms are small but clean and freshly decorated; most overlook the lawn and the hills beyond. There's not much sitting space inside the building, for almost all the ground floor is given over to the restaurant, where the food, especially if you sample the local trout or game, is palatable.

Mid-Mar–mid-Nov; closed Sun pm & Mon; 15 rooms

CHAUDES-AIGUES

Auberge du Pont de Lanau ✦✦
Neuvéglise
15260 Cantal   Tel: 71 23 57 76; Fax: 71 23 53 84

This is a friendly, family-run hotel in the depths of the Truyère gorge very close to Chaudes- Aigues. It is a meeting point for locals as well as holidaymakers and there is a bit of a buzz to it. It has the great advantage of a large high-ceilinged room on the ground floor which serves as bar, lounge and thoroughfare. A wood stove helps on cold evenings. The restaurant is large and a bit impersonal, but the food is good – well-flavoured and with some interesting regional dishes on the good-value menus. The bedrooms, well away from the road, are a little poky, but comfortable enough. Towards the end of summer you may be woken at dawn by the roaring of stags in the forest behind. There is a municipal swimming pool opposite the hotel for hot days.

Feb–Dec, closed Tues pm & Wed low season; 8 rooms

MONTSALVY

Auberge Fleurie ✦
15120 Cantal   *Tel: 71 49 20 02*

A rampant Russian vine rather than flowers covers this small inn just outside the medieval gatehouse of this attractive village on the main road south of Aurillac. The *auberge* is cheap, full of local trade and gossip, and absolutely made for those who desire nothing better than to plunge into the thick of provincial life. The huge restaurant is the star piece – full of gleaming copper and bunches of flowers and with hearty, good-value, country cooking. The bedrooms are small, spotless and old-fashioned, with floral wallpaper and bouncy beds but up-to-date showers. The welcome is very friendly, and you are just expected to mix in.

Early Feb–Dec; 11 rooms (5 with bath or shower)

SAINT MARTIN VALMEROUX

Hostellerie de la Maronne
Le Theil
15140 Cantal   *Tel: 71 69 20 33; Fax: 71 69 28 22*

This smartly converted farmhouse makes a good base for the west side of the Cantal mountains. It lies in a small village beneath Salers in the valley of the Maronne, close to beautiful scenery. The exterior preserves the dormer windows and lauze roof of the traditional Auvergnat house, but the inside has been smartly done up, with comfortable lounge and bar and with well-equipped bedrooms. The restaurant, built further down the hillside is reached by a tunnel beneath the lawn. The food is excellent and beautifully presented and it would be a shame to miss out on the crème brûlée in particular. Prices may seem steeper than they would be in other local hotels, but this is a well-run and modestly luxurious place, so they are far from being bad value.

Apr–early Nov, rest closed Wed lunch; 25 rooms; heated outdoor pool, tennis

Worth considering

SALERS

Hôtel des Remparts ✦-✦✦
15140 Salers   *Tel: 71 40 70 33*

A solid family-run inn in a good location within the old city walls.

VITRAC

Auberge de la Tomette ✦-✦✦
15220 Cantal *Tel: 71 64 70 94*

A simple but pleasing hotel lost in the Châtaignerie. Especially good for families.

AUBRAC, TARN GORGES AND WESTERN CEVENNES

The peculiar geology of the southern Massif Central, where the bed of an old sea has been thrust up among hills of granite and schist, has resulted in some of the most spectacular scenery in western France. The Aubrac plateau and the rounded slopes of the Western Cévennes are replaced, from one river bank to the next, by great sheets of flat limestone, high, porous and arid. Rivers with their sources on the slopes of Mont Lozère or Mont Aigoual have carved deep canyons into this limestone, dividing the bed of the old sea into five plateaux – the Grands Causses. Where the rivers have cut their way through, vertical cliffs, pockmarked with caves and coloured white, orange-red or grey from chemicals in the stone, line the banks. Erosion has left extraordinary pinnacles, towers and jumbles of rock on the cliff edges, while the constant passage of water downwards through the rock has honeycombed the *causses* with underground caverns and watercourses – some of striking beauty.

To the north of the *causses*, the high, severe land of the Aubrac rises above the river Lot. This is a country of wide horizons, open pastureland and forest, poor but alluring. It is not as mountainous as the volcanic massifs further north, but it is less restricted by valleys and gorges, with even fewer people and with a curious atmosphere all of its own. It is also the unlikely setting for one of the best restaurants in France.

To the east, the long ridges of the Cévennes divide the rivers flowing towards the Atlantic from those plunging to the Mediterranean. These are curious mountains: their western peaks are rounded and tree-clad, but as you progress east the valleys and the slopes steepen and become rockier, the vegetation scrubbier and the land more barren. Gradually a Mediterranean light and heat creeps into the air, until, at the watershed you perceive the far-off glimmer of the sea and can even make out the unsightly towers of the Languedoc resort of La Grande Motte dimly on the horizon. The Cévennes have always been one of the poorest regions of France – an outpost of persecuted Protestants; a land which the nineteenth-century Scottish writer, Robert Louis Stevenson could only describe as worse than the Scottish Highlands, and a region from which the population migrated as fast as possible. The country is still poor, but modern back-to-nature movements have led to the creation of a great National Park, to increasing tourism, and even to re-colonisation in places by communes and individuals.

It is the contrast between these very different landscapes rather than the beauty of any one of them which makes this such a satisfying area for the holidaymaker. In the central area of the Tarn Gorges between Millau and Meyrueis, there is no lack of diversions and plenty of facilities. It is also just about possible to do without a car, for there are numerous organised excursions to the main sights and the country is ideal for cyclists (provided you stay off the main roads and can cope with some sharp climbs). For walkers too, there is plenty of variety, from terrifying cliff-top paths on the edge of gorges to long rambles across the *causses* or tougher expeditions through the Cévennes. The downside to the wealth of sights and excursions is the degree of overcrowding in summer. The rigours of the landscape confine the transient population (and accommodation) to the river valleys, and there is limited space. For this reason, it is as well to book accommodation in advance if you plan to visit in July or August.

Good bases

● **Laguiole** Capital of the Aubrac, this workaday little town is the obvious place from which to explore the wild plateaux and the upper Lot valley. There are simple hotels in town. Look for cottages on the south-western slopes of the Aubrac rather than the treeless heights above.

● **Millau** A bustling town in the Tarn valley, ideally placed for exploring the gorges. There is plenty of accommodation in town, and a campsite nearby.

● **Meyrueis** This large village at the top of the Jonte Gorge makes an amiable place to stay, with easy access to the gorges and to the Cévennes. There are several adequate hotels in town and a scattering of places outside. Book in advance for July and August.

● **St Enimie/La Malène** These tiny villages are in the depths of the Tarn Gorge. They make sensible bases for a night or two beside the river, or for boating expeditions but touring from them may be a bit of a struggle as the roads up the gorge sides are very steep.

● **Nant** An open, sunny village in the Dourbie Gorge, with good access to the surrounding countryside and the *causses*.

● **Florac** A suitable base for trips into the Cévennes. The town has plenty of shady squares and a river tumbling through the middle.

● **Le-Pont-de-Montvert** A lovely Cévennes village beside the infant Tarn. Accommodation is basic and fairly limited but the excellent information centre can provide details of further possibilities.

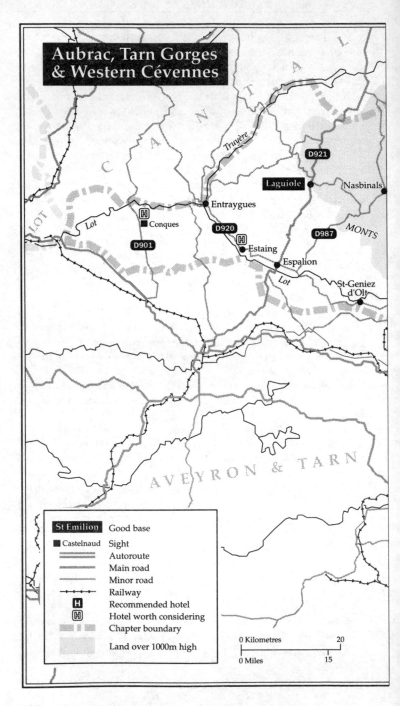

Aubrac, Tarn Gorges & Western Cévennes

CANTAL

Truyère

LOT

Lot

D921

Laguiole

Nasbinals

Entraygues

H Conques

D901

D920

H Estaing

Espalion

D987

MONTS

Lot

St-Geniez d'Olt

AVEYRON & TARN

St Emilion	Good base
■ Castelnaud	Sight
	Autoroute
	Main road
	Minor road
	Railway
H	Recommended hotel
Ⓗ	Hotel worth considering
	Chapter boundary
	Land over 1000m high

0 Kilometres 20

0 Miles 15

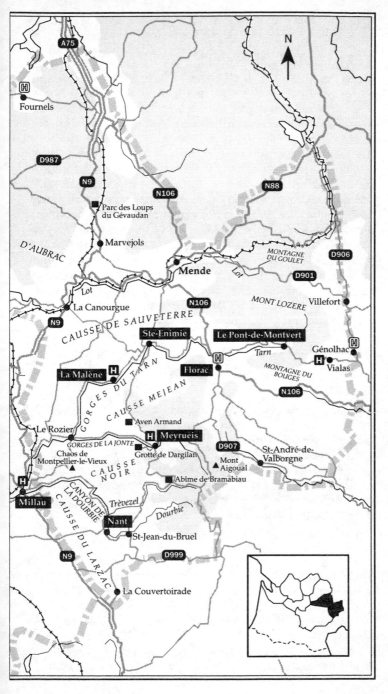

N

A75

D987

N9

N106

N88

Parc des Loups
du Gévaudan

Marvejols

D'AUBRAC

MONTAGNE
DU GOULET

Lot

D906

Mende

D901

Lot

La Canourgue

N106

MONT LOZERE

Villefort

N9

CAUSSE DE SAUVETERRE

Ste-Énimie

Le Pont-de-Montvert

Génolhac

H

La Malène

H

Florac

H

Tarn

Vialas

H

GORGES DU TARN

CAUSSE MÉJEAN

MONTAGNE DU
BOUGES

N106

Aven Armand

Le Rozier

H

Meyrueis

GORGES DE LA JONTE

Grotte de Dargilan

D907

St-André-de-
Valborgne

Chaos de
Montpellier-le-Vieux

CAUSSE
NOIR

Mont
Aigoual

H

Abîme de Bramabiau

Millau

CANYON DE
LA DOURBIE

Trèvezel

Dourbie

CAUSSE DU LARZAC

Nant

St-Jean-du-Bruel

N9

D999

La Couvertoirade

187

THE UPPER LOT VALLEY

The Lot from Figeac to Entraygues

To the east of Figeac, the Lot ceases to be a slow-moving river of the flatlands and comes pouring in a powerful stream through deep-channelled valleys between the uplands of the Massif Central. Between Figeac and Mende, some 150 kilometres to the east, it is rarely possible to see beyond the confines of the steep, wooded banks between which the river runs.

This long stretch of river is little-visited; for it has none of the thrill given to the Tarn by its canyons and limestone cliffs, and there are few riverside spaces for campsites or watery activities. Yet the journey east is not without interest, for not only is the river beautiful, especially in early spring when the trees are coming into leaf weeks before those on the wind-blasted plateaux above, but there are several places well worth stopping for. Chief among these is the great Romanesque pilgrimage church at Conques, but so are the villages of Entraygues, Estaing and St Geniez-d'Olt. Higher up, the wooded scenery which characterises the lower stretches of the gorges gives way to tangles of rock and rearing hillsides until the river becomes positively Himalayan in aspect.

Conques

The pilgrimage church of Conques lies tucked away on the steep side of a small tributary of the Lot, surrounded by a small village of mellow cottages and houses. It is an extraordinarily isolated spot in which to find a large and magnificently decorated Romanesque church, (open all year, daily 7.30 to 7.30). Its position is explained by its origins as an abbey, deliberately remote from temptations and threats, while its size is attributable to the fact that it has become one of the most important stops on the pilgrimage route which ran from Le Puy to Santiago de Compostela.

Pilgrims were drawn here to venerate the relics of Sainte Foy displayed in the church. This young girl was martyred in Agen in the third century and her relics were kept there until a monk from Conques rose high in the favour of the church at Agen and was given the guardianship of the relics. He promptly absconded with them back to Conques. If legend is to be believed, the number of miracles attributed to the saint immediately increased, showing that she was not displeased with her new home and was prepared to connive at the skulduggery involved. Just how much of this story is true, and how much of the plot was premeditated by the then abbot, Bégon, is open to question, but the relics of Sainte Foy certainly came from Agen, and the abbey's wealth was enormously increased by them.

The church was started in the eleventh century and completed in the twelfth. It is built on a shelf of the hillside with the village above, so that on arrival you look down on its three towers. Inside, it is high and light for a Romanesque church, with wide aisles to allow the pilgrims to process past the relics (and to bed down for the night). The stone is light in colour for the Auvergne, and this fact, together with the windows in the clerestory and the unusual delicacy of the pillars combine to make it a compelling place – more Gothic than Romanesque.

The carved tympanum above the west door is unmistakably Romanesque, however, and yet another example of the heights reached by twelfth-century sculpture. The scene is the Last Judgement, and no fewer than 124 different characters are depicted, including Emperor Charlemagne, Sainte Foy and Bégon (among the saved souls of course). The damnation scenes have their usual lurid appeal – the grinning figure of Satan, the pop-eyed demons and a nasty devil trying to tip the balance in which the Archangel Michael is weighing souls – and are all carved with great verve. It is remarkably well-preserved, right down to traces of the original paint-work (blue for paradise, red for hell).

Conques was virtually neglected after the pilgrimage fever had waned, and the building was scheduled for demolition in 1837. Luckily it was preserved and restored, although the cloisters went, leaving only a few arcades.

Church treasures are often among the most tedious of sights, but Conques has managed to preserve such a remarkable collection (everything is well laid out and lit) that the steep entrance fee is worth paying. Much of the collection was made locally, in workshops which continued from Carolingian times to the fourteenth century. The oldest piece on display is a ninth-century reliquary covered with gold leaf and jewels. A tenth-century statue of Sainte Foy, looking like a grotesque doll covered in sequins, is the most prominent piece. It is surrounded by further reliquaries from the eleventh and twelfth centuries, glittering and shining under the lights. It is the age, rather than the beauty of these objects which makes such an impression, together with the fact that they have managed to survive so many centuries of war and revolution. They bear witness too, to a religious enthusiasm which can now seem as strange as it is distant in time.

Conques can get very crowded, so for a leisurely look around it is best to visit either early or late in the day during the height of summer. If you need to stay, there is plenty of accommodation in the village, but much of it is overpriced. The Hotel Sainte-Foy is one of the best places, in a seventeenth-century building (see Where to Stay).

Entraygues

The stretch of the river east from Conques is peculiarly pretty, largely because only a narrow country road (D141/D107) tracks its banks. Poplars and willows grow by the banks, and small farms have colonised the fertile ground close to the river. Entraygues is where the Truyère joins the Lot, virtually doubling the size of the river. The little town is surrounded by hills, and the best views of it are from above, either from the D904 or the D920 to the north. From this angle, the château, poised at the very junction of the rivers, with the roofs of the old quarter clustering around it, exudes the impression of a medieval settlement so strongly that the bright spots of canoes and kayaks by the water seem an aberration from the wrong period.

A walk around the town heightens this sense of belonging to a past time. Its houses lean towards one another and narrow, covered lanes wind into curious dead ends. You expect to find pigs rooting in the gutters, and it comes as a shock to find parked Renaults instead.

For all its sense of the past, Entraygues is not a place to stay for long. Before you leave, however, look for the marks in the Place A. Castanié recording the levels of the floods from which the town used to suffer and wonder that the thirteenth-century Gothic bridge which spans the Truyère has survived.

From Entraygues to Mende

South-east of Entraygues, the first of the limestone begins to appear on the southern bank of the Lot, while to the north-east furrowed valleys lead up to the Aubrac plateau. Between Entraygues and Estaing the river valley is restricted and the road running beside it is plagued with lorries – not the most pleasing stretch. But things improve at **Estaing**. This is another medieval village – a tiny one, with a curious château surrounded by ancient houses. It was the seat of a distinguished French family which lost its status when one of its scions was foolish enough to correspond with Marie Antoinette during the Revolution.

You can be shown round the château by the nuns who now inhabit it, but it is probably more pleasing to wander through the streets and across the ancient bridges, taking a glance at the fifteenth-century church in front of the tiny cobbled square. Estaing also produces wine. The scattered vineyards along the Lot were once more extensive than they now are, but it is worth trying out a bottle while you are here.

There is an utterly simple but clean hotel, Aux Armes d'Estaing overlooking the river and the oldest bridge. It is fine for a night's stay providing you do not expect too much of the food (see Where to Stay).

Espalion is nothing like so picturesque. A widening of the Lot valley has given the town room to expand, and the remnants of its past are well-hidden. The most visible are the lovely eleventh-century bridge over the river and some of the oldest houses in the town ranged along the banks beside it. It is worthwhile making for the **Château de Calmont d'Olt** (open June–end Sept 9–7; closed Thur, Fri), the remains of a feudal castle built high above Espalion on the south bank. The ruins are fairly scanty, but the views are good. The owners have enterprisingly set up full-scale reproductions of medieval siege weapons around the walls. A video shows the trebuchet being fired – its attendants disappearing rapidly in all directions as a huge lump of stone hurtles through the air.

East of Espalion, both **St Côme d'Olt** and **St Geniez d'Olt** merit a pause for the sake of their old houses. So too, if you are interested in archaeology, may the museum at **Banassac** (open 8.30–12.30, 2–6 (5 on Fridays)) 25km further on, where Roman pottery and post-Roman coins are on display. At **Le Villard**, just off the N88, there is a very interesting recreation of a medieval farm, complete with mock-medieval participants. It is aimed at children – although there is not quite enough squalor to suggest the real thing, there are animals in plenty and a blacksmith. Look for signs to the **Domaine médiéval des Champs** (open July–mid-Sept daily 11–7, low season Sun only 11–7).

A good alternative to following the Lot on the traffic-ridden N88 is to cut the corner from La Canourgue to Chanac across the Causse de Sauveterre. In this landscape of stunted pine and small fields there are few habitations but some fine views.

Mende

Mende is not a very attractive place. It is the regional capital, which means that there is a good deal of unpleasing modern building, and its situation is in a peculiarly barren part of the Lot valley, with great rubbly slopes all around. The cathedral is worth a glance however. Its two towers loom over a small square, one garlanded with balconies and encrustations, the other plain, red and sober. The interior is unremarkable, except for the preserved clapper of what used to be the biggest bell in Christendom, destroyed during the Wars of Religion. The original bell is said to have weighed 20 tons, while the clapper is as tall as a man.

THE AUBRAC PLATEAU

The Aubrac plateau is not how one imagines southern France. It is high, windswept and often cold and damp. Hoteliers in the Lot valley will tell you of the modern version of *transhumance*. Instead of the cattle being conducted to the high ground at the start of summer, it is now the tourists who venture up on hot days and rush down to fill the valley's restaurants as soon as the rain sets in. The Aubrac rises steeply to the north of the Lot and drops more gradually into the Truyère valley. Any of the long valleys leading up from the Lot is equally worth exploring – small villages cling to the slopes all the way up. Once on top of the plateau, there is little to see except for the countryside, but this can be quite magnificent. If you venture down the D52 from Nasbinals for example, you are at once in a bare open country of broad skies, small lakes and innumerable birds and flowers in season. There's a waterfall down here too, the **Cascade de Déroc**, where you can actually climb in behind the curtain of falling water and gaze at a constant rainbow if the sun's angle is right.

The chief town of Aubrac is **Laguiole**. It is renowned for its knives which are sold all over Auvergne but are most visible here. These horn-handled implements are not cheap, but will certainly add status to your *casse-croûte* (snack) should you care about such things. Laguiole is small and ordinary, but a good shopping centre and it has a regional folk museum for wet days.

To the west, where the land drops towards the Truyère, a number of sunny villages and good views down the gorges make an attractive half-day's drive. For touring, fishing or aimless pottering among the pine trees and the open moor, try the valley of the Bès, which runs north down from Nasbinals to meet the Truyère. A modern, package-style but comfortable hotel in the middle of nowhere, Les Hameaux de Lozère (see Where to Stay) in the village of **Fournels**, might make a good base for wandering this countryside, especially if you like laid-on entertainment of a kind that you would be hard put to find elsewhere in the Aubrac.

Michel Bras' incredible hotel and restaurant (see Where to Stay) lies on the D15 east of Laguiole. Even if you do not eat here (and it is inconceivable to bypass his weekday 200 franc menu, even if you have to sleep in the car to afford it), the building, like a granite and glass Noah's Ark stranded on the high plateau, is almost a tourist attraction in its own right.

Marvejols and around

To the east of the Aubrac plateau, south of the watershed which divides the Truyère from the Tarn, the land is tormented and rocky. **Marvejols** guards the strategic route north (ignored by the designers of the new A75 motorway). It is not a prosperous country, and Marvejols has few fine buildings, but it is note-worthy for its magnificent fortified town gates and for the strange modern statue of Henri IV, looking like an emaciated Don Quixote, which stands outside the western one. A further statue stands in a square, portraying the Beast of Gévaudan (see below).

Before you reach Marvejols from the north, a turn up the D2 takes you into the **Vallée de l'Enfer** (Valley of Hell), a gloriously rocky gorge with a stately railway viaduct at its end.

Also north of Marvejols (and signposted from all over the region) **Les Loups du Gévaudan** (open June-Aug 10–6; rest of year 10–4.30; closed Jan) is a wolf park built on a slope beneath a very ancient and near-abandoned hamlet. The wolves have all the correct credentials, being sponsored by Brigitte Bardot and being allowed to live in practically natural condi-tions. They loll about in the sun, watching the visitors who puff up and down the slopes between their enclosures or work out on the carefully-provided exercise circuit. Everything you ever wanted to know about wolves is on show in the excellent museum housed in the reception building and there is even a small wolf-den for children. The most fascinating section, for those whose French is up to it, is likely to be the audiovisual show about the Beast of Gévaudan. West Country panthers and such like are put in the shade by this monster, who between 1764 and 1767 made 126 recorded attacks on humans and devoured 50, mostly children. Hunters were dispatched by the court of Louis XV, but attacks only ceased after a large wolf had been shot.

Dispassionate though the commentary is, it throws doubt on the likelihood of the beast having been a wolf, suggesting it was probably a trained war dog run amok.

THE GRANDS CAUSSES

The *causses* take up a huge area of country from the banks of the Lot right down to the edge of the Monts de Lacaune. Their plateaux never fall far short of 1,000 metres, so the height, the aridity of the soil and the extremes of climate mean that they are sparsely inhabited at best. Travelling across them is endlessly pleasurable, for the scenery is prevented from becoming monotonous by the dips and furrows of the land and by the alternation of desert-like grassland with forests of pine, or scrub land full of juniper and broom. All the *causses* have things in common – the soil which is little more than rubble, the outbreak of spring flowers, the sheets of yellow when the broom is out and the occasional carefully tilled field where soil has gathered in a dip in the land. But they also have distinct characters of their own: Sauveterre is the greenest, Méjean the most varied, Larzac the largest and flattest and most like a desert, while the Causse Noir takes its name from the trees which cover it.

The best way to see the *causses* is by bicycle or on foot. Roads are narrow and tranquil, except near the obvious tourist sights. The GR 60 and 62 long-distance footpaths traverse long stretches of the country remote from even the few roads there are. But wandering over the *causses* by car is not to be despised either, provided you do not attempt to rush things and prepare to stop often to look at birds, flowers or views.

The only disadvantage to spending time on the *causses* is the difficulty of getting on and off them. The gorges that cut through them make crossing from one to the next easier said than done. There are some truly terrifying (or exhilarating depending on your taste) roads, made the more so by the fact that Lozère, one of the poorest of *départements*, does not go in much for safety barriers.

The great sights of the *causses* are mostly natural ones – for the limestone offers both underground and surface spectacles. Cave visiting here is rather different from in the Dordogne valley, for prehistoric man has left few traces here, but the rock formations are more extensive and more magnificent. Numbers build up in high summer so you can expect extensive queues at the major sights.

The caves of the *causses* were almost all discovered by the revered E A Martel, a commercial lawyer from Paris who became obsessed by underground exploration. From 1883 onwards he slithered beneath the limestone throughout the region, bringing a new sport, potholing, and a new version of tourism to a neglected area of France.

Aven Armand

If you only visit one cave, let it be this one (open end Mar–end May daily 9.30–12, 1.30–6, June to end Aug 9.30–7, Sept 9.30–12, 1.30–6, Oct–early Nov–5). It is in the south of the Causse Méjean, reached over hillocky, deserted country where tour buses heading in the same direction will be the only sign of life. Unlike other caves where you prowl along courses of old rivers, this is simply a single, huge underground chamber formed by the undermining and collapse of the roof many thousands of years ago.

The absence of any horizon does strange things to your sense of distance and it takes time to realise just how enormous the cavern is. From the gallery high up on the wall from which you catch a first glimpse of it, three-quarters of an hour would seem too long to spend here. But it takes every moment of this time to walk round even once.

All over the floor of the cave great stalagmites have grown. They are not the smooth columns you find in other caves, for the height of the roof means that drips splatter rather than drop, making every stalagmite like a pile of jagged saucers stacked to three or four times human height. There are some bizarre and lovely formations, most of them given names by Martel or his followers. As you walk among the 400 columns, the impression is less of being in a virgin forest (Martel's name) as of being a Lilliputian in a graveyard of church candles.

No other cave in the area matches the beauty of this one. Try to come out of season if possible, for the presence of four or more groups in the cave at the same time is apt to diminish the sense of wonder, while the time spent queuing can easily match your time underground. For all that, the set-up is professional and the guides are chatty.

Grotte de Dargilan

This is not a patch on Aven Armand, but it is a pretty impressive cave even so (open Apr–early Nov, July and Aug 9–7, rest of year 9–12, 2–6). It is burrowed into one side of the Gorges de la Jonte, and one of the thrills is emerging from the constrictions of underground passageways into the airy heights of the gorge. In this cave you follow the old course of an underground river on an extensive journey (with lots of steps). There are some splendid rock formations – for example a single massive column and a whole wall of calcium deposits shaped like a frozen waterfall. The cave is known as the Pink Cavern – but although the iron in the limestone has turned many formations orange, do not expect anything out of the ordinary by way of colour.

This is not a cave for even the mildly claustrophobic, for you penetrate deep and narrow passageways, and it can seem a long way to the surface.

Chaos de Montpellier-le-Vieux

This natural sight is on the Causse Noir, not far from Millau, and is a wonderful place to spend half a day or more. High above the gorge of the river Dourbie, the edges of the cliff have eroded into a fantastic jumble of boulders, precipices, natural arches and towers over a considerable distance. Through this geological tangle wind way-marked paths of different lengths (a leaflet given to you at the entrance describes them all) which lead to the most renowned rock formations or viewpoints. Alternatively, you can take a small tractor-train, where you get the bonus of an informed commentary.

The gaps among the rocks are covered in pine and scrub oak, and the wild flowers are magnificent. April and May are the best months to see them, but they last well into July.

The rocks were given their name by shepherds moving their flocks up on to the *causse* from Languedoc, who saw in the towers and pillars the shape of a ruined city – it is easy enough to see why. For centuries Montpellier-le-Vieux was regarded as the haunt of the Devil, and was infested by wolves. Martel, as ever, was to the fore in mapping it all and giving names to the rocks.

There is ample space here, so crowding is not a problem. Bring a picnic, for it is easy to be enticed into staying longer than you intended, as round every corner of the path something weird or wonderful lies. A warning note – it is easy to get lost in this natural labyrinth, so take heed of the signs suggesting you stick to the marked paths.

La Couvertoirade

The Causse du Larzac is 1,000 square kilometres of rock, dust and scrub – the most uncompromising and the flattest of the Grands Causses. It is less unspoilt than the others, partly because of the motorway which cuts across it and partly because of the military camp and the associated clutter of barracks, tank tracks and warning notices which go with it.

La Couvertoirade belongs to an older military and militant tradition, for it was a *sub-commanderie* of the order of the Knights Templar in the twelfth century. When the order was disbanded in 1312, it passed to the Knights Hospitaller of St John, who fortified the small town in the fifteenth century. When the era of knights was long past, La Couvertoirade lost almost all its population, but being so remote, its medieval fortifications remained intact.

A clever piece of reanimation has happened here, for La Couvertoirade has been turned into a craft village – the artisans setting up their workshops among the ancient stairs and court-yards of the little town. It is a perfect place to spend an hour or two, wandering around the battlements and gateways.

Other traces of the Templars are to be found on Larzac, at Ste Eulalie-de-Cernon, which was their headquarters and at La Calverie, where the modern soldiers have their base.

The **Ecomusée du Larzac** (open July–Sept 9–12, and 5–7), just off the N9, merits a visit. The rural economy of the *causses* (mostly based on sheep and Roquefort cheese) is clearly explained.

THE GORGES

Every river tributary of the Tarn descending westwards from Mont Aigoual has carved a gorge for itself in the limestone. The gorges of the Tarn are the most extensive and on the grandest scale, but are not necessarily the most dramatic or most alluring. Those of the Jonte, the Dourbie and the Trèvezel are close competitors and there are fewer sightseers.

The appeal of these great slashes in the Earth's surface lies in the rock scenery. Curtains of cliffs hang above the roads which cling to the edge of the rivers. Often these roads have had to be tunnelled through buttresses of limestone. Coloured grey, peachy-orange or yellowy-white, the cliffs dwarf the tiny villages, mills or farms which have been crammed into any space where the land is less than sheer. Terraces (mostly abandoned now) show where generations of farmers have attempted to make a living from this unpromising land.

Millau to the west, St Enimie to the north, Meyrueis to the east and Nant and St-Jean-du-Bruel to the south are the best bases for exploring the gorges. Meyrueis has the best setting, but there is something to be said for Millau too with its glove museum and its small town buzz.

It is possible to drive down all the gorges, but be aware that only the passengers will be able to look at the scenery and that the driving is pretty gruelling – especially when the tour buses are out in force. Walking the crests (there are many paths, and plenty of leaflets describing them to be found in tourist offices) is a more pleasing way of seeing the country. Choose your walk to suit your head for heights – some of them (lovingly known as the *Sentiers de Vertige* – Paths of Vertigo) involve ladders stapled to cliff-faces and the like, notably along the section of the Jonte Gorges close to their junction with the Tarn.

Much is made locally of the joys of travelling down the Tarn by water – and this is certainly the most comfortable and tranquil way of seeing the Tarn gorges. You can either paddle yourself in canoe or kayak or else go with a boatman (not that expensive if shared between a party of four). La Malène is the best place to fix up such trips.

Millau

Millau is a junction for roads running north and west and can become a traffic bottleneck in the peak days of July and August. It is an attractive town nonetheless, and if you are caught in a jam it is no hardship to while away an hour or two here. The old centre is not very extensive and has been heavily interlarded with modern buildings, but there is a fascinating **museum** (open Apr to Sept daily 10–12, 2–6; rest of year closed Sun) to discover. This concentrates on the history of gloves and glove-making, which was once Millau's chief industry (cheese production means surplus lambs and hence lamb skins). In a huge room, rigged up as a workshop, you can see all the machines and materials needed to produce gloves, while a video shows the actual process. Glass cases hold examples of gloves of all kinds, from the white elbow-length style worn to the opera at the turn of the century, to boxing gloves or steel-reinforced lumberjack's gauntlets.

Millau is the obvious place from which to explore the lower section of the Tarn gorges and the gorges of the Dourbie and Jonte or from which to drive down the Tarn to St-Rome, up to Montpellier-le-Vieux or to the dry desert of the Causse du Larzac.

The Tarn swings round the town, with pleasantly grassy spaces by its banks and a small municipal campsite. The best place to stay is the Château de Creissels, outside town to the west (see Where to Stay)

The Tarn Gorges

The gorge proper starts at **Le Rozier** where the Jonte joins the Tarn and continues relentlessly to Ispagnac, a distance of 60 kilometres. There are only three spots on the way where it has been possible to create escape roads out of the gorge up the side of the cliffs. For most of its length, the D907 road runs between one precipice and another, and there are a fair number of stopping points where you can gaze up or down in admiration. The waters of the Tarn are a clear blue-green, the limestone every variation of white, orange and grey.

The most renowned stretch of scenery is to be found between Le Rozier and the tiny village of La Malène. The Pas de Souci where the river narrows among giant boulders, Les Détroits, a particularly vertical section of canyon, and the Cirque des Baumes where the cliff edge recedes in a semi-circle from the river are the three chief points on this itinerary. High above the river, reached by a hairpin road, the Point Sublime is a viewpoint on the northern crest.

La Malène, a village huddled beneath the cliff face, is the chief spot on the river for the hire of canoes or *bateliers* (boatmen). You float or paddle down the river (experience is advisable if you take a canoe or kayak) for various distances and are met and transported back to the start.

Touring the full length of the Tarn Gorge is a little monotonous. Aim to travel up to, or down from, La Malène or St

Enimie to see the best sections and forget about the stretch immediately beneath Ispagnac.

The Jonte Gorges

Narrower but not so deep as the Tarn Gorge, the straight trench carved by the Jonte from Meyrueis to Le Rozier is nevertheless almost as spectacular – largely because the erosion of the cliff edges have left a fascinating sequence of pinnacles and rock shapes lining the gorge. The road here is a lot less strenuous to drive than in the Tarn Gorge and less crowded.

The Jonte is popular with fishermen, rock-climbers and cavers, and these days also with bird-watchers. For these last enthusiasts one of the great attractions of the Jonte is the hope of seeing the griffon vultures which were reintroduced to the area in 1982 in the village of Cassagnes on the Causse de Méjean. They are now firmly established and the hundredth bird was born in 1991.

At the head of the Jonte Gorge, **Meyrueis** is a small, very pleasing town – the only place of any size between the *causses* and the Cévennes. After the rigours of the surrounding scenery, the relaxed air of the old houses, the tree-lined streets and the outdoor cafés come as a considerable relief. There are a number of places to stay here, but Meyrueis becomes solidly booked in July and August.

The Canyon and the Gorges of the Dourbie

Despite the fact that its entire course runs through a gorge of one variety or another, the Dourbie varies more between dramatically narrow stretches and sunnier, open passages than do the other rivers of the area. A drive upriver makes an excellent outing, especially in autumn, when the golds, burnished reds and fading greens of the trees combine magnificently with the pastel shades of the limestone cliffs. **La Roque-Ste-Marguerite** is the first place to stop, coming from Millau. This village is built on several levels in the constrictions of the riverside. Nevertheless there is room for a café and a fortified tower built of warm reddish stone, with the Dourbie running clear as gin beneath. A tiny road leads up to Montpellier-le-Vieux from here, offering the possibility of a short round trip.

Above Ste-Marguerite, the Canyon of the Dourbie opens out. There is space for woodland and small fields by the river. At **Cantobre**, a village whose cottages are barely distinguishable from the slabs of rock which surround them, the **river Trèvezel** joins the Dourbie, its gorge a chaos of boulders and forested in its higher reaches.

Between **Nant** and **St-Jean-du-Bruel**, the Dourbie is open and sunny. This is a fertile area sheltered from the biting winds of the *causses*. Both villages have old humpback bridges across the river, and Nant is given a distinguished look by the remains of its old abbey. Either would make a good place to stay and potter for a few days. Nant is probably to be preferred for ease of access, sunny aspect and the luscious strawberries on sale in the grocer's shop.

Above St-Jean lies the most taxing part of the drive, where the Canyon officially turns into a gorge. The walls of the Dourbie close in, and the road on both banks reverts to a *corniche* high above the water, with splendid views down into the depths from a number of look-out points.

THE WESTERN CEVENNES

The Cévennes are split from the Grands Causses by the valley of the river Tarnon flowing northwards from Mont Aigoual to join the Tarn near Florac. Their northern end is composed of three parallel ridges: Montagne du Goulet, Mont Lozère and the Montagne du Bougès. South of these, the mountains degenerate into an extraordinary tangle of rocky heights and deep-cut watercourses, where the watersheds are so mixed up that a river running to the Mediterranean may lie in a valley parallel to one flowing to the Atlantic. Gone are the plateaux and gorges. Instead, there are steep ridges and rocky valleys. The land is just as poor, however, with thin soil over granite or schist instead of the arid limestone. In the past, the Cévennes were sheep country, heavily grazed and heavily eroded. Many of the old *transhumance* paths or *drailles* taken by the flocks are now used by walkers, and the whole region, depopulated and only lightly farmed, has been made into a National Park.

The bare rocks and the scrubby hillsides lie in the middle and the east of the range. The western hills are forested. The trees are a result of a deliberate nineteenth-century attempt to stop erosion after it was discovered that it was mud from Mont Aigoual that was silting up the port of Bordeaux.

When Robert Louis Stevenson crossed the Cévennes from the north with his donkey Modestine in 1878 (a journey recorded in *Travels with a Donkey*) he found a landscape bare bleak and wet, full of uncommunicative peasants and with little trace of the fiery non-conformist religious enthusiasm which had led these same peasants to defy the forces of Louis XV a century and a half earlier. Now the area is perceived as one of the last great wildernesses in southern France, ideal for a sensitive attempt to combine the preservation of the landscape and rural traditions with recreational facilities for tourists.

With these aims in mind, the most interesting sights in the Cévennes have been grouped together into the **Ecomusée de la Cévenne**. They are scattered all over the National Park. You will find a museum of silk and a silk-worm farm, a museum of the chestnut, a mineralogy and mining museum, a museum of the 'Desert' – recalling the history of Protestantism in the region, and several smaller institutions designed to enlighten visitors about the way of life, the architecture or the agriculture of the Cévennes in past times. Tracking down these sights should keep any visitor busy for a week.

The chief information centres for the National Park are at Florac and at Pont-de-Montvert and hold large stocks of leaflets and booklets.

We recommend the English-version 'Touristic Guide Book' for its well-devised car-touring routes, the *Balades et coups de coeur* for its listing of museums and sights, and the series *Sentiers de Découverte des Paysages*, which is ideal for walkers.

To get information before you go, write to Parc National des Cévennes, B.P. 15, le Château, 48400 Florac (Tel 66 45 01 75).

The Northern massifs

Montagne du Goulet

There is not a lot to be said for the Montagne du Goulet. It is unshapely, damp and deserted. The road which penetrates eastward from Mende (D901) runs in its shadow for 59 long kilometres. There are things to see on the way, such as the ruins of the old Château du Tournel, the pleasant village of Le Bleymard and the momentary views from the Col des Tribes, but on the whole there are more pleasing Cévennes journeys. At the eastern end of the road, the artificial Lac de Villefort has improved the landscape, helped by the four-square Château de Castanet, and has become a base for watersports, but the village of Villefort is a disappointment – dusty and uninspiring.

The D906 which twists south from Villefort is a pleasing enough journey, but nothing compared to the road which rises above the western side of the valley of the Palhère (D66).

Almost immediately this becomes spectacular, winding up steep hillsides, with the views broadening out in all directions and the endless humps of Cévennes ridges becoming bluely visible in the distance.

At the top, the road enters a country of gigantic granite blocks, stacked or dropped where erosion has left them. The flat, treeless uplands of Mont Lozère stretch away west, and a little further on, the GR 72 path meets the road close to Mas de la Barque. If you want to walk on this high, scrub-covered plateau, this is a good place to start.

The best is still to come. As the road descends, the Belvedere de Bouzèdes provides genuinely breath-catching views south-east towards the Mediterranean and vertically downwards to the red roofs of **Génolhac** almost a thousand metres beneath. It takes a long time to get down to it from this point, but Génolhac turns out to be a pretty little village, certainly Mediterranean in its heat, its flowers and its close network of lanes and bridges. The railway station here is on one of the most enchanting lines in France. It burrows its way from Alès through innumerable tunnels north through the Cévennes, then through the gorges of the Allier right up to Clermont-Ferrand. If you need to stay the night, the Hotel du Mont Lozère is cheerful and good value (see Where to Stay).

Florac

This small town is pinned in the valley of the Tarnon between the Cévennes and the Causse de Méjean. If you stick to the main road it looks fairly ordinary, but take the time to climb up into the town and it reveals itself as an ideal place to take a break from driving. Through the middle of the sunny streets and small squares tumbles the Source du Pêcher, a stream that emerges from underground to join the Tarnon. The series of basins which hold the water are used to farm trout – great monsters, some of them, which lie poised beneath the bridges, much to the envy of passing anglers. In the old castle you will find the headquarters of the Cévennes National Park (open 8 to 12 and 2 to 6; closed Sat & Sun). It has a huge range of information available and an excellent walk-through audio-visual display about the country and the people. A steep and beautiful road (D16) climbs up on to the Causse from behind the town. There are tremendous views down into the valley from the edge of the escarpment at the top.

If you need a bed for the night, the Grand Hôtel du Parc is large, but with lovely grounds and a good restaurant (see Where to Stay).

Mont Lozère

The D998 (off the N106) north of Florac runs south of Mont Lozère and makes a much more attractive route into the central Cévennes than the D901 described above. The scenery is much more rugged, and the infant Tarn which keeps you company for most of the journey is here a lovely clear trout stream, full of rapids and still green pools. **Le Pont de Montvert** is a definite stopping point. Here you will find another information centre for the Cévennes National Park. Le Pont de Montvert is ancient, huddled and intriguing, with a pointed bridge across the river and small streets of typical Cévennes houses – flattish roofs, sun-baked stone and tiny gardens. A shop here sells breads and cakes made from chestnut flour; for the people of the Cévennes, like those of the Châtaignerie in Auvergne, once used chestnuts as their staple food.

A diversion up into the heights of Mont Lozère can be made by heading north up the D20 and then turning east to Mas Camargues – a large restored farm designed to show visitors how the agriculture of the Cévennes once worked. It is a very narrow road here, but fine country on the way and good walks at the end.

Once past the watershed, the land becomes increasingly rocky and the valleys steeper. **Vialas**, tucked far down under a crumbling peak of white rock is another characteristic Cévennes village – built on several levels on the hillside, with terracing above and below the groups of houses.

The Corniche des Cévennes

South of Florac is the prime tourist route east through the mountains. It runs on ridge tops right through to St Jean-du-Gard, and on a clear day the scenery all the way is unmatchable. The road was built by the troops of Louis XIV in the war against the Camisard rebels (see box page 206). In bad weather this is a high, bleak route and you would be better advised to stick to the valleys, as the landscape of boulders and scrub loses much of its appeal. At St Laurent-de-Trèves at the western end of the road, you can see the footprints of the dinosaurs which once roamed a shallow lagoon where the village now stands.

They were modestly sized carnivores (about four metres long) and their footprints look much as if an overgrown chicken had stepped in wet cement.

North of the Corniche lies the Vallée Française, an isolated, half-hidden place to live or to farm and most attractive to drive through. South of the ridge road, the valley of the Gardon de St-Jean is rocky and equally beautiful; the village of St-André-de-Valborgne, with a café beside its small square and in the shadow of its church, makes an ideal stopping place.

Mont Aigoual

The great lump of schist and granite at the south-western end of the Cévennes is so carved by valleys running in all directions that it is difficult not to become disorientated. The circuit of the mountain is easily made from Meyrueis, and should be, if the weather is clear. At the summit stands a battlemented observatory, and from its windy tower you get the best views in the whole region. If you are lucky with the weather you can see both the Mediterranean and Mont Blanc at the same time, while Mont Ventoux, on the edge of Provence, pokes up out of the haze of the Rhône valley like a slag heap. Your donation of one franc in exchange for this seems more than reasonable as the coin disappears down a rainwater pipe to some underground collecting box. A short way down the mountain a path runs through a rather fine arboretum, stocked mostly with conifers.

Bare ridges, their slopes forested, carry the D18 northwards from the summit. At the windbeaten hamlet of Cabrillac two narrow roads, for the adventurous only, lead east, one down the thick and rocky Trapoul gorges, the other high above the tree line to the Col Salidès. A net of way-marked paths also meet at Cabrillac – if you enjoy ridge walking, this is a good spot to try.

West of the summit (D986) lies the **Abîme du Bramabiau** (open mid-June–mid-Sept 9–7; Apr–mid-Nov 9–6) another cave that merits a visit, said to have got its strange name from the bellowing sound made by its river when in flood. Flat fields give no warning of a sudden precipice where the land just disappears into a gorge. At the top of this long-collapsed cavern, a great slit in the rock has opened, a sizeable stream pours out and over a waterfall. Into this slit you venture along narrow balconies as the underground river hisses beneath (the guide has to use a loud-hailer). In the light of the electric lamps you may be surprised to see a trout swimming beneath – the fish come into the cave from above, where the stream disappears into the ground and seem to be happy enough deep underground.

The pioneer of French speleology, E A Martel, made the first descent of this short underground watercourse, and cavers still follow his footsteps. Ordinary mortals penetrate only a few hundred yards, but the river makes it all worth while.

THE CAMISARDS

'Wool oozes heresy,' runs an ancient saying, and in the Cévennes where vast flocks of sheep traversed the mountains, Protestant doctrines took firm hold. The rebellion of the Camisards (so-called after the white shirts worn by the peasants) was a final, tragic outbreak of religious warfare which did much to set neighbour against neighbour, which led to massive destruction of houses and churches, and whose wounds, it is said, survived well into this century. The act which started the war was the revocation, by Louis XIV, of the Edict of Nantes in 1685, which had guaranteed religious tolerance. The autocratic king saw religious dissent as undermining the unity of his kingdom and determined to enforce Catholicism. (His apologists suggest that he was advised that Protestants formed only an insignificant minority.) Whatever the case, outlawed congregations in the Cévennes took to the hills, and 'desert' churches sprang up in the open air. The enforced billeting of royal troops and the imprisonment and torture of dissenters led eventually to the assassination of the Abbot du Chayla, in Pont-de-Montvert in 1702. Thereafter it was war: it is estimated that fewer than 3,000 Protestants opposed troops ten times that number. Louis XIV resorted to the traditional oppression of a foreign occupier, burning villages where the rebels might have found shelter, executing suspects and terrorising the country. In return, churches were burnt and priests murdered. Although the royalist forces obtained partial victory in capturing or forcing the surrender of most of the Protestant leaders within two years, it was not really until the French Revolution that the Camisard revolt can be said finally to have ended. It was partly this history, so similar to that of the 'Covenanters' in Scotland, which brought Robert Louis Stevenson to the region in 1878.

WHERE TO STAY AND EAT

There are two sections: establishments that we recommend and establishments that are worth considering but which we think do not merit a wholehearted recommendation. Both are marked on the map at the start of the chapter. Unless we say otherwise all have rooms with bath or shower and accept the major credit cards.

Key: ✦ = 0-250FF, ✦✦ = 251-450FF, ✦✦✦ = over 451FF; prices are per room without breakfast, which costs around 40-65FF extra. Some hotels may insist on half-board during high season.

Recommended hotels

LAGUIOLE

Michel Bras ✦✦✦
Route d'Aubrac
12210 Aveyron   *Tel: 65 44 32 24; Fax: 65 48 47 02*

It is easy enough to run out of superlatives for this restaurant set high on the Aubrac plateau, with stunning views into the distant blue haze of the lowlands. The glass and stone building looks like a Noah's Ark stranded by a retreating flood; it is purpose-built, with a tinge of mildly batty dedication, to serve the cause of fine food in the wilderness, and is run partly like a first-class cruise ship and partly like a monastery. Consequently, the ruthlessly efficient serving staff in dark blue Mao jackets, the designer chairs and cutlery, out of Charles Rennie Mackintosh by Ian Hamilton Finlay, and the regional traditions such as keeping your Laguiole knife from beginning to end of the meal can seem a little imposing. But the food – well, you are most unlikely to eat better anywhere in France, especially if you are a fan of finely-flavoured food as close to nature as possible. Strange herbs gleaned from the Aubrac pastures, wild mushrooms from the woods, vegetables of a crisp fineness which suggests daily watering and feeding – these are the sorts of things that appear on your plate in combinations that would be inimitable in your own kitchen. And there is bound to be a plate of Aligot – the sticky mixture of potato and cheese which traditionally keeps the Auvergne farmer going from breakfast until bed.

The weekday F200 lunch menu costs about the same as a tank full of petrol: you will get far more pleasure from it. Bedroom wings extend beyond the restaurant; rooms are sparse, modern and comfortable but small for their price.

Nov–mid-Oct; closed Mon, Tue lunch exc July and Aug; 15 rooms

LA MALENE

Manoir de Montesquiou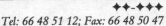
48210 Lozère   *Tel: 66 48 51 12; Fax: 66 48 50 47*

This creeper–clad, towered manor house seems to grow directly out of the cliff face at the bottom of one of the most impressive sections of the Tarn Gorge. It makes an excellent base for boat trips or exploration of the river. This is a comfortable hotel whose owners have a good eye for choosing pieces of furniture to suit the period of the house (sixteenth and seventeenth century). One of the suites has a huge four-poster with Satan carved into the footboard and the local saint combating him from the head, but even the smallest room has something of interest. The large restaurant serves very reasonably priced food from a comprehensive set of menus.

Apr–mid-Oct; 12 rooms

MEYRUEIS

La Renaissance et St-Sauveur
rue de la Ville
48150 Lozère   *Tel: 66 45 60 19; Fax: 66 45 65 94*

A pair of hotels of long-standing run by the friendly Bourguet family, which are very much the centre-piece of this attractive town at the head of the Jonte Gorges. The Renaissance is the classier of the two, set up in a fine old house with a carved doorway. There is a comfortable sitting room and polished floors. The St Sauveur, a few steps away, has very simple bedrooms with fairly old-fashioned bathrooms, but is cheap and not in the least grotty. The restaurant for both hotels takes up most of the ground floor of this building and is very much a local institution. The food is probably the best value you will find in the region, with four-course menus, good home-cooking and some interesting regional dishes.

Early Apr–mid-Nov; 35 rooms

Château d'Ayres
48150 Lozère   *Tel: 66 45 60 10; Fax: 66 45 62 26*

The large manor house lies a few hundred yards outside Meyrueis. It is doing its best to provide a country-house atmosphere for its numerous English guests, despite being the kind of building which was never meant to be a hotel. The public rooms – hall and two sitting rooms – are well furnished, with stripy chairs, gilt mirrors and high windows. Bedrooms at the cheaper end are not large; furnishings are pretty simple for the price although the comfort is gradually increasing. The

208

welcome is warm and friendly. It's worth booking in advance; the hotel is much used by up-market tour operators.

Apr–mid-Nov; 26 rooms; outdoor heated pool, tennis

MILLAU

Château de Creissels ♦♦
Route de St-Affrique
12100 Aveyron   Tel: 65 60 16 59; Fax: 65 61 24 63

Just downstream from Millau, this amiable hotel is ideal for families. It is no beauty – the old château is a maze of corridors and crumbling dead-ends, but has plenty of character. There's a barrel-vaulted cellar where the food is served, a billiard table in an ancient library and a huge variety of bedrooms, some about a hundred yards from the nearest bathroom, others more conventionally equipped. A very friendly place, often with a room or two to spare in high season, and good for an overnight stop.

Mid-Feb–end Dec, low season closed Sun pm, Mon lunch; 33 rooms

VIALAS

Hôtel Chantoiseau ♦♦♦
Le Pont-de-Montvert
48220 Lozère   Tel: 66 41 00 02; Fax: 66 41 04 34

An unbeatable setting at the top of a straggly village under a Cévennes peak of silvery rock is one of the chief attractions of this isolated hotel. Early mornings here, with blue woodsmoke drifting over the rocky valley from the red-roofed cottages below are something to remember. This small hotel is where Patrick Pagès runs one of the region's best kitchens and certainly the best wine cellar. His menus are uncompromisingly Cévenol in inspiration, and you will find such unpromising-sounding ingredients as cabbage sausage or calves brains turned into delicacies in a restaurant of formal splendour. Bedrooms are tiny, comfortable and all have good views. There is a small swimming pool. The hotel and its food are on the expensive side, no doubt about it, but it is a worthwhile indulgence for a night or two.

Easter–mid-Nov, closed Tue pm, Wed in low season; 15 rooms; outdoor pool

Worth considering

CONQUES

Hôtel Sainte-Foy
12320 Aveyron   Tel: 66 69 84 03; Fax: 65 72 81 04

This has the most character among the over-priced hotels of Conques.

ESTAING

Aux Armes d'Estaing ✦
12190 Aveyron   *Tel: 65 44 70 02; Fax: 65 44 74 54*

A simple, clean *auberge* in the Lot valley with a good view of the river.

FLORAC

Grand Hôtel du Parc ✦-✦✦
47 Avenue Jean Monestier,
48400 Lozère   *Tel: 66 45 03 05; Fax: 66 45 11 81*

This large hotel has lovely grounds and a good restaurant; can get busy in summer.

FOURNELS

Les Hameaux de Lozère ✦-✦✦
48310 Lozère   *Tel: 66 31 67 67, low season 42 82 13 98*

A curious package-style hotel in the middle of nowhere on the edge of the Aubrac plateau. Lots of facilities.

GENOLHAC

Hôtel du Mont Lozère ✦
30450 Gard   *Tel: 66 61 10 72*

A little plagued by traffic, but a pleasant family-run inn on the edge of this Cévennes village.

AVEYRON AND TARN

The huge area drained by the Middle Tarn and the Aveyron is less obviously given to superlatives than the deep-cut valleys of the Lot or Dordogne. The limestone *causses* (high plateaux), with their abrupt cliffs and canyons, hang on the fringes of the region, but for the most part the rivers here pursue their courses through valleys, which although steep and rocky are not as obviously magnificent as the gorges to the east or north. In consequence the country is considerably less flooded with tourists in pursuit of scenic wonders and left more to those who enjoy baking in the rich sun of the Midi among quiet medieval towns and undulating hills.

The complicated geology of the area means that there is plenty of variety in the scenery. There is granite to the south-east in the Sidobre and the Monts de Lacaune, red clay and sandstone around Albi, the high infertile schist of the Lévézou plateau and an outbreak of coal near Carmaux. To tour the area is to traverse between villages of pale sandstone, towns of flat red brick, valleys full of beech trees or sweet chestnuts, fields of sunflowers and high grassy pastures. The architecture reflects the countryside: the closer to Toulouse you venture, the more the close-walled farmsteads of Quercy are replaced by the red-tiled, sun-warmed buildings of the Mediterranean.

As usual, it is the rivers that provide much of the interest. The Tarn escapes from its tourist-infested canyons only to plunge into a further gorge of monumental scale below the Plateau de Lévézou which remains virtually deserted, before emerging at Albi to become a slow, powerful river of the flat-lands in its final stretch to the Garonne. The Aveyron, sheathed by steep, tree-covered hillsides for much of its course, opens up now and again and gives a suddenly sunny aspect to the otherwise dour town of Villefranche-de-Rouergue. The Viaur runs deep and hidden; the Rance is sunny and enchanting, while the Agout is slow and green. The waters of all of them arrive, sooner or later, at the Garonne, a river of no great beauty, but of immense importance throughout history as a route for commerce, and the centre-piece of the city of Toulouse.

All these river valleys, with the exception of the Viaur, can be followed on small back roads (the main roads stick mostly to the ridges). The best expedition is along the Tarn above Albi; the best area for quiet exploration is the secret valley of the Aveyron upstream from Villefranche. The valley of the Agout (comparatively flat) is excellent for cycling.

Toulouse itself, around which most of the life of the agricultural basins of the Lower Tarn and Garonne circulates, is a large, amiable city, full of youthful energy and bouncing with self-confidence. For a touch of urban life in the centre of a predominantly rural area, it makes an ideal stopping-point for a night or two.

Almost all this region was once the central fiefdom of the counts of Toulouse, and in addition to the devastations of the Hundred Years' War and the Wars of Religion which it shares with the other areas covered in this book, it had its own earlier purgatory to put up with – the Albigensian Crusade of 1209. At an even earlier date this was one of the most Romanised parts of Gaul, as witnessed by the collection of remains unearthed around Toulouse and displayed in the St-Raymond museum there. It is an area rich in *bastides*, the new, fortified towns of the Middle Ages, and has its share of ruined fortresses and tumbled villages. Toulouse, Albi and Castres were made rich and beautiful by the *pastel* (woad) trade, while linen and leather brought an outburst of prosperity to Cordes, leaving the town with

Good bases

● **Villefranche-de-Rouergue** An ancient and prosperous *bastide* on the edge of the *causses*, with the Aveyron flowing through its centre, Villefranche is very much a crossroads town. The Aveyron valley to the east is gentle and very quiet – a good place to find a hotel or cottage.

● **Albi** A city built of warm red brick, with a strange cathedral, streets of flat-roofed medieval houses and plenty of history, Albi makes an excellent base for exploring the Gaillac vineyards or the Tarn valley to the east.

● **Millau** Millau is well-positioned between the canyon country of the Tarn Gorges and the high, bare Plateau de Lévézou. It is a busy but friendly town, with some excellent high country immediately to the north-west. Accommodation in high season may be hard to find.

● **Revel** This little *bastide* town, set in the sunflower-growing flatlands east of Toulouse, would make a good base for exploring the tiny villages along the river Agout. It is less busy than Castres to the north, and has all the attraction of a small country town.

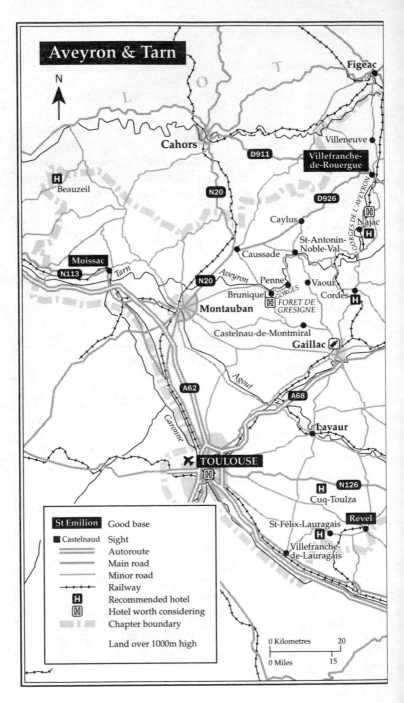

Aveyron & Tarn

N

Figeac

Villeneuve

D911

Villefranche-de-Rouergue

Beauzeil ⊞

N20

D926

GORGES DE L'AVEYRON

Caylus

Najac ⊞
⊞

St-Antonin-Noble-Val

Caussade

Moissac

N113

Tarn

N20

Aveyron

Penne

Vaour

Bruniquel ⊞ GORGES FORET DE GRESIGNE

Cordès ⊞

Montauban

Castelnau-de-Montmiral

Gaillac ✐

A62

Agout

Garonne

A68

Lavaur

✈ **TOULOUSE** ⊞

N126

Cuq-Toulza ⊞

St-Félix-Lauragais

Revel

⊞

Villefranche-de-Lauragais

St Emilion	Good base
■ Castelnaud	Sight
	Autoroute
	Main road
	Minor road
┼┼┼┼	Railway
⊞	Recommended hotel
⊞	Hotel worth considering
	Chapter boundary
	Land over 1000m high

0 Kilometres   20

0 Miles   15

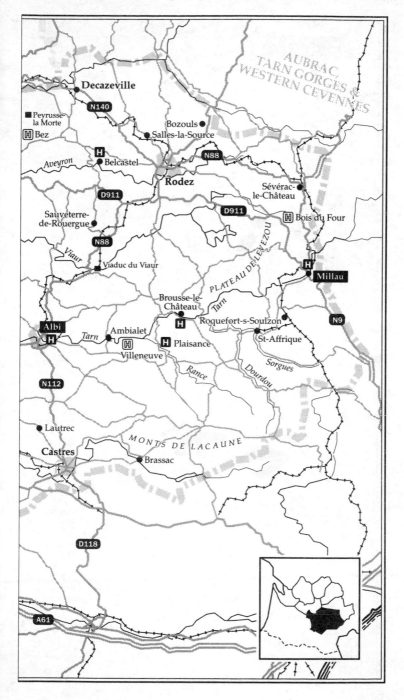

AUBRAC, TARN GORGES & WESTERN CEVENNES

Decazeville

N140

■ Peyrusse-la-Morte

Ⓗ Bez

Aveyron

Ⓗ Belcastel

Bozouls ●
● Salles-la-Source

N88

Rodez

Sévérac-le-Château

D911

D911

Ⓗ Bois du Four

Sauveterre-de-Rouergue ●

N88

Viaur

● Viaduc du Viaur

PLATEAU DE LÉVÉZOU

Ⓗ Millau

Brousse-le-Château

Tarn

Ⓗ

Roquefort-s-Soulzon

Albi

Ⓗ

Tarn

Ambialet

Ⓗ Plaisance
Villeneuve

St-Affrique

N9

N112

Rance

Dourdou

Sorgues

● Lautrec

MONTS DE LACAUNE

Castres

● Brassac

D118

A61

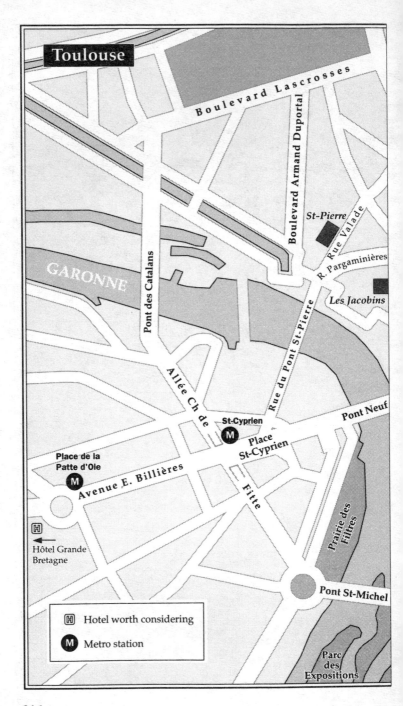

Toulouse

Boulevard Lascrosses

Boulevard Armand Duportal

GARONNE

Pont des Catalans

St-Pierre

Rue Valade

R. Pargaminières

Les Jacobins

Allée Ch de

Rue du Pont St-Pierre

St-Cyprien

M

Pont Neuf

Place
St-Cyprien

Place de la
Patte d'Ole

M

Avenue E. Billières

Fitte

Prairie des
Filtres

Hôtel Grande
Bretagne

Pont St-Michel

Ⓗ Hotel worth considering

Ⓜ Metro station

Parc
des
Expositions

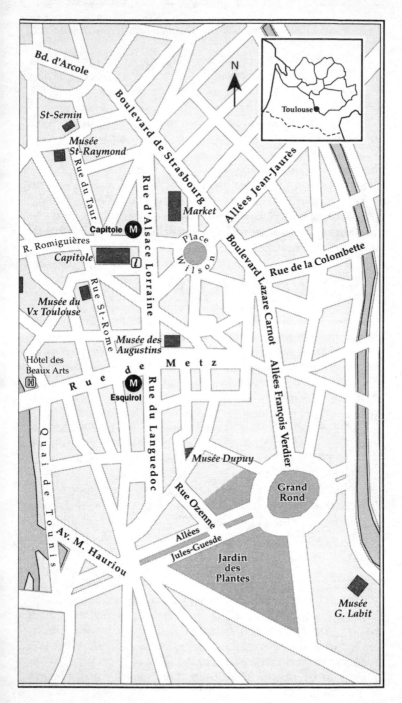

N

Toulouse

Bd. d'Arcole

St-Sernin

Musée St-Raymond

Boulevard de Strasbourg

Rue du Taur

Allées Jean-Jaurès

Market

Rue d'Alsace Lorraine

Capitole Ⓜ

R. Romiguières

Capitole ⓘ

Place Wilson

Boulevard Lazare Carnot

Rue de la Colombette

Rue St-Rome

Musée du Vx Toulouse

Musée des Augustins

Metz

Hôtel des Beaux Arts Ⓗ

Rue de

Ⓜ Esquirol

Rue du Languedoc

Allées François Verdier

Quai de Tounis

Musée Dupuy

Rue Ozenne

Grand Rond

Av. M. Hauriou

Allées Jules-Guesde

Jardin des Plantes

Musée G. Labit

wonderful Gothic houses from the thirteenth and fourteenth centuries.

This is a region for the visitor with time to wander. You will not find such a concentration of sights or activities as in the more popular areas, but there is plenty of variety. There are good areas for walking, a wine region (Gaillac) to explore, and some fine cathedrals, churches and museums which are worth the journey in themselves. Albi is an especially lovely city; Castres and Rodez repay a visit, while Cordes, Najac and Cayouls are outstanding among the small medieval towns. Gastronomically it is not an exceptional area, unless you are fanatical about *cassoulet* or a fan of Roquefort cheese, but the peaches, apricots and strawberries ripen early here, and the warmth of the sun seems to make them taste even better than they do further north.

FROM FIGEAC TO ALBI

The main north-south route in the region runs from Figeac across the *causse* to Villefranche-de-Rouergue, then down the Aveyron valley towards Albi. It is not a route to hurry, for many of the area's best sights and most interesting towns are to be found along it. You can easily spend a day visiting Villefranche, Najac and Cordes, while Albi is a city of such delight that it may delay you for longer.

After crossing the Lot, the main road south (D922) runs fast and level over the north-eastern edge of the Causse de Limogne. A slower, much more pleasant route runs parallel along the Diège valley to the east (D40). The Auberge de la Bouriatte near Bez is a comfortable and peaceful place to stay here (see Where to Stay). Whichever way you come, take the short detour to the old *bastide* of **Villeneuve** for its church and for the general air of well-being which pervades its streets. Most of the church is Gothic, although some of the bell-tower is Romanesque. However, it is the frescoes that make the visit special, for, fragmentary though they are, they clearly show Christ in Glory set above the figures of medieval pilgrims on the road to Santiago de Compostela. Three figures remain intact, looking like an illustration from *The Canterbury Tales*, and providing a rare contemporary glimpse of the travellers you would have seen everywhere in the region had you been here in the twelfth century. Away from the church, Villeneuve is a village of pale lemon stone, with well-restored streets and houses and a bulky fortified gateway above its square.

To the east of the Diège valley, on a rocky promontory above the Audiernes river, the remains of a medieval town (Peyrusse-la-Morte) lie scattered below the cemetery of the current village, **Peyrusse-le-Roc**. Peyrusse was once a large place, protected by two small watch-towers on a vertical slab of rock, which made its living by mining silver. When this became uneconomic in the eighteenth century, the town contracted to its current size, leaving behind its church, synagogue and fortified entrance-gate. Around the remains of these buildings (some being slowly restored), old walls and houses crumble away beneath ivy. You get the best view from the old towers by climbing to them via steep (but well-protected) stairs up the face of the rock.

Further to the north-east, **Decazeville** is an old coal and iron town which you can bypass unless you want to get a bird's-eye view of an open-cast mine. If so, a gallery on the edge of a huge pit has been organised for visitors (visits once a week in July and Aug. Rest of year groups only on request. Tel 65 43 18 36).

Villefranche-de-Rouergue

Villefranche is a large *bastide*, dating from 1252. It is a steep town, crammed into a bend of the Aveyron. All the ditches and fortifications which once ringed the medieval town are long gone, but the grid pattern of streets and the central square typical of *bastides* remain.

Because of the hillsides around and the narrowness of the old streets, Villefranche can seem rather a gloomy town, an impression not helped by the huge bulk of the church of Notre-Dame, which towers over the central square – indeed thrusts out into it. The massive proportions of this church go back to medieval rivalry with Rodez over the height of steeples. The architects at Villefranche had ambitious plans, to judge by the massive base, but the tower itself was never finished and remains capped off half-way up, giving it a curious, stumpy appearance. Inside, make a beeline for the choir stalls – the misericords are carved with a succession of animals, rotund monsters and fabulous beings.

Down at the bottom of town winds the Aveyron, and here, by the Place de la République, is the most pleasant area to look for a café or a snack lunch. Parking is also easier here, and the ancient bridge over the river which you cross to reach the town centre, is elegantly Gothic in style.

Villefranche a diverting town in which to browse. You won't find much that is unusual, but there are a couple of antiquarian booksellers, rows of lingerie shops, and a modern covered market behind the church.

The **Chartreuse St-Saveur** (open July–mid-Sept, daily exc Tue 9.30–12 and 2.30–6; rest of year by appointment. Tel. 65 45 13 18) stands on the left bank of the Aveyron on the road south out of Villefranche. This fifteenth-century Carthusian foundation is now a hospital – well worth a brief visit to enjoy the sunny open space of the large cloister and the beautiful flamboyant carving of the small one.

Najac

Despite having the most beautiful setting of any village in the Aveyron valley, as well as one of the most majestic medieval castles, Najac is relatively little visited. The fact that it is slightly off the main road (D922) may deter those in a rush, but it is a place to spare some time for if you can.

The village is strung along a high promontory formed by a meander of the Aveyron in its gorge beneath. The ridge is too narrow for more than a single street on its top, and it dips and narrows further to a neck of rock, beyond which the keep and heavy curtain walls of the thirteenth-century fortress rise.

The history of medieval Najac is in many ways typical of the region. The little town grew up around the castle – one of a string of fortifications lining the Aveyron. The castle itself was pretty well impregnable in medieval times, but this did not stop the town changing overlords with bewildering frequency. From belonging to the count of Toulouse, it became part of the English possessions in France under Henry II, reverted to Toulouse when his daughter married the then count in 1196, was ceded to the French crown for five years after the Albigensian Crusade, went back to Toulouse, back again to the French king on the death of Raymond VII in 1249, became English after Poitiers (1356) but liberated itself in 1368 and finally became a French possession again.

The arcaded square on the eastern edge of Najac draws you into the narrow street which leads to the castle. Few of the houses on either side pre-date the sixteenth century, their air of great antiquity no doubt owing something to the fact that they are built of stones plundered from the castle. At the far end of the street the plain Gothic church was built by the inhabitants of Najac as a penance for being infected by Catharism.

From the village square to the **Château de Najac** (open April–Sept, daily 10–12, 2.30–7 in July and Aug; in Oct by appointment), is about a 500-metre walk and steep in places. From the esplanade of the castle there are marvellous views of the Aveyron far beneath. The castle, ruined though it is, merits exploration, for much of the interior of the keep remains, as do various stairs and passageways within the walls. There is a guide, if you want one, who can explain the functions of the various rooms.

Najac's street is too narrow for many expansive bars or restaurants, but it has an excellent hotel (see Where to Stay) and makes a good base.

Around Najac

The steep gorge of the Aveyron, tracked by the D115 to Montauban, is the fastest route south. The medieval town hall and the clumps of ancient houses overhanging narrow lanes at **St Antonin-Noble-Val** are worth pausing for. Beyond this town, the gorge narrows and the road shuttles from side to side of the river, plunging through tunnels and running beneath precipices of bleached white rock. Wider views and less traffic can be found by taking the D958 on the right bank of the river or the scary corniche of the D115B on the left.

In the countryside north of the gorge, the thirteenth-century abbey at **Beaulieu-en-Rouergue** is being restored after long neglect. The plain Gothic church and the chapter house are the most important remaining buildings. Art exhibitions take place throughout the summer.

Caylus, nine kilometres to the north-west of the abbey, lies just off the main D926 to Montauban. Most of its cafés and shops have gravitated to the roadside, leaving a tumble-down old quarter lower down the slope, where nothing much stirs among the medieval buildings. There's one lively bar by the market-place, however, in which to regain strength after walking down to the dark fortified church with its sculpture of an agonised Christ by the Cubist artist Zadkine. Beneath the church, one ancient house has its façade decorated with wolves. The castle, like the one at Najac, is built on a narrow promontory, but is too ruinous to be very rewarding and is best seen from high above.

Cordes

Built on an oval rocky hillock rising above the river Cérou, this old *bastide* was spared the worst of the Hundred Years' War and became extremely wealthy in the thirteenth and fourteenth centuries thanks to trade in linen and leather. Its prosperity waned in later years, and outbreaks of plague drove many inhabitants away. The result is a small town full of grand Gothic mansions which has barely outgrown its original ramparts. Tourism has replaced some of the missing trade, and the town is now full of galleries and dubious curiosities such as a museum of sugar sculpture.

You can see the best of Cordes by walking from one end of the main street to the other, passing under the remaining gates from what were once four concentric lines of ramparts. Unfortunately, this same street runs right up and down each end of the oval outcrop on which the town is built, letting you in for some extremely steep walking at the extremities. The western end is the less steep, and you should park your car here if you only aim to go to the top and back again. The best of the Gothic mansions line the Grande Rue close to the market-square at the top of the town. The three most worth seeing are the **Maison du Grand Veneur**, the **Maison du Grand Fauconnier**, and the **Grand Ecuyer** (which is now a good, if pricey, hotel and restaurant – see Where to Stay). The details of the window ornamentation and the various sculptures which decorate the walls of all three repay a careful look. There are wild boars, huntsmen, a half-human figure devouring a fruit, and various animals stuck on to the façades like gargoyles.

The covered market has pillars of stone rather than wood – a testimony to the town's richness – and from under its shelter the thirteenth-century well plunges deep into the rock. Into this were precipitated, according to legend, three of the inquisitors sent to find whether the townsfolk were guilty of the Cathar heresy. In fact, although the town was certainly caught up in Catharism, the only penalty it suffered was the enforced building of a chapel inside two years.

Pause at the market-square to look at the view from the ramparts and perhaps to explore some of the side lanes, where the houses take on a more genuinely medieval look among ancient walls covered with aubrietia. The church is worth a glance, though most of it was rebuilt in the fifteenth century. The **Musée Charles Portal**, inside the gatehouse of the Portail Peint (open Apr–Oct, Sun only 2–5; and July and Aug, daily 2-6) has an archaeological collection from the district, and bits and pieces salvaged from the town.

ALBI

Albi is a southern town down to its last ochre brick. For a lasting image, stand in the garden of the bishop's palace and watch the swifts screaming and dipping over the river Tarn beneath. The flat bricks from which the town is built seem to burn orange in the heat, fading to crimson as the sun sinks. The great bulk of the cathedral – God's aircraft carrier, as it is sometimes called – rises above the whole city. Beneath it, towers poke up above a skyscape of red-tiled roofs, and the Pont Vieux (built in 1040 and still going strong) spans the river in a series of gently pointed arches.

This is a delightful place to explore for a couple of days. It is a manageable size with an extensive old quarter of narrow lanes and interesting shops, especially art galleries (the Galeries du Tilleul opposite the cathedral has good exhibitions), and is well placed for outside expeditions too. There is a music festival in summer. Tourism ranks high, but you are most unlikely to find great crowds.

Albi was founded by the Romans and owed its subsequent prosperity to a number of factors: the river trade on the Tarn, its position as a crossroads between Toulouse and the north, but above all to the trade in *pastel* (woad), which was the only blue dyestuff known to the fifteenth and sixteenth centuries (see box). For an important town in the orbit of the count of Toulouse, it escaped lightly in the crusade against the Cathar heresy; it is all the more strange that this is commonly known as the Albigensian Crusade, since Albi put up no resistance to the crusaders and suffered no destruction. Nor did it suffer much from the Hundred Years' War, being on the fringe of the action. So although its medieval fortifications were demolished in the eighteenth century, Albi's centre remains very close to what it might have been in the high Middle Ages, and is all the more pleasing for it.

Sights in Albi

● **Cathédrale Ste-Cécile** (1281) This should be the starting-point of your sightseeing, for it is one of the strangest cathedrals in France. It is worth walking right round the outside to get a true impression of its daunting, unadorned bulk. Curious brick buttresses, rounded and smoothed like missile tubes, support the walls, which are pierced between each buttress by tall, narrow rounded windows. The roof is entirely hidden by a parapet (constructed in 1849), while the tower, carved into five distinct storeys and also devoid of ornamentation, rises abruptly from one end, slightly off-centre when viewed from behind. There's only one break in the uniformity of this odd design, where the sixteenth-century portico juts out from the main door. This, a superbly over-decorated construction of grey stone in best Flamboyant style, could hardly provide a more bizarre contrast to the severity of the remainder.

After the fortress-like exterior, the interior of the building comes as a surprise. The Gothic is enlivened by superb paint-work, the vaults covered in rich blue and gold scenes of saints surrounding Christ in Glory, the walls in patterns reminiscent of painted tiles. Under the organ, at the far end from the altar, one of the largest frescoes in the world was painted in the sixteenth century. The torments of the damned (it shows the Last Judgement) are uncomfortably close to the visitor's eyes; the blessed souls rise almost out of sight. Unfortunately, where Christ should sit in judgement, there is only an arched doorway, a wretched piece of vandalism dating from 1693, which ruins the effect of the whole.

The rood screen is the other great work of art inside the cathedral. For stone carving marked by fantastic encrustations and traceries there can be few better examples. The original statues which all the decoration once framed were destroyed during the Revolution. To pass beyond the screen you have to contribute a few francs towards cathedral upkeep, but it is worth it to have a peek inside the choir, where further beautifully carved stonework shelters some lively and richly bearded prophets and saints.

● **Palais de la Berbie** (open Apr–May, daily 10–12, 2–6; June–Sept daily 9–6; Oct–Apr, daily exc Tue 10–12, 2–6) The bishop's palace stands between the cathedral and the Tarn, built in much the same style as the former and with its gardens overlooking the latter. It is an immense fortress-like place, with high towers and hostile curtain walls, and the efforts of various bishops to soften its prison-like aspect have not had much effect. This is the unlikely building chosen to house Albi's collection of Toulouse-Lautrec paintings and drawings. Henri de Toulouse-Lautrec was born in Albi (you can visit his birthplace), and it was his mother who left her collection to the city.

Several portraits of her hang prominently among the scenes of rakish Paris night-life, making an odd contrast between the raffish and the puritanical. There is a lot to look at here – drawings and paintings from Toulouse-Lautrec's youth as well as the more familiar Parisian scenes. These, crowded with dancers, singers and goatish gentlemen off for a night on the tiles, cumulatively catch the feeling of the morning after the night before more vividly than any single work of the artist's can do. The museum can become fairly crowded, and it is as well to get there early.

● **Eglise St-Salvy** This is Albi's oldest building: parts of it go back to 1080. It is a curious structure, tucked away amongst a maze of passageways and brick walls, and a bit of a muddle when you eventually find the way in. Much of the Romanesque section is built in stone, while the Gothic parts are in brick – no more pleasing a contrast than at the cathedral, but the watchtower rising above the belfry and the small peaceful cloister are both magnificent.

TOULOUSE

It may be only the sixth largest city in France, but Toulouse feels a good deal larger as you negotiate the frenetic ring roads in rush hour. It is not a place to try to drive around without a map. That said, the centre of Toulouse, once you reach it, has a lot going for it, and it is unwise to regard the town as simply a place with a convenient airport. It is a cheerful, youthful city, buoyed up by the prosperity of the aviation business and with plenty to see and enjoy. Its one disadvantage for the British visitor is that it is not at its best in July and August – like other large French cities, it half closes down when the population leaves for the beaches.

For many years Toulouse was virtually the capital city of an independent state – that part of France running from the Castillian border as far as Provence, which spoke the *langue d'Oc* (still the basis of the native patois) as opposed to the *langue d'Oil* of the north. Before that, it was a flourishing Roman city, as the wealth of golden objects in the Musée St-Raymond testifies. It was under Charlemagne, when it became part of the kingdom of the Franks, that the first count of Toulouse was created; thereafter Toulouse became the focus of a courtly culture, symbolised by the famous troubadours of the southwest. To read some of the more romantic accounts of this golden period, Toulouse would appear to have been well in advance of the relatively barbarous northern courts, while the Cathar version of Christianity (see box at end of chapter), lacking the stern vision of judgement espoused by the Roman church and seeing the world and its products as illusory at best, the products of an evil principle at worst, would seem to have had a gentleness to it which accorded well with the comparatively egalitarian system of government adopted by the counts.

All this came to an end with the Albigensian Crusade of 1209 which effectively saw the end of Toulouse and the regions of the *langue d'Oc* as a separate power. In 1229 Count Raymond VII did penance at Notre-Dame in Paris, and by 1271 Toulouse became part of the French crown. It remained a prosperous place, thanks to *pastel* and to its position on the Garonne, and it is notable, if you browse in the bookshops, that the *langue d'Oc* is still alive, even if only between the pages of specialist publications.

A car is only a bore in the city centre, and the best tactic is to leave it close to one of the métro stations (Place de la Patte d'Oie on the south bank is convenient for the airport) and explore the city using the single métro line and your feet. The triangular area between the Place Esquirol, the Basilique St-Sernin and the river contains the best sights and many of the best shops. The Rue d'Alsace Lorraine is the smart shopping boulevard (with a branch of Marks & Spencers if you cannot go without sandwiches); the pedestrianised Rue St-Rome is the place for street life, boutiques and old houses, while the Rue du Taur has bookshops, antique shops, cafés and bars. The Place Esquirol is busy and full of fast food outlets and chemists, while the Place Wilson has some of the smarter cafés. For window-shopping and browsing, try also the Rue de la Garonnette close to the Pont Neuf. The market, near the Place Victor Hugo, is admirably suited for stocking up on provisions before setting off into the country.

Toulouse, like other big regional cities, is short on places of character in which to stay. The big hotels round the Place du Capitole are very expensive; the smaller town-centre hotels are much of a muchness and parking is often a problem. The Hotel des Beaux-Arts has a good ambiance and a lovely traditional brasserie next door. There are a couple of places worth considering out towards the airport, notably the friendly Grande-Bretagne (see Where to Stay). The best restaurant in Toulouse is Les Jardins de l'Opéra, attached to the grandest hotel, but it closes for most of August.

The main sights

● **Taxiway** If you have ever wished to see an aeroplane being built, this is your chance. Taxiway is a kind of mini-lecture tour put on by Aérospatiale (the French company that assembles the Airbus components) in their huge blue and white building out beyond Toulouse airport. Tours run twice a day in high season, and you need to reserve in advance (tel 61 15 44 00) and have your passport to hand. Head out beyond the airport to Colomiers and go north through the suburb until you see the unmistakable building ahead.

The tour is excellent, but in French and not cheap. A bus runs you round the various buildings and past lines of Airbuses done up in the livery of whichever airline has bought them. You will catch a glimpse of the bizarre 'Super-Guppy' aircraft (soon to be replaced by an even bigger plane) which brings fuselage and wing sections here from factories in Germany, Britain and Spain. From a gantry high above the factory floor you gaze down on the machines which join all the pieces of aircraft together. The workforce has to travel around on bicycles, so huge is the workspace. There are plenty of gee-whizz statistics to go with the view, a good film and a souvenir picture or two. The tour lasts an hour and a half, and there should just be time to squeeze in the afternoon session before catching the British Airways flight to Gatwick (though check the timetable before taking this course).

● **Basilique St-Sernin** At the time of writing St-Sernin was still wrapped in scaffolding; the renewal of the roof has been going on since 1990, and there still seems some way to go. This somewhat spoils the impression of this magnificent Romanesque pilgrimage church which was started in around AD 1080. It was designed to be used by huge crowds – it was a stop on the road to Santiago de Compostela as well as being famous in its own right for the relics it contained – so the interior is cavernous and can seem a bit gloomy when there are only a few tourists around. But the very scale is remarkable for a Romanesque church. The two entrance-doors have some good carving. One shows the usual gruesome sequence of tortures associated with the story of the rich man and the beggar Lazarus.

● **Musée St-Raymond** (closed for restoration at the time of writing). Much of the material on show in this excellent archaeological museum was excavated from a huge Roman villa at Chiragan, not far from Toulouse. The star piece is a Roman copy of a Venus by Praxiteles which stands imposingly on its own. Also remarkable is the collection of busts of the Imperial Roman family, which were discovered in Béziers in 1844. Here are Augustus, Livia, Germanicus, Agrippa and Julia as well as several others – all life size. Then, in a separate room, appears the labours of Hercules, badly damaged (probably from a temple). Chiragan yielded at least four cartloads of sculpture, and much is on display.

Although the Roman work is the best part of this museum (and there are cases full of golden and bronze objects from Roman Toulouse) there are relics from the Merovingian period too, as well as some beautifully decorated Greek vases – with Hercules again featuring strongly.

● **Les Jacobins** (open Oct–June, Mon–Sat 10–12, 2.30–6, Sun 2.30–6; July–Sept Mon–Sat 10–6.30, Sun 2.30–6.30) This is the mother church of the Dominicans, for St Dominic, after founding his order to combat the Cathar heresy, set up its first monastery in Toulouse. St Thomas Aquinas lies buried here. The church is an echoing Gothic structure with a row of thick pillars down the middle effectively creating two naves. The vaulting which these pillars support is wonderfully complex, especially at the eastern end, where all the ribs supporting the roof of the curved ambulatory converge on to a single pillar. Much of the internal decoration of the church has survived, and there are some interesting uses of colour to suggest stonework. The stained glass is modern but very attractive.

The cloister lies to the north of the church (some of it reconstructed), with the fourteenth-century chapter house and the Chapel of St Anthony opening off it. The surviving murals (the Apocalypse and the Legend of St Anthony) in the latter are worth a look. The Grand Refectory, again to the north, was built in 1303 – a huge room, perhaps a little too reminiscent of a Gothic-revival railway station for comfort. It is used for exhibitions of contemporary art, the bright colours going well against the pale ochre walls.

● **Place du Capitole** This large square is the heart of Toulouse, and a massive programme is under way to confine the traffic and to make the square more user-friendly for pedestrians. The Capitole, an eighteenth-century building on the east side of the square, is the town hall. It takes its name from the old councillors (*capitouls*) who used to govern Toulouse at the time of the counts. If you are in the mood for some grandiose – indeed pompous – paintings you can tour the interior and gaze upon scenes from the history of Toulouse which cover the galleries (open all year, Mon–Fri 8.30–12, 2–5).

● **Musée des Augustines** (open daily exc Tue in low season 10–5 (7 on Wed); July and Aug 10–6). The importance of this museum lies in its collections of Romanesque sculpture salvaged from churches and abbeys throughout the region of Toulouse. The building is an old monastery – much damaged, but still very beautiful – and here are displayed row after row of carved capitals and pieces of elaborately decorated stonework. The formality of the Romanesque is relieved by some later, Gothic work. The collection of paintings, mostly by Toulousian artists, is less outstanding, but there are some good paintings from Flanders and Holland.

Other Toulouse sights

If you have the time or inclination you can visit a further six museums. The **Musée Georges Labit** has a large and very good collection of works from the Far East and from Ancient Egypt. The **Musée Paul Dupuy** has a more general collection – musical instruments, arms, coins and costumes. The **Musée du Vieux Toulouse** is an assembly of fragments from the town's history, which could be truly wonderful if the presentation were made livelier.

There is also a natural history museum (old-fashioned), and a museum of transport (very educational). If your interest in the Romans extends to applying in person at the Catholic Institute, a long section of Roman wall lies under the building and you can be taken down to see it.

THE AVEYRON VALLEY EAST OF VILLEFRANCHE

Running in a steep-sided valley which is never deep enough to be a true gorge, the Aveyron is at its most beautiful between Villefranche and Rodez. This is an unfrequented stretch of country, sandwiched between two main roads, and following the river slowly either upstream or downstream makes a lovely half-day's drive. Not that it is possible to follow the river closely – a criss-cross route is necessary.

Of the small villages here, **Belcastel** is outstanding for its situation. A pointed bridge arches over the river, while old houses crowd the northern bank. As you come down to the village you see the ruins of the château first, then the curve of brown cottages beneath. The river here is clear and slow, and great trout can be seen around the piers of the bridge. There is an excellent *auberge*, Le Vieux Pont, and a newly opened hotel to go with it (see Where to Stay). A shady patch of green lawn beside the river makes a good picnicking spot and extends into a prettily situated campsite.

Compolibat and **Prévinquières** are also pretty, though not in the same league. If you end up at **Rieupeyroux** on a southward tack, a tiny chapel on a nearby hillock might have been built to take advantage of the view, which stretches in all directions.

Rodez and around

The importance of Rodez as a commercial and industrial centre is underlined by the system of modern ring roads, which swing you round and through the line of the old ramparts, and by the modern-day precincts and squares, which have been built in the middle of the old town. After pottering through medieval villages, Rodez can be rather disconcerting to visit.

The cathedral at Rodez is a great bare fortress of a place. Its most distinctive feature, indeed its most attractive one, is the detached bell-tower, which in contrast to the cathedral itself is heavily ornamented, mostly in Flamboyant style. There are turrets, pinnacles and niches; the apostles guard the bays beside the windows.

Other sights in Rodez are limited to a couple of towers remaining from the old fortifications and a baroque Jesuit chapel. The regional collection of archaeological artefacts in the Musée Fenaille is closed for restoration. This is not to say that Rodez does not have other charms. The shops are a cut above others in the area, and it is an especially good place to come in search of antiques. There are some fine houses among the narrow lanes, and curious pieces of modern municipal architecture.

Bozouls

This village is known for its *trou* (hole), in fact a kind of mini-canyon carved by the river Dourdou out of the limestone, which lies just north of Rodez. It is not so much the canyon that is remarkable as the way the village is built around its very edge – the residents of the closest houses must be immune to vertigo. Curiously, the canyon takes a bit of finding, for the village looks very ordinary when you arrive, and it is not until you have poked about behind the main street that you suddenly realise that you are actually on the edge of a cliff. You can drive down to the bottom of the hole to see the rushing water and to look up at the houses high above.

Salles-la-Source

A pleasing village on a steep slope of the Causse du Comtal north-west of Rodez, which draws visitors because of the odd waterfall near the centre, where an underground spring emerges to fall down a cliff into a dark pool. In summer the fall is no more than a trickle (the hydro-electricians have got at it too), but after rain or in the autumn it comes into its own and gushes satisfactorily out of the cliff.

Of rather more interest is the **Musée des Arts et Métiers** (open May, June and Sept, daily 2–6; July and Aug daily exc Sat am, 10–12.30, 2–7) in an old mill building up behind the waterfall. The trades and machines of rural life are well displayed; the remains of a large steam engine lie outside, in company with an ancient travelling still.

Plateau du Lévézou

East and south-east of Rodez the land gradually rises to a height of about 1,100 metres, and the landscape becomes bleaker and given over to upland pasture. The Aveyron and the Viaur have their sources on this plateau. There is nothing much to see (apart from the wild flowers) until you come to the eastern edge, where the plateau drops away in an abrupt escarpment. This marks the end of the granite country: in the distance, like cut-outs against the sky, rise the quite different sharp-edged limestone cliffs above the Tarn and Jonte Gorges. The views from the edge of the Lévézou plateau are superb. The D2 road which runs north from the D911 towards Sévérac-le-Château along the edge of the escarpment makes an excellent route from which to sample the ever-changing scenery of distant cliffs and valleys.

Sauveterre-de-Rouergue

South-west of Rodez beyond Baraqueville in the lost country of shallow valleys and low hills known as the Segala (from *seigle* (rye)) is this very pretty *bastide*, dating from the thirteenth century and seemingly little changed since then. A picturesque combination of water, old towers and houses, plus a large and open, arcaded square make this a good goal for an outing. To the south runs the river Viaur, the least accessible of all the rivers of the area. Its gorge is deep, steep and thickly forested, and neither road nor village is to be found in its depths. The best spot from which to catch a glimpse is at the Viaduc du Viaur (off the N88) where the railway spans the gorge on a narrow and rather frightening arch of steel.

THE TARN VALLEY WEST OF ALBI

Gaillac and the Forêt de Grésigne

Gaillac, some 22 kilometres down the Tarn from Albi, is the centre of the local wine-growing district. (Gaillac is said to be the oldest wine region in France.) Travelling west from Albi, you can gaze your last on the distant cathedral from the viewpoint of the ruined Château de Lévis. Gaillac vineyards mostly lie to the north-east of the town itself, in a country of rolling fertile hills without a great deal of scenic interest apart from the odd tucked-away river valley and the beauty of the oldest farmhouses. Explore the roads around Cahuzac, Vieux and Montels for the best of these. On the other hand, those growers offering *dégustation* are well signposted. Gaillac produces an excellent sparkling white wine, and you should not tour the area without sampling some.

The town is busy and very much dominated by the wine trade, so that after Albi the lorries and the warehouses come as a shock. However, there is an unspoilt old centre, with clusters of red-brick houses and narrow lanes.

In the forested hills between Gaillac and the Aveyron, the Forêt de Grésigne, there are some splendid unrestored *bastide* villages. Much the best is **Castelnau de Montmiral**, whose tiny arcaded central square is just the right size to contemplate in comfort from the well-placed cafe to one side. **Puycelci** lacks the square (it was not a *bastide*) but the view of it as you come up to the cluster of old houses from beneath is fine. **Larroque** is a tiny village tucked under a monstrous orange precipice.

Bruniquel

Bruniquel guards the mouth of the Aveyron Gorge, where the river emerges on to the flatlands in its final run to join the Tarn. This is a strange and lovely village, mounting in tiers up a hillside to a castle at the top. On the side from which you approach it there is no hint that the castle and the houses at the top of the village stand poised on the edge of the cliff which drops vertically down to the river.

It is a steep climb from the gatehouse at the bottom of the village (trying to get a car up is not recommended), past houses with geranium-filled windows and a useful *auberge* with rooms (l'Etape du Château; see Where to Stay) to the **château** (open Easter–June and Oct, Sun only, 10–12.30, 2–6; plus Apr, June and Sept, Mon–Fri 2–6; July–Aug, daily 10–12, 2–6). The buildings are far gone in places, but there is a rusty old kitchen, a vertiginous gallery over the gorge and a few furnished rooms which you can see only on a guided tour. Restoration is happening, but slowly.

Penne

This is another village on the edge of the Forêt de Grésigne high above the Aveyron gorge, and an even stranger place than Bruniquel, for here a whole village has been crammed on to a tiny precipitous neck of rock. Cottages cling to the cliff face, with their gardens vertically beneath, and a single narrow path between them, which acts as a main street. Yet somehow there is still room for a church and the remains of a château, although the only café lies outside the village. It is a place which takes only ten minutes to see, but which you are unlikely to forget.

Montauban

In contrast to those villages that have scarcely expanded beyond their medieval walls, Montauban is a *bastide* that has gone on to better things. It was founded in 1144 by the count of Toulouse and rapidly became an important trading centre for the low-lying, fruit-growing area all around. The town's chief claim to fame was as a stronghold of Protestantism during the Wars of Religion. It resisted three attempts to take it, frustrating Louis XII himself in the process. Less reputably, raiding parties from Montauban were responsible for much of the pillage and destruction in the Catholic towns of the area.

There is not much left of the old medieval foundation apart from the grid-plan layout of streets. The central square of the *bastide* has survived, however, albeit utterly transformed. In the seventeenth century it was rebuilt in red brick (keeping the arcades) into a series of elegant town mansions.

The chief reason to penetrate to the centre of Montauban is to see the **Musée Ingres** which is in the old bishop's palace on the edge of the Tarn (open mid-Oct–Easter daily exc Sun am and Mon 10–12, 2–6; Easter–June, Sept–mid-Oct, daily exc Mon 10–12, 2–6; July and Aug, daily 9.30–12, 1.30–6). Ingres was a native of Montauban and studied here before going to Paris and becoming David's pupil. The works collected in the museum were left to the town by the artist himself. It is a well-laid-out display, with paintings by David, Géricault and Delacroix to complement those by Ingres himself. *Roger délivrant Angelique* is only a reproduction of the painting in the Louvre, but here you will find the huge *Jésus parmi les docteurs* and the *Songe d'Ossian* as well as Ingres' violin and a display of his drawings from among the thousands owned by the museum.

The gaunt fortified church of **St-Jacques,** with its octagonal belfry can be seen from miles away, and indeed is actually more interesting from a distance than it is inside.

Moissac

No one who is interested in the Romanesque period can afford to miss Moissac, for the abbey here preserves some of the best carving from that period in the whole of France. Modern-day Moissac is a small town that would be sleepy if it were not for the heavy traffic heading downstream towards Agen. The landscape around it could be half a planet's distance from the high, bare uplands of the Aveyron valley. This is a prime fruit-growing area and orchards of pears, apples and plums are laid out on either side of the river. It is also an area famous for dessert grapes. Stick to the smaller roads on the northern bank of the Tarn for the best impression of the area.

The remains of the old **abbey** lie just to the north of Moissac's central square, and consist of the abbey church, the cloister and one or two of the conventual buildings. Only the western end of the church – the tower and the narthex – are Romanesque; the remainder is Gothic. The outstanding carving of the western doorway dates from around 1100 and is in a very good state of preservation. The theme is the apocalypse of Saint

John, and Christ, with staring eyes and neatly combed hair and beard, gazes imposingly at you as you approach. The symbols of the Evangelists surround him, and the 24 elders mentioned in the Apocalypse cluster on either side, regarding Christ with some astonishment. The central pillar of the doorway beneath is carved with six lions curling around each other, while scenes from the life of Christ decorate the right-hand side of the door and demons torture damned souls on the left. Although heavily stylised, there is a remarkable liveliness and humanity about the whole composition, which is hugely satisfying.

Round the corner from the doorway is the entrance to the cloister (open May–Oct, daily 9–12, 2–6; July and Aug–7 Nov–end Apr 9–12, 2–5). There are guides to explain every detail of the carving which decorates the capitals of the pillars which form the arcades, but unless your appetite for scholarship is exhaustive, it is just as satisfactory to contemplate them on your own. Right round the cloister, animals, foliage, scenes from the Old and New Testaments, saints and geometric patterns are carved without any apparent logical sequence. Larger pillars at the corners and the centre are clothed with marble from old Gallo-Roman sarcophagi and are carved with abbots in bas-relief. All these marvels almost disappeared for good in the last century when the route chosen for the railway was drawn through the cloister's centre. This extraordinary piece of vandalism was halted at the last minute; even so, some of the old abbey buildings were lost. Do not miss the stairways in the corner which conduct you to the upper storeys of the church tower and eventually on to the roof. Even up here the pillars are decorated and you can gaze out on the red roofs of Moissac and the river beyond

TOULOUSE TO MILLAU

Le Pays de Cocagne

The Land of Cockaigne, that mythical country of luxury and ease, actually exists. East of Toulouse, between the Garonne and the Tarn, lies the low fertile country, broken by shallow ridges of hills, which was the centre of *pastel* production in medieval times. The *pastel* was formed by hand into round balls or *cocagnes* (see box below), from which the area takes its name.

This area is off the tourist trail and a day or two spent wandering through this countryside can bring pleasure and contentment. The higher outcrops of land are crowned by old villages, whose churches, with their huge brick 'Toulousian' belfries, are worth a glance, and there is much gentle beauty in the slow undulations of the hillsides scattered with ancient red farmsteads. Pick your way among the following (ordered south to north).

● **Villefranche de Lauragais** A thirteenth-century *bastide*, quite big and busy and on a main road, but with one of the best Gothic belfries in the area.

● **St-Félix de Lauragais** A pretty village with a wide and sleepy market-square lined by half-timbered houses.

● **Revel** On the edge of the Montagne Noir, this is a hemmed-in market town, once a *bastide*, with an appealing central square and fourteenth-century covered market. It is a good place for browsing through small shops and for picking up information from the very efficient tourist office. There are a couple of simple hotels, while Le Lauragais restaurant on the southern outskirts serves good meals in rustic surroundings (tel 61 83 57 22).

● **St-Julia** A tiny fortified village, still with its ramparts and narrow gates. A very fine eleventh-century belfry crowns the church.

● **Magrin** The ruined château here has been turned into a museum of *pastel* (open Easter to Oct, Sun 3-6; July and Aug daily 3-6). There are display panels about the trade and the techniques of manufacture, and some helpful guides.

● **Lavour** The river Agout curls around the western side of this largish town in a deep valley. It is a curious red, rather modern-looking place with carefully nurtured flower-beds in the gardens where the old bishop's palace once stood. It was a stronghold of Cathar resistance to the Albigensian Crusade, and its original church was destroyed in the siege of 1211. The replacement cathedral (1254) is a fine red-brick Gothic building with an imposing nave and a sixteenth-century clock (*jacquemart*) whose wooden mannikins beat out the hours.

● **Lautrec** A village with two long streets of ancient houses leading up to a knobbly hillock (fine views) which once was crowned with a château and now is home to a restored, creaky windmill.

Castres

This is a pleasant, unassuming town on the western edge of the Monts de Lacaune, poised between hills and lowlands, with the river Agout running a semi-canalised course through its centre (boat-trips from the Pont Vieux). It was the birthplace of Jean Jaurès, a famous socialist politician who was assassinated on the eve of the First World War. The town has a museum of his life and work.

However, most foreign visitors come to see the **Musée Goya** (open July and Aug daily exc Mon 9 (10 Sun)-12, 2-6; rest of year 9-12, 2-5). More Spanish painters than Goya are represented, Murillo among them, but it is the Goya works that are the main attraction. The best painting is the exquisite self-portrait, while there are numerous engravings, among them a complete set of *Les Désastres de la guerre*, and a set of *Les Caprices*, full of curious surreal monsters and grotesques. The collection is housed in the old bishop's palace (now the town hall), a suitably magnificent background to this excellent gallery.

Everything else is a bit of an anticlimax. The cathedral is attractive from the outside but gloomily baroque within. The gardens of the bishop's palace are bright with bedding plants, and there are photogenic old houses clustered along the river. Otherwise, Castres is a town for gentle window-shopping. There are two good bookshops with lots of regional histories and folklore. The central square is small – just room for a small market and several cafés.

The Sidobre

Immediately to the east of Castres, forested hills rise to a height of about 700 metres. This western edge of the Monts de Lacaune is known as the Sidobre. The underlying rock is granite, and it is an infertile region of few villages, apparently good for little else than raising conifers and chestnuts or quarrying the rock for memorial headstones. It is not an ideal spot for touring – the views are limited and the villages either hang-dog and dismal or else modern and dull. The chief curiosity of the region is its balanced rocks – huge monoliths poised precariously on top of one another, left that way by the slow process of erosion of the surrounding material. Many of the roadside quarries have set up their own imitations. Another phenomenon is the 'chaos' or 'rock river' where the massive boulders have tumbled together in heaps. The most accessible of these stony sights is probably the rocks at **Sept Faux,** just off the D622 from Castres to Brassac, where two giant rocks lie in balance just outside a cottage garden (carefully padlocked to prevent you from attempting to move them).

Brassac is good to look at, chiefly because of its Gothic bridge where you can still see the old hooks from which lengths of linen were hung to bleach. The **Lac de Raviège**, formed by a dam on the Agout has a small watersports centre if you are in need of some cooling off. At **Ferrières** there is a ruined château and a museum of Protestantism, commemorating the strong Huguenot tradition of the area.

As you drive north-east on the fringes of the hills the country becomes less heavily forested and more interesting, but this is still very much a forgotten part of France and tourists are few and far between. Make for the Rance valley at **St-Sernin-sur Rance** for the best scenery. The river runs in a series of deep-cut loops through sunny pastures down to the Tarn. The main D999 to Millau cuts east from here, and is the quickest route out of the Monts de Lacaune. If the Rance valley pleases, stay at Les Magnolias in the village of **Plaisance** (see Where to Stay).

Roquefort-sur-Soulzon

Around the dusty town of **St-Affrique**, crystalline rock gives way to limestone and you have reached the edges of the *Grands Causses*, those barren plateaux which separate the Tarn basin from the Mediterranean (see 'Aubrac, Tarn Gorges and Western Cévennes').

An extremely pleasant touring route southwards runs from St-Affrique up the valley of the river Sorgues, passing through several tiny villages and ending up on the **Causse du Larzac**. On the edge of one of these villages, **Lapeyre**, with only a rusting sign to give any indication of it, you will find the churchyard where Lord Byron's daughter, Medora, lies buried. She was born of the incestuous relationship between Byron and his half-sister, and herself led a tumultuous and unhappy early life (being seduced by her brother-in-law) before eventually finding peace as a farmer's wife in this remote and unlikely spot. Her grave is marked by a simple headstone, and overlooks the deep valley and the limestone hills beyond.

The *causses* are sheep country, for only the floppy-eared *brebis* find nourishment on the sparse vegetation of the uplands. What keeps huge flocks of sheep economically viable, in a typically French combination of good fortune and enterprise, are the peculiar caverns and rock-faults around **Roquefort** – the home of one of the more famous and pungent of all French cheeses. Without these caves and fissures, which keep humidity and temperature constant, there would be no *penicillium roqueforti* to give the cheese its characteristic blue veining.

Roquefort is not the most attractive of villages. Squeezed beneath a sheer escarpment, the road through it runs past large factories – dedicated to the village's one industry. However, there is a good tour through the caves of the **'Société'** (the chief co-operative), and large car parks show how popular this activity is. (Tours: July and Aug, daily 9.30–7; rest of year, daily 9.30–11.30, 2–5.)

The legend (all good food products have a legend behind them) runs that a shepherd eating his *casse-croûte* (lunchtime snack) of bread and cheese in a cave spied his favourite shepherdess from afar and abandoned his lunch in pursuit of greater delights. When his road took him past the cave again some time later he found that the cheese in his discarded crust had turned into – well, Roquefort. The tour describes all this, places you in front of a diorama of the local landscape which dramatically jolts and shatters to illustrate the geological convulsions which formed the caves, and then leads you, via a maze of ladders and tunnels, through the huge underground warehouses where the cheese is stored during the ripening process. It is noticeable that the visitors are kept carefully separated from the cheese – whether the cheese would contaminate the tourists or the tourists the cheese is not stated. There is, however, the opportunity to sample and to buy. It is cold under ground; take extra layers of clothing.

The main roads in this area meet at **Millau** (for a full description, see 'Aubrac, Tarn Gorges and Western Cévennes' chapter). It is a busy but friendly town, and an obvious place to stop before heading east to the gorges, north to Sévérac-le-Château or west again down the Middle Tarn valley.

Sévérac-le-Château

This village, 31 kilometres north of Millau, will soon be bypassed by the A75 autoroute. Start by driving up to the ruins of the château on the hilltop. The building is an ugly mixture of styles, but the views from the courtyard are magnificent. The village's winding lanes beneath are flanked by very beautiful old houses from the fifteenth and sixteenth centuries, many with turrets and imposing windows. Sévérac is also a good centre for numerous short walks (none of them particularly strenuous). A leaflet describing them is available in the town.

If other hotels in the area are fully booked (not uncommon in an area rather short of good places) try the Relais du Bois du Four, 21 kilometres north-west of Millau on the D911 (see Where to Stay).

THE MIDDLE TARN

The famous Tarn Gorges, where the river cuts through the limestone of the *causses*, draw all the tourists, leaving the section between Millau and Albi more or less neglected. Yet the scenery beside this part of the river, while not quite so over-whelming, is on a grand scale, and you are unlikely to regret driving down this section of the river.

In a deep, if seldom precipitous, gorge, the Tarn cuts through the high ground of the Lévézou plateau, leaving rocky banks of heather and conifers on either side. The river is dammed in several places meaning that you gaze down on still, dark lakes from the road high on the valley side. Follow the D73 and the D200 for the best views. Occasional small hamlets beside the river or suspension bridges hung above dams punctuate the first half of the journey, but beneath Le Truel, where the valley opens out a bit, there are campsites and picnic spots and two villages well worth the journey.

PASTEL

Pastel, or woad as it is known in Anglo-Saxon countries, is an undistinguished-looking plant, one of the 4,000 members of the Crucifer family along with cabbage, mustard and radish. Until the discovery of indigo, however, this humble vegetable was the best – indeed the only – source of high-quality, long-lasting blue dye.

During the Middle Ages coloured cloth was in demand for vestments, robes and even tapestries and thus *pastel* was an essential commodity for the cloth-producing countries of northern Europe, notably Flanders and England. It flourished in the countryside east of Toulouse, where mild winters, wet springs and hot summers provided ideal growing conditions.

Turning the leaves of the plant into dyestuff was a laborious process. Leaves were cut as they matured, dried and then ground in a mill, the resulting mash being left to ferment before being rolled into fist-sized balls or cakes (*cocagnes*). These were then dried again, broken up, water added and allowed to ferment a second time. The

Brousse-le-Château

This is a place which, once discovered, may be hard to leave. In a little side valley, the ruins of a castle sit perched on a crag with just a few ancient houses clustered around it and a small stream tumbling through the middle. An extremely pleasant roadside *auberge* Les Relays du Chasteau (see Where to Stay) with a couple of tables set out in the sun make it a spot tempting beyond endurance. A narrow cobbled lane leads to the castle ruins, which take only a few minutes to explore and are populated by hens. A small shop sells postcards and soft drinks.

Ambialet

This is a more conventional sight. A loop of the river has created a narrow peninsula – so narrow that only a skinny neck of rock prevents the river from running straight. The houses of the village are photogenically strung out along this neck and into the peninsula beyond. A power station, disguised as a Gothic mansion, sits at the narrowest point. An old priory occupies the highest point, with a little Romanesque chapel outside it – well worth finding for its carved doorway and the small-scale beauty of the place. A short way upstream there is a

glutinous, foul-smelling mixture had to be stirred every three days as it fermented (the breaking down of the glucose released the pigment). The final result – about five per cent of the original weight of the leaves – was a kind of granular paste, which was formed into small cubes.

The marketing of the *pastel* and its shipment to northern Europe demanded a sophisticated monetary system to make the trade flourish, especially as the period between harvesting the leaves and the final production of the dye was almost a year. To begin with, Albi and Bayonne were the centres of the export market, but Toulouse gradually replaced them. The city had the necessary capital and the banking network to be able to finance the trade more efficiently.

The market started to decline in around 1561. Partly it was competition from indigo that caused the eventual disappearance of the *pastel* trade, but the Toulouse merchants' failure to invest, and the Wars of Religion helped it on its way. Now there is not a single field of *pastel* growing anywhere near Toulouse.

THE CATHAR HERESY

In the years following the millennium the Christian church in Western Europe was in a turbulent state. In reaction to the perceived wealth and sluggishness of the Catholic priests and prelates, a number of small evangelical movements arose, with the ideal of imitating the poverty of Christ and taking the gospel directly to the people. While sharing these ideals, the Cathars, or 'Good Christians' went further. They constructed what was effectively a different Christian religion from that of the established church, and rejected that church and all its works.

In the gospel of St John (I.iii), the Latin Bible (Vulgate) has *et sine ipso factum est nihil quod factum est* ('and without him was not any thing made that was made' – King James Bible). The Cathar Bible ignored the 'quod factum est' and translated into the *langue d'Oc e senes lui es fait nient* ('and without him was made the nothingness)'. This little difference in translation had huge implications, for it suggested a dualistic creation – the 'real' world made by God and the 'nothingness' made in the absence of God. Once the principle of dualism is established, there is plenty of supportive quotation in the Gospels. Indeed, much of the difficulty that the Catholic Church had in its struggle with the Cathars was the force of their logic, founded, as was so much of medieval debate, on the words of the Evangelists or the Apostles.

To the Cathars the visible world and everything in it was created in the absence of God. It was a product of the evil principle, illusory and corrupt. This included the Old Testament, the established church and all the works of man. To them, Christ did not die on the cross to expiate original sin. Their rituals did not include the Eucharist, with its bizarre idea of transubstantiation. Christ was sent by God to awaken the divine spark slumbering in its chains of flesh in everyone and release it to its destiny. For the Cathars the crucial sacrament was the baptism by the Holy Spirit by the laying on of hands, the *consolamentum*. By thus being baptised, they became *parfait* or perfect – given the chance of salvation.

It was this strict adherence to the laws laid down by Christ that led the Cathars to call themselves the Church of the Good Christians, and their ideals, and the logic behind their ideals, posed a terrible threat to the Catholic Church.

The response was twofold. The Dominican and the Franciscan orders were sanctioned by the Roman Church, the first to counter the Cathars by active preaching, and the second to imitate Christ's life of poverty. But a more direct method was sanctioned in 1209: a crusade against the Cathar heresy.

For Pope Innocent III, calling a crusade against people who were nominally Christian was a difficult step to take, and for King Philippe Auguste, allowing a crusade to be mounted against his subjects was equally hard. For a time the king resisted the papal pressure, but at the end of 1208 he allowed the crusade to commence.

The count of Toulouse, who was the primary target, took evasive action by submitting to the Pope, promising to pursue the heretics, and signed up for the crusade. Thereafter, he did nothing, but since he was nominally under the protection of the church, the crusade turned against Raimon Roger Trencavel, another protector of heretics, and took the towns of Carcassonne and Béziers, with terrible massacres and communal bonfires of the heretics. The dukes of Burgundy and Nevers, possibly worried about the results of their actions, then left the crusade in the command of a minor noble – Simon de Montfort.

During the years between 1211 and 1229, the crusade went on. Scarcely a town or castle throughout the domains of the count of Toulouse remained untaken or free from siege. In 1229, the count of Toulouse signed a treaty in Paris, which left him only with the core of his former possessions and furthermore forced him to marry his only daughter to the King's youngest brother. If he had no other heir, the lands of Toulouse would belong to the French Crown.

In 1242, the Count, having spent years forming alliances, called upon the Cathar nobility in exile in Castille and attempted to regain his lost lands. The power of the French King was too great, however, and once more he was forced into submission. In 1249 he died, and the days of Toulouse as an independent power were over. The Inquisition raged over the south of France, burning heretics and hearing the testimony of informers. The last great Cathar strongholds in the Pyrenees fell one by one: Montségur in 1244, Quéribus in 1254. The Cathar Church was reduced to a few congregations worshipping in secret in the mountains.

promising small hotel at Villeneuve-sur-Tarn in the shape of the newly renovated Hostellerie des Lauriers (see Where to Stay).

WHERE TO STAY AND EAT

There are two sections: establishments that we recommend and establishments that are worth considering but which we think do not merit a wholehearted recommendation. Both are marked on the map at the start of the chapter.

Key: ✦ = 0-250FF, ✦✦ = 251-450FF, ✦✦✦ = over 451FF; prices are per room without breakfast, which costs around 40-65FF extra. Some hotels insist on half-board during high season. Unless we say otherwise all have rooms with bath or shower and accept the major credit cards.

Recommended hotels

ALBI

Hostellerie Saint-Antoine   ✦✦-✦✦✦
17 rue Saint-Antoine
81000 Tarn   *Tel: 63 54 04 04; Fax: 63 47 10 47*

Certainly the best place to stay in Albi, and blessed with air-conditioning for hot summer nights, this is a family hotel, run with some charm and a good deal of slick organisation. The building is mostly modern without any pretence to be other than a functional place, but there is a small green garden between the wings on to which most rooms face. Bedrooms are fitted out with a good deal of style – bathrooms are especially luxurious, brightly lit and with lots of space. The food in the rather barn-like restaurant is reasonably priced, and well presented, if not yet in the gourmet class. The wine list is a little sparse. It is a friendly and welcoming place, worth the slight premium it commands over Albi's other hotels.

All year; restaurant closed Sat lunch, Sun lunch; 44 rooms

BELCASTEL

Hôtel Le Vieux Pont   ✦✦
12390 Aveyron   *Tel: 65 64 52 29; Fax: 65 64 44 32*

The sisters Fagegaltier have recently opened this hotel to go with their well-reputed restaurant, which lies just across the Old Bridge. The hotel is a smart conversion of a large stone house. Inside it is stark and modern, with white everywhere, recessed lights, supremely comfortable beds and radiators which look like *objets d'art*. The river Aveyron runs just below the windows and you can gaze straight out on to the street of russet cottages and the château high above which compose the village of Belcastel. The restaurant pays a great deal of heed to regional specialities.

End Feb–Dec, closed Sun pm, Mon (only in July and Aug); 7 rooms

BROUSSE-LE-CHATEAU

Le Relays du Chasteau ◆
Broquies
12480 Tarn   Tel: 65 99 40 15

Location is everything. This small inn lies right in the centre of a tiny, grey, medieval village with a crumbling castle on a spur opposite. There's a plain dining-room, a bar which serves as a meeting point for the village and a sequence of tiny, spotlessly clean bedrooms with good modern showers. Best of all, there is a small sunny terrace right beside the trout stream where you can eat regional food at low prices.

End Jan–end Dec, closed Fri pm and Sat am low season; 12 rooms

CORDES

Le Grand Ecuyer ◆◆-◆◆◆
rue Voltaire
81170 Tarn   Tel: 63 56 01 03; Fax: 63 56 18 83

An expensive hotel, but worth it for the glory of the building, one of the most beautifully decorated in Cordes, and for the beauty of the antique furniture with which the house is carefully outfitted. Massive simple cupboards, gilded mirrors and enormous stone fireplaces are everywhere and every room has something wonderful to look at. There is a whole sequence of sitting rooms; the dining-room is cool and supremely elegant, and the bedrooms (some with air-conditioning) are memorable. The food too is some of the best in the area.

Mid-Apr–mid-Oct, closed Mon, Tue lunch exc July and Aug; 13 rooms

CUQ-TOULZA

Hôtel Cuq en Terrasses ◆◆-◆◆◆
Cuq le Château
81470 Tarn   Tel: 63 82 54 00; Fax: 63 82 54 11

A sunny, old *maison du maître* in the Pays de Cocagne near Toulouse is the setting for this venture by Tim and Zara Whitmore. Tim's background as architect and interior designer has led to the transformation of the house – every bedroom is different and decorated with interesting fabrics and antiques. Breakfast is beautifully presented on dark blue tablecloths. There could hardly be a better place to unwind for a few days.

All year; 8 rooms; outdoor pool, badminton

MILLAU

Château de Creissels
Route de St-Affrique
12100 Aveyron   Tel: 65 60 16 59; Fax: 65 61 24 63

Just downstream from Millau, this is an ideal hotel for families. It is no beauty – the old château is a maze of corridors and crumbling dead-ends, but has plenty of character. There's a barrel-vaulted cellar where the food is served, a billiard table in an ancient library and a huge variety of bedrooms, some about a hundred yards from the nearest bathroom, others more conventionally equipped. A very friendly place, often with a room or two to spare in high season, and good for an overnight stop.

Mid-Feb– end Dec, low season closed Sun pm, Mon lunch; 33 rooms

NAJAC

L'Oustal del Barry
Place du Bourg
12270 Aveyron   Tel: 65 29 74 32; Fax: 65 29 75 32

This hotel is situated at the end of the main street, overlooking the old square and with a lovely romantic garden across the road on a steep slope down to the Aveyron. Bedrooms are small, and shower rooms can be miniscule. But many rooms overlook the ruins of the *château*, and in the moonlight this makes up for a lot. So does the really excellent food. Jean-Marie Miquel uses fresh herbs in imaginative combinations. The marinaded duck breast will refresh you, and the rhubarb tart tastes wonderful.

End Mar– end Oct, closed Mon in Apr to June and Oct; 21 rooms (17 have bath or shower)

PLAISANCE

Hostellerie Les Magnolias
12550 Aveyron   Tel: 65 99 77 34; Fax: 65 99 70 57

An excellent hotel, with all the right things going for it: a fourteenth-century house, a tiny antique hillside village and a restaurant where a roaring fire (in autumn) combines with exquisite smells wafting from the kitchen to give the diner a delightful sense of anticipation. The rooms vary according to the age of the part of the building in which they are situated, but you can expect to find antique furniture, thick curtains and tiny bathrooms. There is a small garden at the back in which to relax on hot days.

Apr–end Dec; 6 rooms

SAINT BEAUZEIL

Château de l'Hoste
Route Agen
82150 Tarn-et-Garonne   *Tel: 63 95 25 61; Fax: 63 95 25 50*

Miles from anywhere, on the borders of Quercy, 42 kilometres north-east of Agen, this white, eighteenth-century manor house stands at the end of an avenue of shady trees. The rooms are large and scattered along various wings. There is a sunny courtyard, a small swimming pool, tables on the terrace (the food is very pleasant) and a small, plush bar. It makes an excellent place in which to tuck yourself away for a night or two.

Mid-Mar–mid-Feb; closed Sun pm and Mon Oct to end Apr; 32 rooms; outdoor pool

SAINT-FELIX LAURAGAIS

Auberge du Poids Public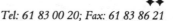
31540 Haute-Garonne   *Tel: 61 83 00 20; Fax: 61 83 86 21*

On the road from Toulouse towards Revel and Castres, this is a useful and efficient hotel, popular with weekenders from the city. It is sufficiently far from the main road to be peaceful and there is a pleasant terrace at the rear with views of rolling fields. Bedrooms are fairly standard, but everything works and it is comfortable enough. The food is rather good – the salads notable for the use of a very good walnut oil. There's a strong regional wine list. The dining-room, which takes up most of the ground floor, is a bright and airy, marred only by the automatic door to the kitchen which sounds exactly like a snoring labrador!

Feb–Dec, closed Sun pm Oct to Apr; 13 rooms

Worth considering

BEZ (NEAR VILLENEUVE)

Auberge de la Bouriatte
12700 Aveyron   *Tel: 65 64 67 16; Fax: 65 64 65 64*

An isolated hotel in an unfrequented valley, with beautifully decorated rooms, swimming pool and friendly host. The food is not always reliable.

BRUNIQUEL

L'Etape du Château
82800 Tarn-et-Garonne　　　　　　　　*Tel: 63 67 25 00*

A jolly, simple inn with a few rooms of its own and some *chambres d'hôtes* opposite. Fine views from the restaurant and a good-natured proprietor.

NAJAC

Hôtel Longcol
12270 Aveyron　　　　*Tel: 65 29 63 36; Fax: 65 29 64 28*

On the edge of the Aveyron valley a little way north of Najac, this is a posh and fairly pricey hotel. It is an old farmhouse, beautifully converted and full of flowers and interesting furniture. A good hideaway.

SEVERAC-LE-CHATEAU

Relais du Bois du Four
Saint-Léons
12780 Aveyron　　　　*Tel: 65 61 86 17*

A rambling roadside inn, with long corridors and creaky stairs. It is a little short on comfort, but standards in the kitchen are very high, and it may have a room free when nowhere else does.

TOULOUSE

Hôtel des Beaux-Arts　　　　　　　　♦♦-♦♦♦
1 Place du Pont-Neuf
31000 Haute-Garonne　　　*Tel: 61 23 40 50; Fax: 61 22 02 27*

The hotel has tiny rooms and parking is impossible, but it has more character than most of the city centre hotels.

TOULOUSE

Le Grande-Bretagne　　　　　　　　　　♦♦
298 Avenue Grande Bretagne
31000 Haute-Garonne　　　*Tel: 61 31 84 85; Fax: 61 31 87 12*

Very convenient for the airport, this hotel is on the west bank of the Garonne on a long anonymous street. It is friendly, if a little scruffy.

VILLENEUVE-SUR-TARN

Hostellerie des Lauriers ◆-◆◆◆
81250 Aveyron *Tel: 63 55 84 23*

Newly renovated bedrooms and a fine river view make this otherwise simple hotel rather different from its nearby competitors. Reports on the food would be welcome.

PRACTICAL
INFORMATION

TRAVEL

Air

Air France flies direct from Heathrow to Toulouse and Air Inter from Gatwick to Bordeaux. British Airways flies direct from Gatwick to Bordeaux and Toulouse.

There are many direct flights to Paris from most UK regional airports, with onward connections to the south-west of France. A good travel agent or flight specialist should be able to find you some special offers. Make sure the agent selling you the ticket is covered by an ATOL bond.

From Paris, there are flights to Limoges, Clermont-Ferrand, Albi, Brive, Castres, Rodez, Bergerac and Périgueux (Air Inter, TAT and Air Littoral).

● Air France, Colet Court, 100 Hammersmith Road, London W6 7JP; (tel 0181-742 6600). Air France acts as agent for Air Inter and Air Littoral.

● British Airways, 156 Regent Street, London W1R 5T (personal callers only) or credit-card bookings on (0345) 222111. British Airways act as agents for TAT.

Crossing the Channel with a car

Sea routes

Journey times given are for day and night crossings respectively.

● Brittany Ferries, tel (01752) 221321 or (01705) 827701: Plymouth to Roscoff (6–7 hours), Portsmouth to St-Malo (9–10¼ hours), Portsmouth to Caen (6–7 hours), Portsmouth to Santander (33–35 hours).

● Hoverspeed, tel (01304) 240241: Dover to Calais (35 mins on hovercraft, 55 mins Seacat); Folkestone to Boulogne (55 mins Seacat only).

● P&O Ferries, tel (01304) 203388: Dover to Calais (1¼ hours), Portsmouth to Cherbourg (5–7 hours), Portsmouth to Le Havre (5½–7½ hours).

All French phone numbers listed in this book include the area code for dialling from anywhere in France, except for Paris. To dial from Paris add 16. To dial from the UK simply add 0033 at the front of the number.

● Sally Line, tel (01843) 595522: Ramsgate to Dunkerque (2½ hours).
● Stena Sealink UK, tel (01233) 647047: Dover to Calais (1½ hours); Newhaven to Dieppe (4 hours); Southampton to Cherbourg (5–9 hours).
● Truckline (part of Brittany Ferries); tel (01705) 827701: Poole to Cherbourg (4½–6 hours).

There is likely to be stiff competition between the ferry lines and the Channel Tunnel, and it is worth keeping an eye open for incentives. The overnight crossings on the longer routes are especially advantageous for those living north or west of London; the convenience of being able to sleep and travel simultaneously may outweigh the faster journey times offered by the Channel Tunnel.

Tips

● You need to book months in advance to secure car space in high season, particularly on night sailings
● A cabin is a blessing on night sailings
● Fares are at their most expensive for sailings during weekends in July and August, particularly on overnight or early morning crossings
● Special return fares (for three, five or 10 days) cost from half the price of a standard fare.

The Channel Tunnel

A vehicle shuttle service, Le Shuttle, runs from Folkestone to Calais and takes 35 minutes. The intention is that the service will run 24 hours a day, every 15 minutes – teething problems and delays were still occurring at the time of going to press. Tickets can be obtained from toll booths at the terminal, and passengers will take the next available train. Alternatively, you can book through a travel agent or through Le Shuttle customer service centre (0990) 353535. The price varies seasonally and is set per car (regardless of the number of passengers).

Rail

Direct train/boat daily services to Paris start from London Charing Cross and take ten hours when using a ferry or 8 hours by Seacat. Double the cost but more than half the time is the Eurostar train through the Channel Tunnel – a three-hour non-stop service between Waterloo and Paris is currently running twice a day. There are 'Apex' return tickets (must be booked two weeks in advance), in addition to standard and first class. Tickets can be booked in advance from Eurotunnel (01233) 617575 and both first- and second-class tickets are refundable with no advance notice required. Fares on this service are likely to remain competitive with the London-Paris air fare.

The chief railheads within the south-west are Brive-la-Gaillarde, Bordeaux and Toulouse, and French Railways (SNCF) operate direct services from Paris to all of them. The railway network within the south-west is extensive by British standards, and there are few towns without a station.

There are motorail services from Calais and Paris to Bordeaux, Brive, Narbonne and Toulouse.

Tourist offices

French tourist office (*Maison de la France*), 178 Piccadilly, London W1V OAL Tel: (0891) 244123.

Nearly every small town has its own *Office de Tourisme* or a *Syndicat d'Initiative*.

Aquitaine

Regional tourist office (*Comité Régional de Tourisme*): 23 Parvis des Chartrons, 33074 Bordeaux; tel 56 01 70 00
Departmental tourist offices (*Comités Départementals du Tourisme*):
● **Dordogne**: 25 Rue Wilson, 24009 Périgueux; tel 53 53 44 35
● **Lot-et-Garonne**: 4 Rue André Chénier, B.P. 304, 47008 Agen; tel 53 66 14 14
● **Gironde**: 21 Cours de l'Intendance, 33000 Bordeaux; tel 56 52 61 40

Limousin

Regional tourist office: 27 Boulevard de la Corderie, 87031 Limoges; tel 55 45 18 80
Departmental tourist office:
● **Corrèze**: Maison du Tourisme, Quai Baluze, 19000 Tulle; tel 55 29 98 70

Travel passes called Euro Domino allow you three, five or ten days' unlimited rail travel within a month. Under-26s and over-60s can travel on French railways at reduced rates. People travelling with children may find the Kiwi Card (similar to a family railcard) worth enquiring about – adult reductions of up to 50 per cent are available. To get further details or to apply for these passes, contact the London branch of SNCF, at 179 Piccadilly, London W1V OBA; tel (0345) 300003 for credit-card bookings and (0891) 515477 for information. SNCF can also provide information for those wishing to take bicycles on trains.

● French Motorail; tel 0171-409 3518 for information and bookings.

● British Rail International, International Rail Centre, Victoria Station, London SW1V 1JY; tel 0171-834 2345.

Midi-Pyrénées

Regional tourist office: 54 Boulevard de l'Embouchure, B.P. 2166, 31022 Toulouse; tel 61 13 55 55

Departmental tourist offices:

● **Lot**: 107 Quai Cavaignac, B.P. 7, 46001 Cahors; tel 65 35 07 09

● **Tarn**: B.P. 225, 81016 Albi; tel 63 77 32 10

● **Aveyron**: 33 Avenue Victor Hugo, 12000 Rodez; tel 65 73 63 15

● **Tarn-et-Garonne**: Hôtel des Intendants, Place du Maréchal-Foch, 82000 Montauban; tel 63 63 31 40

Auvergne

Regional tourist office: 43 Avenue Julien, B.P. 395, 63011 Clermont-Ferrand; tel 73 93 04 03

Departmental tourist office:

● **Cantal**: B.P. 8, 15018 Aurillac; tel 71 46 22 00

Languedoc-Roussillon

Regional tourist office: 20 Rue de la République, 34000 Montpellier; tel 67 22 81 00

Departmental tourist office:

● **Lozère**: 14 Boulevard Henri-Bourrillon, B.P. 4, 48001 Mende; tel 66 65 60 00

Coach services

Eurolines (tel 01582 404511) operates regular coach services
(daily in peak season) between London, Victoria Coach Station
and Bordeaux, Toulouse, Brive and Cahors. Overnight journey
time is 16 hours between London and Bordeaux.

Car travel

Driving regulations

You must have with you: your UK driving licence; the vehicle
registration document (plus a letter of authorisation if the vehicle is not registered in your name) and insurance documents.
Your car must carry a GB sticker.

The minimum age for drivers in France is 18. You are not
allowed to drive on a provisional licence. Seat-belts must be
worn by the driver and all passengers. Under 10s may not travel
in the front unless in a specially fitted seat facing backwards.

It is compulsory to carry a warning triangle if your car does
not have hazard warning lights. Headlamp beams on right-hand
drive cars must be adjusted; if you imagine the headlamp is a
clockface, stick adhesive black tape over the area between seven
and nine. Alternatively, conversion kits are available in many
garages and at most ferry terminals. Yellow-tinted headlights
are no longer compulsory in France.

Rules of the road

Stop signs mean stop – crawling slowly rather than coming to a
complete halt is an offence. *Priorité à droite* (priority to the right)
continues in many built-up areas; usually it no longer applies
elsewhere. Visual confirmation of a priority road is displayed in
yellow and black diamond-shaped signs; the same sign with a
diagonal black line indicates the end of a priority stretch. At
most roundabouts outside built-up areas you must now give

Further information is available from The Automobile
Association (AA), Fanum House, Basing View, Basingstoke,
Hampshire RG21 2EA; tel (01256) 20123. (For driving regu-
lations in Europe tel (01256) 493751/3.) The Royal Auto-
mobile Club, RAC House, PO Box 100, Bartlett St, South
Croydon, Surrey CR2 6XW; tel 0181-686 0088. (For
European driving regulations tel (0345) 333222.)

way on approach (as in the UK); but take extreme care, not all French drivers follow the rules. Also take care on the outskirts of towns or villages, where small lanes meet the main road – it is all too easy to forget that traffic (especially tractors) joining the main road may have right of way. If a car flashes its head-lights it is indicating that it has priority and you should give way.

The speed limit on motorways is 130kph (wet roads 110kph), on dual carriageways 110kph (wet roads 100kph), on other roads 90kph, and has now been lowered to 50kph in towns (the town name marks the beginning and end of the limit).

Note: A sequence of approaching cars flashing their lights at you usually indicates a police trap ahead rather than anything wrong with your driving!

For route-planning telephone the AA on (0171)-930 8242 or the RAC on (01345) 333222. For a recording of European Traffic Information call either the AA on (0336) 401904 or the RAC on (0891) 500241.

Insurance and Green cards

British insurance policies provide cover for accidents that occur in EC and other selected countries. However, the cover normally extends only as far as is necessary to comply with the legal minimum in the particular country through which you are motoring. So even if you have comprehensive insurance in the UK, you may not automatically get the same standard of cover abroad. If you give your insurance company notice (allow at least two weeks), it should extend your comprehensive cover to include Europe. Some companies will do this free, others will make a charge. Although not a legal requirement, you are advised to take a Green Card (ask your insurance company for one) as it may prove more effective than a UK insurance certifi-cate to show you are insured to the minimum level.

Breakdown cover

There are many companies that offer breakdown cover abroad. It is worth telephoning around as rates and the extent of cover vary considerably. As well as the AA and the RAC, there are other large breakdown companies including Europ Assistance (tel (01444) 442442), National Breakdown (tel (0113) 239 3939) and Mondial Assistance (tel 0181-681 2525).

Petrol

Petrol in France is a few pence more expensive per litre than in the UK. There are surprisingly few petrol stations on N- and D-roads, so remember to fill up in towns. Petrol in supermarket stations can be 15 per cent cheaper than on autoroutes. Eurocard/Mastercard and Visa are the most widely accepted credit cards for petrol. Unleaded is *sans plomb* in French.

Route planning

Both the AA and RAC can tailor-make route plans for you for a standard fee, but you need to apply at least three weeks in advance. Maps showing the *Bis* network are available free from roadside information kiosks or the French Tourist Office. *Bis* is short for *Bison Futé* (wily bison) and is a government scheme that picks out fast through-routes (usually D-roads) for holiday traffic.

The route most commonly used by British drivers from the ferry ports of Caen or Le Havre is the N20, which runs south from Châteauroux to Montauban. Notorious for its bottlenecks in holiday season, this road is gradually being upgraded but is still worth avoiding at peak weekends. The A75 motorway from Orléans to Clermont-Ferrand is being rapidly extended south towards Montpellier, and this provides a convenient and comparatively uncrowded route into the eastern side of the area covered by this book. The A10 motorway from Paris to Bordeaux is the obvious route to take into the western end of the region.

To circumvent Paris on the western side (necessary from Caen or Le Havre), the route from the A13 motorway at Mantes-la-Jolie down to Rambouillet (D191/N10) is recommended as being faster than the route via Evreux and Dreux and not subject to the bottlenecks in the Forêt de Marly, which plague the route via Versailles. On the eastern side, from the A1 (Calais motorway), the Paris *périphérique* (ring road) is probably still the fastest through-route except during rush hour or week-end mornings or evenings – take a good map and watch for the electronic signs that warn of traffic jams (*bouchon*). The network of motorway and dual-carriageways further out, which takes you round the city via Evry, can sometimes be even slower than the long cross-country route from Senlis via Meaux and Melun (N330/N36). An alternative is to stay on the Reims motorway (A4/A26) until Troyes and then make your way across country, but this is only a feasible route for those in no hurry, or who want to travel through eastern France.

Within the south-west, the Bordeaux–Toulouse motorway (A62) is the best west–east through-route. The northern route (N89) from Bordeaux to Clermont-Ferrand is very crowded and often very slow. In general, it is better to stay off the main roads in the region wherever possible; driving is far more pleasurable on the D-roads, and using them can often prove just as fast a method of getting from A to B.

Car parking

Do not park where kerbs are marked with yellow paint or where you will cause an obstruction, as your car may be towed away. Parking is not allowed on open roads unless the car is off the tarmac. Parking on one side of the road on alternate days is shown by a sign saying *Côté du stationnement, jours pairs* (even days) or *impairs* (odd). In major cities there is a blue zone, where parking discs must be used (obtainable from tourist offices).

Car hire

Avis (tel 0181-848 8733), Budget (tel (0800) 181181), Hertz (tel 0181-679 1799) and Europcar (tel (0345) 222525) have offices in many of the larger towns, and at Bordeaux or Toulouse airports. It is worth comparing prices available direct from the main companies with those quoted by your travel agent, who may have access to advantageous discounts. Check what is included when comparing prices – you may find you are charged extra for things like theft insurance on arrival with some companies and not with others. You should also check your car for any scratches or damage both on arrival and on handing it back, as companies charge for the first £100 worth of damage. Prices for car hire vary according to destination and season, although it is generally cheaper to book in advance rather than on arrival in France.

Common road signs

Absence de glissière no crash barrier
Absence de marquage no road markings
Cédez le passage give way
Déviation diversion

Marquage effacé no road markings
Parking gratuit free parking
Péage pay-booth on motorway
Priorité aux piétons give way to pedestrians
Ralentir slow down
Rappel literally 'remember': usually under speed signs
Route barrée closed road

Emergencies

Police and ambulance tel 17
Fire brigade tel 18

Fines

You can be stopped and fined on the spot for driving offences up to 2,500FF. Fines for not wearing a seat-belt range from 230–600FF, for speeding 600–4,000FF and for drink-driving (alcohol limits are same as in the UK) 2,000–30,000FF.

PACKAGE HOLIDAYS

Independent travel to France is straightforward and often cheaper than taking a package. However, large numbers of tour operators do offer packages. Most involve the use of your own car, although fly-drives and coach-based packages are also available. Self-catering packages are perennially popular, as are camping packages. Accommodation varies from cottages to villas and castles, many with swimming-pools. A number of operators offer special-interest holidays, with walking, painting, canoeing and art tours being among the choices.

For a complete list of tour operators, get *The Traveller in France Reference Guide* from the French tourist office (address on page 254).

HEALTH AND INSURANCE

EU member states have reciprocal health agreements which entitle you to receive urgent medical treatment and care in a state-run hospital within the EU. In theory, you need the form E111 to prove your entitlement. The E111, and information about it, is contained in the leaflet T2, *Health Advice for*

Travellers, available from main post offices. The E111 does not entitle you to repatriation and should not be considered as an alternative to taking out a holiday insurance policy.

When arranging insurance cover for France:
● make sure that you are covered for medical expenses up to £250,000 and that the insurance includes cancellation or curtailment of your holiday
● make sure any valuable individual items are covered
● always check the exclusion clauses in the small print
● if you hire a car, make sure to take out a collision damage waiver; personal accident cover is only necessary if not already covered by your general holiday insurance.

CUSTOMS AND DUTY-FREE

There are no restrictions on the amount of duty-paid goods (i.e. purchases from local shops) brought from France into the UK. However, these goods should be carried personally and intended for your own use. If you bring back more than the suggested UK guide limits (10 litres of spirits, 20 litres of fortified wine, 90 litres of wine, 110 litres of beer, 800 cigarettes, 400 cigarillos, 200 cigars) you may have to prove that your shopping is for you.

Duty-free shopping – at airports or on ferries – will continue until 30 June 1999. Duty-free allowances will still apply but will be controlled at point of sale not at customs.

ACCOMMODATION

Hotels

In France, hotels are graded from one to four star, depending on their level of facilities. In the south-west, most accommodation outside the large towns will be in the two- or three-star bracket, with a scattering of luxury hotels (usually châteaux) in the more popular areas.

Two-star hotels remain affordable, and are certainly the most characteristically French form of accommodation. Hoteliers usually plough more resources into their restaurant than their bedrooms, and you can expect the latter to be clean and comfortable, but with minimal décor. At the three-star level there is usually a little more luxury, probably with a lounge, cocktail bar, and rather more evidence of modernisation in the bedrooms.

There are numerous hotel chains in France. Two of the more interesting, with accommodation at opposite ends of the price spectrum, are the Féderation de Logis de France, which has over 4,000 small family-run establishments throughout France, and Relais & Chateaux, which incorporates 150 luxury hotels. Guides listing hotels in both schemes are available from the French tourist office. The Logis guide is also available in bookshops.

A complete list of hotels in each region with their star ratings is obtainable from local tourist offices. They also run a reservation service called Accueil de France which can make bookings up to a week ahead. There is a small charge, and you must visit the office in person.

French hotel-keeping differs from that in Britain in several respects, and it is worth remembering a few simple points. Chief among these is the fact that washing facilities rather than size usually govern the room price, and if you choose a shower rather than a bath, or can manage with a basin and WC, you can save disproportionate amounts of money. It is seldom worth paying the extra for a bath anyway, since many tubs are half-sized. Second, the price you are quoted rarely includes breakfast and the local café may provide cheaper and better morning fare. Third is the fact that many hotels have family rooms with plenty of space and three or four beds, and these may well be cheaper than hiring two rooms for self and children. Finally, if you are faced with a bed that appears only to have a bolster, look in the bedroom cupboard. Pillows are almost always to be found there.

If you book within a few days of your intended arrival, most hotels will be happy to take your word that you will turn up, without bothering to take credit card numbers. The downside of this is that they will feel free to re-let your room if there is no sign of you by 6.30pm. If you are going to be later, always telephone; it can save tears. On the same subject of late arrival, most hotel restaurants take their last orders at 9.30pm, and you will be lucky to find anything to eat thereafter.

Gîtes

Gîtes are houses, often converted farmhouses or cottages, in rural spots. They are classified by ears of corn – from one to four depending on how well-equipped they are; the emphasis is on simplicity rather than sophistication. The Dordogne basin is one of the most popular areas for *gîte*-based holidays, and you should book as early as you possibly can no matter when you plan to go. Outside the Dordogne basin, holidays for July and August should be booked far in advance but there is less problem at other times of year.

There are two ways of booking a *gîte*. The French tourist office can provide addresses and telephone numbers for booking offices in any *département* in France, as can the Fédération Nationale des Gîtes de France. Each office has a complete guide to *gîtes* in the area; you can then book direct with the owner, or in some cases the local office will act as a booking agent. A simpler alternative, especially if you are concerned about your linguistic abilities, is to leave all the arrangements to Gîtes de France in this country and choose a *gîte* from their brochure. This has a more limited selection than those available in France, but still details 2,500 cottages countrywide. *The Gîtes Guide* is available in UK bookshops (FHG Publications) and lists a large number of *gîtes* and gives details of booking procedures.

● Gîtes de France, 178 Piccadilly, London W1V 9DB; tel 0171-493 3480.

● Fédération Nationale des Gîtes de France, Maison de Tourisme Vert, 56 Rue St-Lazare, 75009 Paris; tel (1) 49 70 75 85

Chambres d'hôtes

Chambres d'hôtes – similar to B&B in the UK – come in all shapes and sizes, from châteaux downwards. Many will provide an evening meal, given advance notice. There is not the same difference in price between these establishments and hotels as there is in Britain, but standards of accommodation are often as good, if not better. The welcome and the 'family atmosphere' vary, but in the best of them you will be received very warmly indeed. Local tourist offices have lists of *chambres d'hôtes*, usually detailing those whose owners speak English. Almost all *chambres d'hôtes* are marketed through the Gîtes de France group, who publish a guide in English (available from bookshops or from their London office – telephone number and address above) called *French Country Welcome*. This lists 12,000 B&Bs and *Chambres d'Hôtes de Prestige* (magnificent country houses in rural France). Gîtes de France also offers a selection of *chambres d'hôtes* on a package basis.

Gîtes d'étape

Gîtes d'étape are large farmhouses, often with dormitory lodgings, like hostels, intended primarily for walkers or riders. *Gîtes d'étapes* (available from Gîtes de France) gives details of such lodgings across France.

Youth hostels

To be able to use youth hostels in France, you need to be a member of the UK's Youth Hostel Association (tel (01727) 855215), or obtain a membership card in France. The French Government Tourist Office produces a leaflet, *France Youth Travel*, which gives details of youth hostel organisations. Local tourist offices also have information on youth hostels in their area.

Camping

The French regard themselves as the most sophisticated campers in Europe. Campsites in France are graded from one to four stars. All are required by law to have a source of purified water, are expected to have running water (some one-stars do not have to offer hot running water), a daily refuse collection and a public telephone. The main differences and improvements, as you progress through the ratings, relate to the general range of amenities, how crowded they might get and the minimum size of pitch. Many French campsites are municipal; these are often more basic than privately-owned sites, but just as likely to be well-maintained. Some sites now have *campéolettes*, Swiss-style chalets.

Ways to go camping

A package camping holiday provides you with a tent in a three- or four-star site and a courier to look after you. You can pay up to twice as much for this service than if you make your own arrangements, but you obviously save on buying or transporting your own equipment.

If you take your own equipment, a reservation agency (a service offered by some tour operators and by membership organisations) will take care of bookings and you may get a wider choice of smaller sites.

Equally, there is no problem about making your own arrangements, and this brings the advantage of being able to choose a pitch away from those reserved for groups. To book, write (or telephone) direct to the campsites.

● Some sites will not accept an independent booking without a camping *carnet*, others offer a reduction if you have one. The *carnet* is available to members of the the the AA, RAC, the Caravan Club (tel (01342) 326944), the Camping and Caravanning Club (tel (01203) 694995) and the Cyclists' Touring Club (tel (01483) 417217). Memberships cost from around £25 a year. If you are not a member of any of these organisations, you can also get a *carnet* from the GB Car Club (tel (01794) 515444) for a small fee.

● If you want to stay at any site in July or August, book in advance. In May, June or September many advertised facilities (e.g. bar or shop) are shut.

● If you are camping independently, the Michelin guide *Camping Caravanning France* is indispensable. Other camping guides include *Camping à la ferme* (Gîtes de France)

WALKING

Grandes Randonnées (GRs) are long-distance paths across the whole country. *Petites Randonnées* are local footpaths – from two hours' long to a day's walk. They usually have the advantage of being circular. The Institut Géographique National (IGN) produces the best series of maps for walkers. The *Série Verte* (1:1,000,000) maps are useful for planning your route, but for the walk itself use the larger scale *Série Bleu* (1:25,000). You may have to buy several if you are covering a long distance. Topo Guides, published by the Fédération Française de Randonnée Pédestre, describe walks in French. Some of these guides exist in English, called *Footpaths of Europe* (published by Robertson McCarta). If you have difficulty getting maps or Topo Guides try Stanfords, 12–14 Long Acre, London WC2E 9LP (tel 0171-836 1321) or Daunts, 83 Marylebone High Street, London W1M 3DE; tel 0171 224 2295. Paths are usually way-marked, but the less frequented paths can get overgrown and markings can be sporadic and unreliable.

● French ramblers' association: Fédération Française de Randonnée Pédestre, 64 rue de Gergovei, 75014 Paris; tel (1) 45 45 31 02

WEATHER CHARTS

	Jan		Feb		Mar		Apr		May		June	
	°C	R	°C	R	°C	R	°C	R	°C	R	°C	R
Bordeaux	9	16	11	13	15	13	17	13	20	14	24	11
Clermont-Ferrand	7	12	8	11	13	9	16	12	20	12	23	12
Toulouse	9	14	10	12	14	11	17	12	20	13	25	10
Millau	7	14	9	12	13	13	16	12	20	13	24	11
London	6	15	7	13	10	11	13	12	17	12	20	11

°C=Average daily maximum temperature in °C
R=Average number of rainy days per month

	July		Aug		Sep		Oct		Nov		Dec	
	°C	R	°C	R	°C	R	°C	R	°C	R	°C	R
Bordeaux	25	11	26	12	23	13	18	14	13	15	9	17
Clermont-Ferrand	25	9	25	10	22	10	17	11	11	12	7	12
Toulouse	27	9	27	9	24	10	18	11	13	12	9	15
Millau	27	8	27	10	23	10	17	13	12	13	8	15
London	22	12	21	11	19	13	14	13	10	15	7	15

°C=Average daily maximum temperature in °C
R=Average number of rainy days per month

IMPORTANT DATES

Festivals

The following is a selection of the main spring and summer festivals in the Dordogne basin. Regional tourist offices will have comprehensive lists with exact dates, which vary from year to year in most cases. For an overview, send for the booklet *Nouvelles de France* available from the French tourist office.

26 February–5 March, **Albi**, Carnival
May, **Bordeaux**, Music Festival
12–18 May, **Albi**, Jazz Festival

12–28 May, **Cahors**, Photography and Visual Arts Festival
28 May, **Aubrac**, Seasonal movement of animals to higher pastures
4 July–31 August, **Toulouse**, Classical Music, Jazz and Folklore Festival
8 July–16 August, **St-Céré**, Lyrical and vocal music Festival
11 July–25 August, **Conques**, Classical and Baroque Music Festival
12 July–7 August, **Cordes**, Classical and Contemporary Music Festival
14–17 July, **Villeneuve-sur-Lot**, Jazz Festival
15 July–19 August, **Vallée de la Vézère**, Classical Music and Opera Festival
15–31 July, **Castres**, Spanish Arts Festival
18–23 July, **Montignac**, International Folklore Festival
24 July–27 August, **Montignac**, Music concerts
5–6 August, **Gaillac**, Wine Festival

Public holidays

1 January: New Year's Day
Easter Sunday and Monday
1 May: Labour Day
8 May: Victory in Europe Day
20 May: Ascension Day
Whit Sunday and Whit Monday
14 July: Bastille Day
15 August: Assumption Day
1 November: All Saints' Day
11 November: Remembrance Day
25 December: Christmas Day

School holidays

Some school holiday dates can vary in different parts of France.
All Saints: 21 or 22 October to 2 November
Christmas: 20 or 21 December to 3 or 5 January
Winter: 2½ weeks between 11 February and 20 March
Spring: 2½ weeks between 9 April and 15 May
Summer: 3 or 6 July to 4 or 6 September

Market days

This list gives the weekly market-days for many of the bigger towns and villages in the region. Local tourist offices will have full listings. Most towns with markets also have a monthly or bi-monthly fair (*foire*), which is a bigger and more comprehensive version of the weekly market. In some towns at various seasons of the year, these fairs may specialise in particular local produce (chestnuts, truffles, *foie gras*, poultry or mushrooms, for example).

Albi Saturday morning
Aurillac Wednesday morning, Saturday morning
Belvès Saturday
Bergerac Wednesday, Saturday
Brantôme Friday
Brive Tuesday, Thursday, Saturday morning
Bugue Tuesday, Saturday morning
Cahors Wednesday, Saturday morning
Cajarc Saturday afternoon
Castres Tuesday morning, Wednesday to Saturday
Excideuil Thursday
Les Eyzies-de-Tayac Monday
Figeac Saturday
Gourdon Tuesday, Saturday morning
Hautefort Wednesday
Jumilhac-le-Grand 2nd & 4th Wednesday of each month
Martel Wednesday, Saturday morning
Meymac 2nd and 4th Friday of each month
Millau Wednesday morning, Friday morning
Moissac Saturday, Sunday morning
Monpazier 3rd Thursday of each month
Montauban Wednesday morning, Saturday
Montignac Wednesday
Nontron Saturday
Périgueux Wednesday, Saturday
Ribérac Wednesday, Friday
Rodez Wednesday morning, Saturday morning
Salignac-Eyvignes 2nd Thursday, last Friday of each month
Sarlat-la-Canéda Wednesday, Saturday
St Antoine-Noble-Val Sunday morning
St-Cyprien Sunday
St-Emilion Sunday morning
St-Flour Saturday morning
Toulouse Wednesday, Saturday
Villefranche-du-Périgord Saturday

BOOKS AND MAPS

Maps

Michelin Motoring Atlas, France (1: 200,000): essential for touring in France.

Michelin yellow maps (1:200,000) are the most reliable and give excellent detail. Large sheets 234, 235, 239 and 240, and small sheets 71, 75, 76, 79, 80, 82 cover the area.

General guides

Dordogne (Philips Travel Guides, 1992): a coffee table book with impressive colour pictures.

The Which? Guide to France (Consumers' Association/Penguin 1994): plenty of descriptive detail on the whole of France.

Le Lot – Helen Martin (Columbus Books, out of print) is a readable and useful guide to the *département*.

Nouveau guide du Périgord-Quercy – Jean-Luc Aubarbier et al (Ouest France) is the most comprehensive guide (in French) to the sights of the Dordogne and Lot – available in most good French bookshops.

The Wines of Bordeaux – David Peppercorn (Mitchell Beazley).

Accommodation guides

Red Michelin, France (yearly guide): the most authoritative hotel and restaurant guide, but all in symbols.

Gault Millau, *France* (yearly guide); written in florid French (but available in most good UK bookshops), with a wide selection of hotels and restaurants throughout France; its famed restaurant choice favours those that offer regional or modern cuisine.

Gault Millau, *The Best of France* (RAC): a selection of the above, but abbreviated descriptions in English.

Guide to Hotels and Country Inns of Character and Charm (Rivages). An authoritative guide to good places to stay in the French countryside.

Specialist reading

The Hundred Years' War – Christopher Allmand (Cambridge Medieval Textbooks).

Le Vrai Visage du Catharisme – Anne Brenon (Loubatières): A scholarly account of the Cathars and their history (in French). Available from good bookshops in the region.

The Troubadours and their world – Jack Lindsay (Muller, out of print).

Das Reich – Max Hastings (Papermac): A highly readable account of the progress of a German armoured division through the Dordogne basin in 1944, and of the tragic consequences.

General reading

The Sons of the Generous Earth – Philip Oyler (Hodder, out of print): The Dordogne 'classic' – a lyrical description of the region in the post-war years.

Three Rivers of France – Freda White (Pavilion Books).

The Colossus of Maroussi – Henry Miller (Minerva).

Bonjour Tristesse – Françoise Sagan (Penguin).

INDEX

THE WHICH? GUIDE TO BRITTANY AND NORMANDY

Ideal for anyone taking a seaside holiday, camping, touring or walking in Brittany and Normandy, this discriminating guide covers two of the best-loved and most accessible regions of France. From rocky coastlines and unspoilt beaches to the pastoral landscape that is home to Camembert and Calvados, famous tourist attractions such as the dramatic island fortress of Mont St Michel, the Bayeux tapestry and Monet's house in Giverny, the area has a great deal to offer. This guide explores all the possibilities, including many lesser-known places. It also provides practical advice on travelling, shopping, food and the weather, and the *Holiday Which?* team picks out the best bases and recommends resorts, hotels, campsites and places to eat at, whatever your budget.

Paperback   210 x 120mm   304 pages

Available from bookshops
and by post from
Consumers' Association, Dept SSW,
Castlemead, Gascoyne Way, Hertford X, SG14 1LH.

Access/Visa card holders can phone FREE on
(0800) 252100 to place their order,
quoting Dept SSW.

THE WHICH? GUIDE TO FRANCE

Rural peace, cosmopolitan cities, tranquil country towns, fine sandy beaches and breathtaking mountain scenery . . . France has so much to offer its visitors. In this, the fifth edition of *The Which? Guide to France*, the team from *Holiday Which?* brings together all the essential information you need, both for planning a trip and to use while travelling within France.

As well as a profile of each area, including Corsica, the book has features on history and architecture and on food and drink. Throughout, background details are provided on the churches and cathedrals, museums and châteaux with which France is so liberally endowed. The guide also lists recommended restaurants in Paris and includes an invaluable practical information section.

Detailed maps and a hotels index help you pinpoint any of the 300-plus hotels which have been independently inspected and selected for this guide as being the best value for money.

'Arguably the best of the mid-range guides.'
The Daily Telegraph

Paperback   210 x 120mm   640 pages

Available from bookshops
and by post from
Consumers' Association, Dept SSW,
Castlemead, Gascoyne Way, Hertford X, SG14 1LH.

Access/Visa card holders can phone FREE on
(0800) 252100 to place their order,
quoting Dept SSW.

THE WHICH? GUIDE TO WEEKEND BREAKS IN BRITAIN

What do you look for in a short holiday break? Beautiful countryside to walk in, perhaps stopping off at the occasional hostelry? Somewhere you can pursue an interest, like Britain's industrial heritage or natural history? Or simply relaxation in lovely surroundings, with some memorable meals and a spot of shop-browsing?

This new guide to mini-breaks in Britain will provide you with inspiration aplenty, plus all the practical data you are likely to need, with addresses, phone numbers and opening times. It covers England, Scotland and Wales, and includes touring routes through areas such as 'Constable country', Snowdonia and the Yorkshire Dales; the best seaside resorts and historic cities; and special sections on subjects as diverse as gardens and vineyards, bird-watching, Hadrian's Wall, fossil-hunting in Dorset, and the Boswell/ Johnson trail on Skye.

Paperback   210 x 120mm   512 pages

Available from bookshops
and by post from
Consumers' Association, Dept SSW,
Castlemead, Gascoyne Way, Hertford X, SG14 1LH.

Access/ Visa card holders can phone FREE on
(0800) 252100 to place their order,
quoting Dept SSW.

THE GOOD WALKS GUIDE

Edited by Tim Locke

This new ringbound edition features 150 great walks – some taken from earlier walks guides published by Consumers' Association – in outstanding locations throughout Britain; each is self-contained on its own looseleaf page so that it can be removed, placed in the plastic folder provided and carried on the walk.

The walks, all between 3 and 8 miles long, are within the scope of occasional walkers but offer plenty of interest even for seasoned walkers. Each walk is accompanied by a full-colour map showing all the details and landmarks for following the directions easily; these divide the walk into manageable sections, so that you can see how you are progressing. There are masses of full-colour photographs to inspire you, and places of interest, geological features, flora and fauna to note along the way are highlighted.

Ringbound   297 x 210mm   320 pages

Available from bookshops
and by post from
Consumers' Association, Dept SSW,
Castlemead, Gascoyne Way, Hertford X, SG14 1LH.

Access/ Visa card holders can phone FREE on
(0800) 252100 to place their order,
quoting Dept SSW.